Initiating Change in Highland Ethiopia
Causes and Consequences of Cultural Transformation

In a rural community in southern Ethiopia, there are two types of rituals performed by the same people. Historical evidence suggests that one has shown remarkable stability over the years, while the other has undergone massive transformations. External factors are the same, so how is this to be explained? Dena Freeman focuses on new ethnographical and historical data from the Gamo Highlands of southern Ethiopia to tackle the question of cultural change and transformation. She uses a comparative perspective and contrasts the continuity in sacrificial rituals with the rapid divergence and differentiation in initiations. Freeman argues that although external change drives internal cultural transformation, the way in which it does is greatly influenced by the structural organisation of the cultural systems themselves. This insight leads to a rethinking of the analytic tension between structure and agency that is at the heart of contemporary anthropological theory.

DENA FREEMAN is Research Fellow of Queens' College at the University of Cambridge. She is the co-editor, with Alula Pankhurst, of *Peripheral People: The Excluded Minorities of Ethiopia* (Hurst & Co.), and her essay, *From Warrior to Wife: Cultural Transformation in the Gamo Highlands of Ethiopia*, won the Curl Essay Prize in 2000.

Initiating Change in Highland Ethiopia

Causes and Consequences of Cultural Transformation

Dena Freeman

Queens' College
Cambridge

DAMAGED

CAMBRIDGE
UNIVERSITY PRESS

PUBLISHED BY THE PRESS SYNDICATE OF THE UNIVERSITY OF CAMBRIDGE
The Pitt Building, Trumpington Street, Cambridge, United Kingdom

CAMBRIDGE UNIVERSITY PRESS
The Edinburgh Building, Cambridge CB2 2RU, UK
40 West 20th Street, New York, NY 10011-4211, USA
477 Williamstown Road, Port Melbourne, VIC 3207, Australia
Ruiz de Alarcón 13, 28014 Madrid, Spain
Dock House, The Waterfront, Cape Town 8001, South Africa

http://www.cambridge.org

© Dena Freeman 2002

First published 2002

Printed in the United Kingdom at the University Press, Cambridge

Typeface Plantin 10/12 pt   *System* LᴬTEX 2ε   [TB]

A catalogue record for this book is available from the British Library

Library of Congress Cataloguing in Publication data

Freeman, Dena.
Initiating change in highland Ethiopia: causes and consequences of cultural
transformation / Dena Freeman.
    p.   cm.
Includes bibliographical references and index.
ISBN 0 521 81854 0
1. Gamo (African people) – Rites and ceremonies.   2. Social change –
Case studies.   3. Gamo (African people) – Social conditions.   I. Title.
DT380.4.G19 F74   2002
303.4′0963–dc21   2002022273

ISBN 0 521 81854 0 hardback

Contents

Illustrations

Plates

Figures

Maps

Acknowledgements

This book has evolved out of a doctoral thesis written while I was a graduate student at the London School of Economics. The research was made possible by grants from the Leverhulme Trust, the Economic and Social Research Council (ESRC) and the London School of Economics, and its rewriting has been possible courtesy of a Research Fellowship from Queens' College, Cambridge.

Many people have helped make this book. Extra special thanks must go to Maurice Bloch and James Woodburn, who carefully supervised my doctoral research. I am also grateful to Wendy James and Mike Rowlands, who examined my thesis and asked many difficult questions and raised several interesting points. Their input has helped me improve this work considerably. Thanks also to Eshetu Chabo, Don Donham, Peter Loizos, Jackie Scott, Dan Sperber, Marilyn Strathern, Harvey Whitehouse and Tadesse Wolde, who have all commented on earlier drafts of various sections of the manuscript.

In Ethiopia I was affiliated to the Institute of Ethiopian Studies and the Department of Social Anthropology at Addis Abeba University. My grateful thanks go to all the people there, particularly Abdussamed Ahmed, Bahru Zewde and Alula Pankhurst. I must also offer my sincere thanks to the people of Doko who welcomed me into their houses and their lives. Their tolerance and continued goodwill was phenomenal. I am especially grateful to Shagire Shano, Wale Washo and their family for offering me a home and becoming my family. I would also like to thank my assistants Alemayehu Adamo, Abera Gum?a and Mattios Maja.

Select glossary

A NOTE ON TRANSCRIPTION OF GAMO TERMS

ch', k', p', t' and *ts'*	all explosives (also in Amharic)
d'	an implosive that has a sound between d and t
?	a glottal stop
e	at the end of a word, pronounced like the French é

GAMO TERMS

ade	father, owner, boss, senior
angisa	lineage head
atuma	type of *halak'a* in some *deres*
ayle	slave
bekesha baira	head of sub-lineage, i.e. senior to four generations of patrilineal descendants
bitane	type of *halak'a* in some *deres*
dana	initiate in the large *dere* of Doko
degala	caste-like group of artisans who do not have full status in the *dere*; mainly work as tanners and blacksmiths today
dere	Gamo community
demutsa	type of sacrificer
dubusha	assembly place
ek'k'a	sacrificer; *dere* senior
guyhatets	ceremony of togetherness which establishes formal relations between wife-givers and wife-takers
halak'a	initiate in a small *dere*
hudhugha	initiate in a medium-sized *dere*
gach'ino	state in which one must rest, eat well and do no work; women are *gach'ino* after marriage and childbirth, men are *gach'ino* after circumcision and during part of the *halak'a* initiations

gatuma	stick given to *halak'as* in Doko Masho
gazo	large bamboo poles erected in *halak'a*'s compound
gome	transgression of a traditional rule, which is thought to lead to misfortune
gufe	wooden walking stick
guʔa	gift taken to father-in-law after wife has reached menopause and all *kumets* gifts have been taken
horoso	ceremonial staff carried by *halak'as* and *ades*
k'ach'ina	men who have not been initiated as *halak'a*
kallacha	metal phallus, worn on the forehead during ritual occasions by *hudhughas*, *danas* and, in some *deres*, *ek'k'as*
kawo	senior sacrificer in the *dere*; ritual leader
korofine	clan head
kumets	full, complete: name given to gifts taken to certain people, particularly fathers-in-law
k'olla	private part of the house
lashuma	stick given to *halak'as* in Doko Gembela
lazantsa	intermediary in wedding negotiations and *halak'a* initiations
maaka	type of sacrificer
maggana	offerings made to the spirits
mala	farmers and citizens in the *dere*; not *mana* or *degala*
mana	caste-like group of artisans who do not have full status in the *dere*; work as potters
Mesqalla	Gamo New Year Festival; name derives from Amharic, *Mesqal*
perso	wheat beer
p'oʔets	horn blown by *mala*
shaʔa	plot of farmland by the house
sofe	public parade that marks a change of status
ts'omma	general term for the artisan castes, *mana* and *degala*
uʔe	intermediary in *halak'a* initiations in Doko Gembela; also the name for small flies
uts'uma	*stellaria media*, a common grass that grows well anywhere
woga	law, tradition; the right way to behave
zurra	neighbourhood work-group in which one man from each house must participate

AMHARIC TERMS

balabbat	administrative position in the Imperial government; intermediary between the state and local communities; position given to *kawos* in the Gamo Highlands
gebbar	tenant farmer who had to provide food and labour for Amhara settlers during the Imperial period
neftenya	Amhara soldier-settler
zamach (zamacha)	campaigners; students who were sent to the countryside to teach Socialism, nationalise land, improve schools and clinics, and ban traditional practices at the beginning of the Derg period

1   Introduction: theorising change

In a remote part of southern Ethiopia there is a small farming community which has two forms of politico-ritual organisation. One is based on
animal sacrifices and the other is based on initiations. The same people
participate in both these systems. However, over the course of the past
century or so the two systems have undergone very different types of
change. The sacrificial system has retained more or less the same overall
form although its practices have become less frequent and less elaborated;
whereas the initiatory system, in contrast, has undergone a fairly radical
transformation so that the form of the initiations is now quite different
from how it was a hundred years ago. All the external factors are the
same, indeed it is the very same people carrying out both these practices,
so why do the two systems change in such different ways?

This ethnographic puzzle provides us with an opportunity to try to understand cultural change. The unusual situation of two cultural systems
changing in different ways in the same circumstances will force us to tease
apart the mechanisms that bring about change. We will need to look at
causality, at individual action, at systemic organisation and at communal
decision-making. These, then, are some of the issues that this book will
address as it seeks to formulate a model of cultural change that will allow
us to comprehend this unusual Ethiopian ethnography.

Anthropological approaches to change

Anthropological approaches to cultural change can be broadly divided
into two camps. There are those that prioritise structural or systemic factors and there are those that prioritise individual action. Much of the
history of anthropology can be seen as a series of attempts to bring together these two perspectives. And it is arguable that this synthesis has
yet to be fully achieved. However, in order to explain our ethnographic
case, where the actions of the same individuals lead to one system transforming and one system not, it will be necessary to understand both the
individual and the systemic factors of change. This book then represents

another attempt to synthesise individualist and systemic approaches to social life and to cultural change. Before outlining the approach taken in this book, it will be useful to take a look at some of the different varieties of systemic and individualist analyses that have been instructive in the development of anthropological theory.

The systemic mode of analysis

The systemic mode of analysis offers a way to understand the patterning of society or culture. By focusing on social and cultural systems, systemic analysis can offer insights as to how different parts of the system fit together and how changes in one part of the system will lead to changes in another part of the system. It allows us to take a holistic perspective and make some generalisations about the different forms of cultural life in different societies. Many different types of anthropological analysis can be classified as systemic analyses, but perhaps the two major anthropological traditions that fall into this category are functionalism and structuralism. Neither of these traditions is particularly noted for its focus on cultural change, but several anthropologists whose ideas have derived from these traditions have generated useful insights into the way in which cultural systems change over time.

Approaches derived from the functionalist tradition   One approach to the study of cultural change has been to try to elucidate causal variables that determine the form of different cultural variants, which are seen to be transformations of each other. These variables in turn are generally seen to be driven by one particular independent variable which forms the base of the structural system. Within this broad functionalist framework, various independent variables have been suggested, most frequently either various elements of social organisation, such as property transmission or residence patterns, or environmental factors such as ecology or the technology of production.

Studies of cultural variation and transformation in the structural-functionalist framework (e.g. Nadel 1951; Goody 1962) posit some aspect of social organisation as the independent variable and then try to correlate changes in other variables with changes in this base variable. Jack Goody explains the position clearly: '[We must proceed by] comparing the standardised modes of acting in the two communities, in order to see where the differences lie. Having established the covariations, we have then to try to determine which are the dependent, which the independent variables' (Goody 1962:8). In his study of mortuary rituals among the LoDagaa of northern Ghana, Goody establishes correlations between a number of variables, including form of mortuary ritual, form of kinship organisation and the nature of father–son relations. He then suggests that the independent variable, which is thought to drive all the other variations, is in fact the system of inheritance. Among the LoWiili all property is transmitted agnatically, whereas among the LoDagaba immovable property is transmitted agnatically while movable property is inherited by uterine kin. So, for example, tense father–son relations are 'caused' among the LoWiili by the fact that the son is dependent on his father for his inheritance, and more relaxed father–son relations among the LoDagaba are 'caused' by the fact that the son is not so dependent on his father because much of his inheritance will come from his mother's brother. It follows then that one variant is a transformation of the other: start with the LoWiili variant and change the inheritance pattern and you will end up with something very similar to the LoDagaba variant. Goody in fact suggests that this is what happens in LoWiili/LoDagaba border areas where, through intermarriage, sons of LoWiili men and LoDagaba women can choose to inherit either from their father or from their mother's brother. If, for whatever reasons, they choose to inherit from their mother's family then changes in the way they propitiate the ancestors and hold their mortuary rites, etc., will soon follow.

Goody is more subtle than many functionalists in that he explicitly repudiates the notion that all variations in social behaviour interlock with each other in a holistic manner (Goody 1962:419). However, the course of the transformation he suggests is still based on an essentially organistic view of culture, and there is little discussion of mechanism, beyond the initial choice made by borderland youths about their inheritance. Most of the work concentrates on drawing up structural correlations, and the issues of causality and the direction of change are only addressed briefly in the final discussion of borderland youths. Goody's problem with causality is essentially that he wants to give structure causal efficacy, but because he also believes that structure is not a 'thing' that 'exists' he can find no way to ground his intuitions about change in any actual social mechanisms. Although Goody tackles this problem again in later works, it is not one that he successfully overcomes. In *Production and Reproduction* (1976), for example, he uses the statistical tools of linkage and path analysis to try to determine the direction of causality between a set of correlations regarding plough agriculture and diverging devolution. His use of these statistical tools is a brave attempt 'to get a little beyond the circularity of structural-functionalism and the much simpler unilineal, single-factor hypotheses that dog so much work in the social sciences' (Goody 1976:37), but ultimately it tells us little about the micro-mechanisms of change and how it actually takes place on the ground.

The materialist approaches of ecological anthropology, cultural materialism and cultural ecology see cultures as adaptive solutions to environmental givens (e.g. Steward 1955; Sahlins 1958; Sahlins and Service 1960; Rappaport 1968, 1979; Harris 1979, 1980). They differ in the degree to which they acknowledge the importance of technology and the organisation of production (Thin 1996:186) and in the extent to which they include other societies as part of the 'environment', but they all share a view of causality that considers the material 'base' (or 'infrastructure') to determine the cultural 'superstructure'. In other words, they consider 'culture' in functionalist terms, as a coherent whole that adapts to its environment, much as a biological organism adapts to its environment. Within these approaches there are two related perspectives on cultural change. One seeks to understand culture as a homeostatic system that changes in order to keep its population in balance with its environment (e.g. Rappaport 1968), and the other seeks to understand the transformation of culture in response to changing environmental conditions.

Perhaps the best example of this latter perspective is Sahlins' comparative look at social stratification in Polynesia (Sahlins 1958). In this early work Sahlins looks at a number of Polynesian societies and attempts to understand gross variations in the form and degree of their social stratification as functional adaptations, or transformations, driven by different ecological and technological conditions. His causal model starts from environmental conditions and then extends to considerations of the organisation of production and exchange, then to social stratification, and finally, rather weakly, to vague extrapolations to other elements of cultural and ritual life. He writes:

Degree of stratification is directly related to surplus output of food producers. The greater the technological efficiency and surplus production, the greater will be the frequency and scope of [food] distribution [centred around chiefs] . . . Increase in scope, frequency and complexity of distribution implies increasing status differentiation between distributor and producer. This differentiation will be manifest in other economic processes besides distribution, and in sociopolitical and ceremonial life. Thereby the hypothesis: other factors being constant, the degree of stratification varies directly with productivity. (Sahlins 1958:5)

Through a fairly detailed look at fourteen Polynesian societies and their environments, Sahlins shows that this hypothesised correlation more or less holds. However, by simply comparing static, idealised structures he is unable to show that it is anything more than a correlation. By ignoring mechanism or process, or any real consideration of history, he is, like Goody, unable to prove his suggested causality, and unable to explain convincingly how the suggested changes actually occur. His analysis is devoid of subjects or agents, and thus causal mechanisms are implicitly considered to work at the level of 'structure', wherever this may be. As in many other models in ecological anthropology, 'the system' is imbued with causal efficacy while there is no adequate discussion of the ontological status of such a system. The causal model that results is as a consequence either teleological or downright mystical.

If, for the sake of argument, we were to accept his model of causality, then the explanation of cultural change that we are left with is essentially linear and evolutionist. The basic cultural structure is elaborated to a greater or lesser extent according to the amount of surplus available. Implicit in this argument is the idea of reversibility: if one of the less stratified societies were to become more productive then they would evolve into a form like that of the more stratified societies existing in its vicinity, and if one of these more stratified societies were somehow to become less productive they would devolve into a form like their less stratified neighbours. In a later publication Sahlins expands his set of factors which might cause devolution to include greedy chiefs, status rivalry and other non-environmental factors (Sahlins 1963:297–300), but the essentially linear nature of his model remains the same. There is no room in this model for structural transformation, or what we might call non-linear change.

Edmund Leach's study of political systems in highland Burma suffers a similar problem (Leach 1981 [1954]). Although purporting to be a model of 'structural change' and 'historical transformation', it is in reality a linear model which sees variants of Kachin culture forever oscillating between two fixed ideological points. The stumbling block for Leach is his analytical separation of the 'system on the ground' from the 'system of ideas'. By this analytical twist Leach can ignore the spiralling effects brought about because, on the ground, 'the facts at the end of the cycle are quite different from the facts at the beginning of the cycle' (1981 [1954]:xiii), and instead concentrate on the supposed cyclical oscillation of the 'system of ideas'. By ironing out these on-the-ground differences, he implies that they have no causal power to *interact* with the system of ideas and, perhaps, transform it. Instead they can only *drive* the system into more (*gumsa*) or less (*gumlao*) hierarchical form, while the system itself is untransformable.

Leach's model is thus linear for different reasons than Sahlins' (1958) model. Sahlins' model is linear because it is essentially unicausal. Productivity determines all. Whenever there is more than one causal variable the rest are 'held constant' so that the linear variations with one variable can be seen. But Leach's model ostensibly embraces multicausality, as he looks at the causal effects of ecology, political history and the actions of individuals (1981 [1954]:228–63). However, by rendering the system of ideas off-limits to any effects of these factors, and yet imbuing these ideas with causal power over the actions of individuals, Leach short-circuits the multicausal model of complex interactions between different factors, and effectively ends up with a linear model.

There are, I think, two major reasons for the weaknesses in Leach's model which are pertinent to this discussion. One is that Leach was arguing against the functional holism that was common at the time, and exemplified, for example, by Sahlins' (1958) book. However, he does not fully manage to step out of this framework, for although he insists that the system 'on the ground' is full of incoherencies, he still feels the need to posit a 'system of ideas' that is a coherent whole. The other reason for the incoherence of Leach's own model is that he is ultimately unsure whether to place causality in the realm of structure or in the realm of individuals. On the one hand he sees the structural contradictions between the *mayu-dama* marriage system and both *gumlao* and Shan ideology as driving 'structural change', and yet on the other hand he states that 'every individual of a society, each in his own interest, endeavours to exploit the situation as he perceives it and in so doing the collectivity of individuals alters the structure of the society itself' (1981 [1954]:8). Leach is thus acutely aware of the ontological problems of seeing structure as causal, and is trying to incorporate a more ontologically sound individualist view into what is essentially a structural account. While this is definitely a step in the right direction, Leach does not quite succeed in combining these two approaches in a rigorous manner. I will return to this below, but first let us take a look at another set of approaches to cultural variation, those that take their inspiration from Claude Lévi-Strauss and structuralism.

Approaches derived from the structuralist tradition For Lévi-Strauss, studying cultural variation and transformation is fundamental to any study of culture. Whether looking at kinship organisation or myth (1963, 1994 [1964], 1981 [1971]), his works proceed not by generalisation into 'ideal types', but by the explication of numerous variants, of which no one is more 'true' than any other. He is interested in the way that different versions of a cultural element represent transformations of its basic structure. Thus he looks for underlying patterns which form the 'structure' of all variants, and at the same time seeks to understand the logic by which one can transform into another.

Lévi-Strauss's conception of 'structure' is thus radically different from that of the structural-functionalists. He sees structure not as the holistic, organically functioning backbone of society, but rather as the logical patterning of principles existing behind surface variations in cultural elements. This structure is 'deep', and can only be uncovered by the study of surface variation. Furthermore, it never forms coherent wholes, but is a matter of continual communication and modification (Bloch 1996:535).

His notion of 'transformation' is also more complicated. He considers that myths, for example, are genetic, as well as formal, transformations of other myths (Sperber 1985:84). By this he means that when a myth-teller recounts a myth he is transforming a myth that he himself heard earlier – transforming the version that he heard by forgetting bits, adding new elements, changing the order, and so on. This is genetic transformation, transformation in its genesis. Formal transformation, which is the notion of transformation more commonly associated with structuralism, refers to the processes of opposition, inversion, symmetry, substitution and permutation by which different variants can be logically related to each other (D'Anglure 1996:335). Since it is difficult to follow the actual genetic transformations which myths undergo in their telling and retelling, he suggests that it is possible to try to reconstruct this history by taking 'formal transformations between related myths as hypothetical models for genetic transformations' (Sperber 1985:84). Thus although Lévi-Strauss's study of myth is for the most part synchronic, much of his causality lies in the realm of history, as he sees one variant generating another through time, in response to changing external conditions.

For the most part Lévi-Strauss does not attempt to explain how myths actually transform in practice, but limits himself to showing how variants of myths can be seen to be logical transformations of each other. Near the beginning of the first volume of his magnum opus on Native American myth he states the case plainly:

By demonstrating that myths from widely divergent sources can be seen objectively as a set, it presents history with a problem and invites it to set about finding a solution. I have defined such a set, and I hope I have supplied proof of it being a set. It is the business of ethnographers, historians and archaeologists to explain how and why it exists. (Lévi-Strauss 1994 [1964]:8)

Many anthropologists working in the structuralist tradition have followed this path, and thus stuck to formal analyses of variation which are ahistorical and non-causal. Thus, to cite but one example, Nur Yalman provides a formal analysis of Sri Lankan and South Indian kinship systems, showing how they are all variations of one underlying structure (Yalman 1967).

Another branch of Lévi-Strauss's intellectual descendants, however, have sought to ground such formal analysis of structure and variation in the external world, by trying to look at the causal effects of politics, ecology and what have you, as they transform structures through history (e.g. Sahlins 1985; Piot 1995). These efforts differ from Leach's model in that external factors are considered not just to drive structure into greater or lesser elaborations of its basic form, but actually to transform it. In this way the short-circuit between the external world and symbolic ideas that doomed Leach's model to linearity is opened out, and these historical structuralist models take on a non-linear nature. In other words, they try to model the recursive way in which the external environment affects structure, and in turn how structure affects the form of interaction with the external environment. Structure and history become analytically inseparable.

Thus Sahlins, to cite a well-known example, suggests in his later work that external events, such as the arrival of Captain Cook in Hawaii, are initially understood through local cultural structures and then transform these structures, as cultural categories take on new meanings and connotations in the new context. And Piot suggests that the symbolic structure of Kabre society in Togo both influenced the way in which large numbers of immigrants were absorbed in the seventeenth to nineteenth centuries, and in turn was itself transformed by these politico-historical events. The innovation in these models is that causality is not seen as unidirectional, and the insights of both Marx and Weber are brought together to understand cultural change. In this way they attempt to transcend the distinction between materialist and idealist approaches, and between structure and history. Thus Sahlins' notion of the 'structure of the conjuncture' focuses on neither 'structure' nor 'history', but compounds the two to focus on the 'practical realization of the cultural categories in a specific historical context, as expressed in the interested action of the historic agents' (Sahlins 1985:xiv).

Bruce Knauft uses a similar approach to great effect in his book on south coast New Guinea cultures (Knauft 1993). But in contrast to Sahlins' formulation, Knauft does not require the influence of foreign forces or events to set change into motion. Rather, he focuses on 'how structures feed upon changes that they themselves generate' (1993:11). Through a detailed look at the variations between the many cultures of south coast New Guinea, he argues that structure should be seen not as a synchronic entity that might be revalued as the historical context changes, but rather as an entity that might *itself* transform. He shows how the unintended consequences of some actions will 'act as irritants' and lead to structures 'self-transforming from the inside as they respond dialectically to their own prior actualisations' (1993:11, 14). Socio-material factors in the external, or non-symbolic, world feed into this recursive process, offering both constraints and opportunities for development in certain directions.

Knauft goes further than many other theorists in explicitly acknowledging the unpredictability and non-linearity that transformation through such recursive processes generates, and stresses the sensitivity to initial conditions whereby very similar forms can diverge quickly into strikingly different cultural variants. He appears to give symbolic and non-symbolic factors the same ontological status, and thus sees both as causally efficacious. However, because his scale of analysis is large, encompassing the many cultures of south coast New Guinea, he does not attempt to theorise the micro-mechanisms that actually bring about the transformational change that he describes.

This is perhaps the greatest weakness of any form of systemic analysis. Focusing on large-scale systems, studies in this mode tend to lose sight of the individuals whose actions actually generate the social system. Structure tends to become reified and it is often implicitly seen as a causal entity that somehow constrains the actions of individuals. And at its most extreme, individuals become almost like automatons who blindly follow the rules of the social system. Even in less extreme forms it is often unclear how individuals live through the system and how the actions of individuals somehow add up to 'create' that very social system. To explore these types of questions we need to turn to the individualist mode of analysis.

The individualist mode of analysis

The greatest strength of the individualist mode of analysis is that it offers ways to understand the actions of individuals. Analyses in this mode take the individual as the starting point, not 'society' or 'structure'. They are thus far more ontologically rigorous than systemic analyses and they try to explain social or cultural phenomena from the bottom up, rather than the top down. They do not portray individuals in far-away places as exotic 'others' and we can generally sympathise, if not empathise, with the subjects of this type of analysis. The most important traditions within this mode of analysis are transactionalism and what I shall refer to as the cultural transmission tradition.

Approaches derived from the transactionalist tradition A transactionalist approach sees society as the product of the interactions between individual actors. Structure is not considered to be a 'thing' that determines people's actions, but rather is seen as an emergent phenomenon that derives from the cumulative effects of the freely chosen actions of individuals. In order to understand why individuals act in the way that they do, it is instead necessary to consider their motives and goals and then to look at the strategies that they use to accomplish these goals. These strategies will often involve manipulating social values and institutions.

Structure, in other words, can itself be used as a tool, or as a resource, in the negotiations between individuals.

Perhaps the best example of a transactionalist analysis is Fredrik Barth's *Political Leadership among Swat Pathans* (1959). In this account Barth argues that Swat politics can be understood by looking at the relations between leaders and their clients. Individuals choose to become clients when they make the choice to enter into a relationship with a leader. There are various different types of leader, such as chiefs and saints, and various different types of political grouping. Individuals choose which relationships they wish to enter into and, indeed, whether they enter into any relationships at all. Local politics can then be understood as the series of negotiations that take place between individuals, as the various leaders and the many clients try to get into relationships which they believe will be the most beneficial to them. Everyone is acting in their own self-interest and trying to manipulate the accepted social order in the pursuit of their own goals.

This approach to culture provides a dynamic action-oriented perspective. The focus placed on individual choice would seem to offer a useful way to approach the question of cultural change, because if individuals are always choosing what to do, they are always free to choose to do something differently. If we can understand what would make them choose to do things differently, then we would be a long way towards understanding how cultural change actually takes place.

But what this approach does not offer us is a way to understand how systemic change takes place. It is unclear quite how structure 'emerges' from individual actions and why the cumulation of lots of individual actions has a pattern at all. While society or culture may not be as ordered as some of the systemic analyses suggest, there certainly is some degree of coherence in socio-cultural life that cannot be adequately explained by the transactionalist approach. And what happens to this pattern if some people begin to change their individual actions? How does the pattern itself change and why does it not simply fall apart? I will return to these points later, but first it will be useful to take a look at a very different type of individualist analysis.

Approaches derived from the cultural transmission tradition The final group of theoretical approaches to cultural change that I will discuss here focus on the way that incremental transformations take place during cultural transmission. These approaches (e.g. Dawkins 1982; Barth 1987; Sperber 1996) see culture not as some overarching whole, but rather as being made up of units that are continually communicated between individuals. They have a firmly materialist ontology and give little or no analytic weight to the shadowy notion of structure. Instead they seek to explain macro-phenomena in terms of the cumulative effects of micro-phenomena, rather than in terms of other macro-phenomena (Sperber 1996:2). Thus rather than try to explain religion, say, in terms of economic structure, these approaches would seek to explain the distribution of religious ideas in a given population in terms of their mode of transmission.

These approaches do not carve up the world into 'individuals' and 'societies' in the manner of much anthropological theory. Instead they have as their basic unit of analysis cultural elements – memes (Dawkins), representations (Sperber) or ideas (Barth) – and their transmission. Thus for Sperber, for example, there is no separate domain of culture in opposition to the individual, but rather there are representations that are more or less cultural, as they are more or less widely distributed among a population (Sperber 1996:49). These approaches, then, focus their analysis on communication or transmission.

One major difference between the theorists grouped together here, however, is the way in which they consider cultural transmission to occur. Dawkins has perhaps the simplest model. He calls his cultural units 'memes', as a cultural analogue to genes, and suggests that, like genes, memes are mostly replicated through transmission. Only occasionally will mutations occur, and these mutant memes then compete with other memes so that the fittest survive. In this way natural selection is considered to guide the gradual evolution of culture. Sperber strongly critiques the meme model and argues that cultural transmission is far more complicated. He suggests that cultural transmission consists of the complicated process whereby an individual creates a public representation from an individual mental representation, and then a second individual creates a new mental representation from this public representation. Environmental factors influence this process, for example in providing opportunities for the public representation to be spoken or written, as do psychological factors, such as the memory and mood of the individuals, and the relevance of the content of this particular representation to the other representations they have stored in their minds. Thus transmission of representations is rarely simple replication, but is instead transformation, influenced by the cognitive capacities of the human brain.

In *Cosmologies in the Making* (1987), Barth uses a transmission model to explain a particular pattern of cultural variation and transformation in inner New Guinea. Like Sperber, he sees continual transformation occurring as ideas oscillate between public and private versions, but unlike Sperber, he considers that the organisation of these communicative events themselves influences the degree to which transformation or replication occurs. Thus, for Barth, it is the organisational form of Mountain Ok initiations – that they take place only every ten years, that they are shrouded in secrecy and only one ritual leader is thought to know how to conduct them properly, and that people may also attend the initiations of neighbouring communities – that provides the opportunities for their continual transformation, through the individual creativity of the ritual leader. If they were organised some other way, perhaps if they took place annually, or if the knowledge were open to all, then they would transform in quite different ways and to quite different degrees.

This much seems extremely plausible, but Barth is rather weaker in his modelling of the individual creativity which can be either stimulated or constrained by the organisation of communicative events. According to him, the creative imagination of the ritual leaders leads to an unintentional symbolic drift, as the incremental changes in the fan of connotations of symbols, in the saliency of their various meta-levels, and in the scope of certain cosmological schemata add up over time (Barth 1987:31).

When it comes to causality, these approaches again differ markedly from the other approaches discussed above. Both Barth and Sperber are looking for the mechanisms of cultural transformation, and, although they conceive of them a little differently, they both locate them in the workings of the human mind and in the mechanisms of transmission of ideas or representations between human minds. Whereas Barth's discussion of inter-individual transmission focuses solely on social organisational and psychological factors,[1] Sperber's repeated stress that causal factors are both psychological and environmental (e.g. 1996:28, 84) opens up his model to causal influences from all areas, including history, politics, ecology, technology, etc., as they cause particular inputs to particular human minds. And of course, these psychological and environmental factors are themselves affected by the distribution of representations, so that feedback loops result in a causality that is not multi-linear but recursive (1996:84).

The most important shortcoming in these generative approaches to cultural change, however, is their almost total loss of any notion of culture as a system, whether open or closed, simple or complex. Sperber's location of causality in either psychological or environmental (mind-internal or mind-external) factors, while encompassing everything, leaves us with a model of brains in the environment that downplays the significance of the structural interactions between different cultural elements. Barth's explanation of the variation in Mountain Ok ritual does take into account some social organisational factors, such as the frequency of the ritual, but it also avoids any discussion of the actual structure of the ritual, and thus implicitly considers it irrelevant for its own transformation. In other words, whatever structure the ritual has, it will, according to his argument, transform in the way he describes, because the nature of the transformation is caused only by the psychological and social organisational factors he discusses, and not by the structure of the ritual itself. This approach, then, offers us no way to explain why different cultural elements transform in different ways, and to different degrees, when they are performed by the same people in the same cultural setting. While ontologically rigorous, the downplaying of structural factors thus severely limits the usefulness of these approaches in explaining certain features of cultural change.

Towards an integrated theory of cultural change

It is clear that both systemic and individualist analyses offer important insights into the nature of social and cultural life and how it changes over time. The challenge is to find a way to integrate these two perspectives in one analysis so that a more complete understanding of cultural change can be achieved. This task has been attempted by several theorists over the years, including many of those whose works I have reviewed above. While some of them have succeeded in incorporating certain aspects of an individualist approach within a systemic analysis, or vice versa, it has proved difficult to formulate a truly integrated approach.

The most useful attempt in my opinion is one that I have yet to discuss, namely practice theory, particularly the version put forward by Anthony Giddens (e.g. 1976, 1984). This approach to social life brings together insights from both systemic and individualist modes of analysis, particularly structuralism and transactionalism, and seeks to understand social practices ordered across space and time. However, while practice theory goes a long way towards integrating systemic and individualist perspectives on social life, it is rather less successful at modelling cultural change. In order to formulate an integrated theory of cultural change, then, we will need to take practice theory as a starting point and then modify it somewhat. Most importantly, it will be necessary to bring in insights from regional and world systems theorists, from structural Marxists, and from the rather unfashionable field of legal anthropology. In what follows I will build on the practice theory approach in order to formulate a model of cultural change which will then help us to solve the ethnographic puzzle presented at the beginning of this chapter.

Let us start by outlining some of the most important aspects of the practice paradigm. In this approach to social analysis individuals are seen as agents who act in the world in a purposeful manner. They act in their own self-interest and seek to improve their own situation through their interactions with the environment and with other people. They develop strategies to further their self-interest and these strategies often shape the nature of their interactions. These individuals are maximisers and all of them are ultimately trying to maximise the same thing, power. If a researcher can understand how power is constructed in a particular society, then she will be able to empathise with the people of that society and understand the strategies that they use in their interactions.

So in the practice paradigm we have individuals who act purposely in the world in order to maximise their self-interest. So far this is very similar to the transactionalist approach. However, Giddens then complicates the picture by suggesting that all action has both intended and unintended consequences. Thus when I burn some incense I intentionally make the room smell nice but I unintentionally set off the smoke detector, or when I write in English I intentionally communicate something but I unintentionally further the reproduction of the English language. So even though most human action is purposeful and strategic, it will always have unintended consequences that were not part of the original strategy. And in some cases the unintended consequences may turn out to be more important and long lasting than the intended ones.

The concept of structure in the practice paradigm also bears consideration. In Giddens' formulation structure is not an overarching totality, but is rather a set of rules and resources that individuals use when deciding how to act. These rules and resources are not necessarily codified and individuals may or may not be able to formulate them discursively, but they form the tacit knowledge that people use all the time in their everyday life. Thus if I want one of those cakes in the shop window I know that I have to pay for it, or if I want to communicate with you then I know that I have to speak in English. Whether implicit or explicit, these rules can be thought of as the techniques or generalised procedures that are applied in the enactment of social practices. They have no ontological existence in time and space, according to Giddens, other than as ideas and memory traces in people's brains and in the instantiations of their practice. Structure, for the most part, is inside people's minds. It is not something that is external.

With these formulations of structure and agency, Giddens considers how social action takes place. Using the rules and resources available to them, individuals develop strategies of social action in order to maximise their interests. However, the unintended consequences of their actions tend to feed back and create the context of further action. And because this new context is generally no other than the original context, patterns of behaviour are reproduced over time. So the act of standing up when a teacher comes into the room reproduces the idea that students should stand up when a teacher comes into the room and thus constrains other students to stand up when a teacher next comes into the room. 'The moment of the production of action', to quote Giddens, 'is also one of reproduction in the contexts of the day-to-day enactment of social life' (1984:26).

It is at this step in the argument that I have to part company with Giddens. What started out as a flexible and open model of social action has somehow ended up being a circular model for social reproduction. By doing the things that they do, people create the conditions to continue doing the things that they do. This formulation, as it stands, is not going to help us to understand social or cultural change. Let us reconsider the final step of the argument and see if we can find the flaw that dooms his model of social action to one of endless social reproduction.

The flaw is tiny, but terribly significant. When it comes to the unintended consequences of action feeding back to create the new contexts of further action it is not always the case that the new context is the same as the original context. In fact it is extremely *unlikely* that any two actions will take place in exactly identical contexts. For example, the class of students that stood up for their teacher yesterday is in a slightly different context today. The cleaners have cleaned the classroom, one of the students had an argument with his father last night, and the goody-two-shoes who always stands up first is off sick. The unintentional consequences of all of these actions feed back and create the new context for action. In this case, the new context is reasonably similar to the old context and it is likely that the students will again stand up for their teacher.

However, it is also possible that the unintended consequences of the actions of the previous day will lead to a new context that is significantly different. For example, some of the students might have seen a documentary on television the previous night that argued that it was an archaic practice for students to have to stand up when their teacher entered the room. As a consequence of watching this documentary they might have discussed it with their classmates and decided that today they would not stand up when their teacher comes in and they would see what happens. In this example, the unintended consequences of action have fed back to create a new context for action and in this new context the students have chosen to perform a new action.

So we see that in any real-life situation the context is constantly changing and because of this actions do not always reproduce structure every time they are performed. On the contrary, they continually re-create structure, sometimes creating it as it was before and sometimes creating it slightly differently. The reproduction of structure is thus but a limiting case in the continual micro-transformation of structure. It is not the norm, but the exception.

With this modification, we can begin to see how the practice paradigm might offer us the basis from which to develop a model of cultural change. In this type of model we see that, as the context changes, individuals use the available rules and resources (both new and old) to develop strategies of action to maximise their interests. Some of the unintentional consequences of their actions feed back to create slightly different contexts for further action. In these new contexts individuals draw on the now slightly different rules and resources to develop slightly different strategies for action. Some of the unintentional consequences of these actions feed back to create a slightly different context, and so on.

This basic formulation, though, is not yet complete. There are three matters that we need to consider. First, what *types* of contextual change will tend to lead to novel actions? Second, what are the *causes* of these changes in the first place? And third, how is any coherence or 'systemness' created and maintained through the aggregate of constantly changing individual acts?

Let us start by considering the types of contextual change that will lead to individuals changing their actions. It is clear that only contextual changes that offer individuals new opportunities (or resources, in Giddens' terminology) to maximise their self-interest will lead to them changing their actions. Other contextual changes will have little effect. Thus the change in the cleanliness of the classroom or the absence of a particular student in our example did not provide either the students or the teacher with any new opportunities to improve their lot and thus did not lead to any new action. The screening of a particular documentary, on the other hand, gave the students some new information and some new ideas. It gave them a justification for not standing up and thus provided them with the opportunity to contest a rule in order to improve their status and subtly challenge the authority of the teacher.

When a changed context provides this type of new opportunity it is very likely that an individual or a group of individuals will choose to take advantage of the situation and act in a different way. The causation is not determinative. The change in context does not *necessarily* lead to change in action. The students might have watched the documentary and thought nothing further of it. But given that individuals are maximisers who are always trying to improve their lot, it is *likely* that someone at least will choose to act on a new opportunity.

If it is contextual change, or change in the available rules and resources, that provides new opportunities for strategic action, we need to consider what causes these contextual changes in the first place. Other than natural events like earthquakes and changes in the weather, the only thing that can bring about changes in the context is the intended or unintended consequences of the actions of individuals or groups of individuals. If people lived in closed societies that existed as discrete bounded entities, then this argument would be circular and we would be stuck in a chicken and egg situation – which came first, the changed context or the changed action? But since people do not live in such closed societies this circularity does not arise. We do, though, have to consider the nature of the societies or communities in which people live.

The vast majority of people live in some sort of collectivity, whether this is a small-scale local community or a large-scale national society. For want of a better term, these collectivities can be called social systems. But these social systems are not closed systems. They are open systems and they are in turn part of broader regional or world systems (Friedman and Rowlands 1977; Wolf 1985). This is a shorthand way of saying that individuals interact with a large number of other individuals, some of whom live in the same local collectivity and some of whom live further away. The nature of these interactions might be quite different, varying from reciprocal face-to-face conversations to one-way communication via television or newspapers, or from trading partnerships to relations of colonial domination. Most interactions will probably, but not necessarily, take place within the local social system, but it is often through the more infrequent and unusual longer-distance interactions that new ideas are transmitted and new opportunities come about.

Thus in our example we could consider the school to be the local social system. Many of the interactions of the students and the teachers take place with other members of the school, but all of them are also involved in interactions with people outside the school, such as parents, friends, TV presenters, novelists and so on. In our hypothetical case the consequences of the actions of a group of documentary makers, programme schedulers and various other people outside of the school provided the students in the school with some new resources which they used to justify a new action.

Or we could take another example. Consider three small-scale communities, A, B and C. People in A have trading partnerships with people in C and they travel through B's territory as they go back and forth with their wares. At some time, however, the people in society D invade B's territory and start a long-drawn-out war. This action of the people from D will have consequences not only for the people of B, but also for the people of A and C. It is now no longer safe for them to pass through B's territory in their trading activities and they will have to decide whether to look for other routes or new trading partners from other communities, or to give up trading altogether. In this way the consequences of people's action can change the context for other people even though there has been no *direct* interaction between these two people or groups of people.

The point here is very simple, but very important. Because of the complex web of interconnections between individuals, the actions of individuals in one local social system can have consequences for individuals in other local social systems. This is not to say that all change is 'externally generated', for the division between internal and external has become blurred. The open nature of social systems means that 'internal' and 'external' are just matters of degree. Contexts do not only change because external colonisers arrive, they can also change because wars disrupt trade which changes the local opportunities for wealth production, or in any number of other ways. In order to understand change in one locale then it is not necessary to trace back the chain of causes to some ultimate starting point. Such an exercise would in any case be impossible. Going back two or three links in the chain should be more than sufficient to understand the local dynamics that have provided the new opportunities that have led to people changing their actions.

Now that we have seen how contextual change can come about, and the type of contextual change that is likely to lead to individuals changing their actions, we can consider how the aggregate of these changed actions can retain some degree of coherence or 'systemness'. The model so far might seem to imply that everyone just does as they please and that any resulting social or cultural change is simply random. This is not the case for two reasons. First, when individuals try to change their actions these changes are often contested. And second, most collectivities have institutions for making communal decisions and hence communally sanctioned changes. These two types of local interaction tend to have the effect of retaining some degree of 'systemness' in social life.

When there is contextual change this change will not necessarily open up new opportunities for everyone. In most cases some individuals will be able to benefit from the new opportunities while others will not. Some may even stand to lose from the new opportunities that are now available to other people. In our example of the students and their teacher, for instance, the new context provided an opportunity for the students to enhance their status but it thus also opened up the possibility that the teacher's status might be diminished. The fact that changed contexts provide different types of opportunities for differently situated people has been ably demonstrated by several anthropologists, notably those from the Marxist tradition (e.g. Meillassoux 1975; Rey 1975). In this type of situation it is common for conflicts to emerge between individuals who stand to gain and individuals who stand to lose from the change.

The way that these conflicts are handled will affect the way that individual change aggregates and incremental social or cultural change takes place.

Let us return to our example of the students and their teacher. In our hypothetical case the screening of the documentary has provided the students with new opportunities to take action to enhance their status in the school and challenge the authority of the teacher. Let us assume that the students choose to act on this opportunity and that they do not stand up when their teacher next comes into the room. It is extremely unlikely that the teacher will just accept this behaviour and continue as normal. On the contrary, he is likely to contest this new behaviour and try to make the students stand up. The way in which the teacher chooses to contest the new behaviour will depend in part on the rules and resources that are available to him. Thus he might threaten the students with detention. Because the teacher can draw on more powerful resources than the students, such as detentions, it is very likely that he will be able to contest the change successfully and force the students to act in the 'appropriate' way. In this case, then, a one-off change will not aggregate into incremental change in the social system because the change has been successfully contested.

Such cases are not unusual. Because the rules and resources in society are never equally distributed, it is generally the case that one protagonist in a dispute will be able to draw on more powerful resources than the other protagonists. In this way the unequal distribution of power in society can make certain types of change more difficult, such as those that are to the detriment of the power holders. And conversely it can make certain other types of change more easy, namely those that are of benefit to the power holders. So change will not be random after all. Its patterning will be shaped by the distribution of power in society.

Let us imagine for a moment that power is distributed somewhat differently in the school and that the teachers cannot give detentions. In this situation, when the threat of sanctions cannot resolve the conflict, it is likely that negotiation will take place instead. The head teacher might call a special meeting and the teachers and students might get a chance to argue their cases and explain why they think one particular behaviour or the other is appropriate. In such a situation the students have a far greater likelihood of persuading the teachers to accept their new behaviour and it is much more likely that a change will be successful. If the change is agreed by all the teachers and students in the meeting then it will become the new rule. Students in other classes will not have to stand up for teachers and a tiny transformation of the local social system will have taken place.

In this case we have seen a rather different method of dispute resolution. Instead of powerful people using codified rules and sanctions to impose a judgement, we see individuals coming together to resolve their differences through discussion. Both methods of dispute resolution can lead to a change in the rules, but the type of change that is most likely will be different according to the range of interests represented in the decision-making body. School rules are far more likely to change to the benefit of the students if students are involved in the dispute resolution and decision-making processes. The important point here is that methods of dispute resolution and communal decision-making will influence the way that overall incremental change takes place. In order to understand social and cultural change, then, we must rescue the topic of dispute resolution from the backwaters of legal anthropology and place it right at the centre of our analysis.

Let me summarise the argument so far. Social and cultural change will take place in a local social system when the consequences of actions of individuals or groups of individuals in other local social systems provide new opportunities for certain individuals to improve their lot. Being max-imisers, these individuals will probably try to change their actions so as to exploit the new opportunity to their benefit. Other individuals will most likely contest these changes because they stand to lose from them. This will result in conflict and disputes. Each disputant will use all the rules and resources available to him or her to try to resolve the conflict in their own favour. In most cases these resources will not be distributed equally between the two disputants, giving one of them an advantage.

One of the resources available to both disputants in most cases, how-ever, will be the procedures of communal dispute resolution that are used in that local social system, such as courts and judges or informal communal assemblies. The final outcome of the dispute and hence of the initial attempted change will be influenced both by the distribution of resources between the disputants and by the particular procedures of communal dispute resolution and decision-making. The outcome may be either the upholding of tradition (i.e. agreeing to do things the way they were done before) or the micro-transformation of structure (i.e. agreeing to do something new).

This outcome will then feed back to influence further action. If the out-come happened to be the micro-transformation of structure then the new rule agreed upon would form part of the new set of rules and resources that other individuals could then draw upon when deciding how to act. It would thus change the context of further action. If it changed the con-text in a way that did not provide any new opportunities for individuals further to improve their lot then it would not lead to any further change. If, however, it changed the context in such a way that it did provide new opportunities for certain individuals further to improve their lot, then these individuals would probably act so as to exploit these opportunities and the cycle of disputes, resolution and possible micro-transformation would go round again. In this way incremental micro-transformations can iterate and eventually result in overall systemic transformation.

In order to show how this can take place we must now leave abstract theorising and return to grounded ethnography. The series of events that I propose will eventually result in systemic change, or even systemic transformation, do not follow a linear sequence. We cannot start at the beginning and predict what will happen. In any real situation the interplay of changed contexts and changed actions is so complex that we can only understand what happened after it has happened. We need to take a real situation and try to follow through the course of events as they unfold. Let us then return to southern Ethiopia and introduce our ethnographic case in a little more detail.

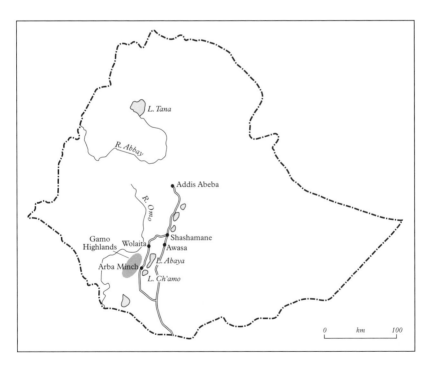

Map 1   Location of the Gamo Highlands in Ethiopia

The Gamo Highlands

The ethnographic puzzle presented at the beginning of this chapter comes from one of the communities of the Gamo Highlands. The Gamo Highlands lie in a fairly remote part of Ethiopia, some 500 km south-west of Addis Abeba. They are located in what was formerly Gamo-Gofa province and is now, with some boundary changes, North Omo Zone. The administrative centre of this zone and the locus of most connections between this area and the central government of Ethiopia is the town of Arba Minch. Founded near the southern shores of Lake Abaya in the late 1960s, Arba Minch is a small town with a population of some 40,000 people (Population and Housing Census 1994:109). Two dirt roads climb the 1,500 m up from hot and dusty Arba Minch into the cool and damp highlands. One road leads to the tiny town of Gerese in the southern part of the highlands and the other leads to the slightly larger town of Chencha in the north. Despite the presence of local government offices, neither of these towns has electricity, running water or a population greater than 6,000 people.

Rising up from the west of Lakes Abaya and Ch'amo, the Gamo Highlands reach altitudes of over 3,000 m and are home to approximately 700,000 men and women (Population and Housing Census 1994:14). The cultivation of cereals forms the basis of subsistence, with barley and wheat being most important in the higher altitudes, and maize and sorghum more important on the lower slopes. *Enset*,[2] or the 'false banana', is also central to subsistence and other crops include peas, beans, potatoes and cabbage. Manure is essential for successful agriculture and thus cattle and smallstock are kept by most farmers. Men hoe the land using the two-pronged hoe and they often farm together in work groups. In some parts of the highlands men have also taken up weaving and trading in recent years.

People live in scattered settlements and are organised into many different communities or *dere*. The national administration further groups these communities together into Peasant Associations, which form the smallest unit of local government. Each Peasant Association will have a chairman, a secretary and various other officers who will generally be local men who have had some school education and become literate in Amharic. This state allocation of power, however, exists alongside local political traditions in which the distribution of power in any community is organised according to two contrasting politico-ritual systems which, in shorthand, we can call the sacrificial system and the initiatory system.

Sacrificial seniority is ascribed and is largely based on genealogical seniority according to primogeniture. Seniors make animal sacrifices on behalf of their juniors at all levels of society: lineage heads for their lineage members, clan heads for their clan members, and community sacrificers for their community. The senior sacrificer of a *dere* is generally known as *kawo*, and, although he is more a symbolic figurehead than a political leader, this term has sometimes been translated as 'king'.

In contrast, initiatory seniority is achieved and is essentially open to anyone. Men are initiated to the position of *halak'a*, with their wives or mothers, through a series of rituals that can span between two months and two years and include a series of feasts for which the initiate must accumulate large amounts of resources. While he is *halak'a* a man is said to 'herd' the community. He has a special role in the communal assembly, he carries out animal sacrifices on behalf of the community and he observes a number of prohibitions in his own behaviour. Once his period of 'herding' the community comes to an end, the *halak'a* discharges these responsibilities to the next *halak'a* and himself takes on the more senior status of *dere ade*, or community father. As a *dere ade* he now commands greater respect and can often become highly influential in community matters.

These two cultural systems are not unique to the Gamo Highlands, but are found in various forms throughout much of south-west Ethiopia. In the areas to the north and west of the Gamo Highlands there are traditional kingdoms and chiefdoms where the sacrificial system predominates, while in the areas to the south and east there are many societies with generation grading systems based on organised series of initiations. What is unusual about the Gamo Highlands, located at the overlap of these two broad 'culture areas', is that here these two systems co-exist alongside each other.

Thus there is no overall leader of any *dere*, and sacrificers, *halak'as* and *dere ades* can all make competing claims to seniority and authority. None of these men, however, has the power to impose his will on the community or to make laws or judgements. Instead all community decisions are made at open assemblies in which all male citizens can participate. Decisions are made after lengthy discussions and only when the assembly can come to consensus.

I lived in the highlands for twenty-one months between 1995 and 1997, and spent most of this time in the community of Doko. Doko is the community which presents the particular ethnographic puzzle that will form the focus of this book. It is a reasonably large community and it is located in the northern part of the highlands, not very far from Chencha town and the road down to Arba Minch. It is currently divided into two halves, Doko Masho and Doko Gembela, and I lived in Doko Masho with a family who very kindly took me into their home and quickly involved

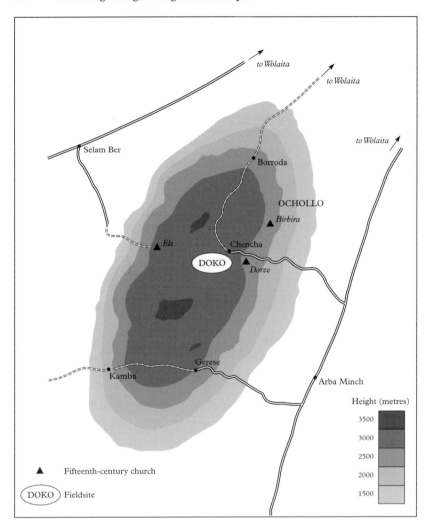

Map 2   Location of Doko in the Gamo Highlands

me in local life. They will appear many times in the pages of this book, and hence deserve some introduction now.

The head of this family was a man named Shagire. In his late sixties or early seventies, Shagire was a respected elder and *dere ade*. He had a reputation for fairness and honesty and he also had a very wicked sense of humour. His wife, Halimbe, was a quiet woman who seemed rather

Plate 1   Shagire (left), Wale (holding Bible) and other family members.

older than her years. She had given birth to four surviving children. The girls, Assani, Shasheto and Tsehainesh, had all married and gone to live with their husbands' families, while the one son, Wale, continued to live with Shagire and Halimbe. Wale was an intelligent man in his thirties. He had six years of school education behind him and was literate in Amharic. He had also trained as a carpenter and thus he spent little time engaged in farming. Much to Shagire's dismay, Wale had refused to be initiated as *halak'a* and had converted to Protestantism some years ago. Instead of participating in many of the ritual activities that his parents felt to be important, he now preferred to go to church on Sundays with his wife, Almaz, and their two young children.

The tensions between the different members of this family will play a large part in our story of social and cultural change in Doko. The story that I am going to tell, though, stretches back in time to the beginning of the nineteenth century and involves a consideration of events beyond the confines of Doko, or even of the Gamo Highlands. In order to understand how the practices of the sacrificial and initiatory systems have changed we will need to consider the causes of these changes and the way in which they have been brought about by the actions of individuals. And in order to understand how the changes in the practices of the initiatory system have resulted in the overall transformation of that system we will need to

Plate 2   Almaz (centre) preparing grain, with Wale's modern house in
the background.

follow through the complicated chain of incremental changes that have
taken place.

Given that I was only in Doko for a short time and given that the micro-
sociological detail that such an analysis requires is unlikely to be retained
in the historical record, it would seem that we have a difficult task before
us. And indeed, reconstructing the precise details of all the events that
actually took place in the past 200 years would be impossible. But this is
not our aim. Our aim, more simply, is to construct a plausible model of
how that change took place.

The structure of the book

In order to construct such a model we will first need to know about the
macro-historical changes that have taken place during the last 200 years or
so, and chapter 2 starts our story by recounting these events. We will also
need to know how these macro-historical changes have changed the local
context in the Gamo Highlands and consider what new opportunities they
have opened up and who was well placed to take advantage of them. This
will be discussed in chapters 3 and 6. In order to understand this fully,
though, we will also need to know something about the distribution of
power in Doko at various times throughout this period and also about the

rules and resources that structure, and have structured, the local social system. This will be discussed in chapters 4 and 5, where the sacrificial system and the initiatory system will be taken in turn.

Having pieced together a picture of the changing context in Doko and of the types of new opportunities that would have become available to certain people at various points in the past 200 years, the analysis then turns to consider how certain individuals would have acted on these opportunities and how other people would have responded to their actions. We will need to look at the types of conflict that would be likely to ensue and the way in which these conflicts would be resolved. And we will also need to consider whether or not the Gamo mode of conflict resolution would be likely to result in decisions to make incremental changes to the 'rules'. All this is the topic of chapter 7.

Then in chapter 8 we can consider how a series of such incremental changes might have iterated and resulted in overall systemic change in the initiatory system. We will piece together a plausible chain of events by considering the change that took place between two known instantiations of the system. With this knowledge of 'before' and 'after' we can extrapolate what is likely to have happened in between. We can construct a plausible model of how the system transformed. Having done this, we must also consider why the changes that took place did not also lead to the transformation of the sacrificial system. And finally, we can discuss more generally why it is that different cultural systems seem to change in different ways.

2   The recent history of the Gamo Highlands

A good starting point for our exploration of the dynamics of cultural change in the Gamo Highlands is to look at some of the large-scale historical changes that were going on in Ethiopia during the nineteenth and twentieth centuries. The nineteenth century saw the increasing involvement of the Horn of Africa in the slave trade and the expansion of the Abyssinian empire southwards towards the vicinity of the Gamo Highlands. This expansion eventually culminated in the establishment of the nation state of Ethiopia at the turn of the century. Since then Ethiopia has seen the development of first a national currency and then taxation, the opening up of new trade and transport opportunities through the increasing use of motorised vehicles, the spread of Protestant ideology by European and North American missionaries, a revolution that brought Marxism to even the remotest parts of the country and, most recently, a new government that has reorganised the country as a federal Republic along ethnic lines.

The nineteenth century: slaves, warfare and internal flux

During the nineteenth century much of the Horn of Africa was involved in the Red Sea Trade. Trade routes extended from the Gulf of Aden port of Zeila southwards through the centre of the Amhara empire and on towards the 'savage' lands of the south. With the exception of only a few periods when political disruption made travel to the south unsafe, merchant caravans had traversed these routes since at least the first century AD. Gold, ivory, precious skins, spices, incense and slaves from the area that is now southern Ethiopia were traded for the salt bar currency known as *amole* and exported across the Red Sea to the Mediterranean countries and Arabia (Abir 1970:119; Bahru 1991:8). During the nineteenth century trade on these routes was flourishing and particularly focused on slaves, as British interference in the East African slave trade had led to a dramatic increase in demand for slaves in Arabia (Abir 1970:123).

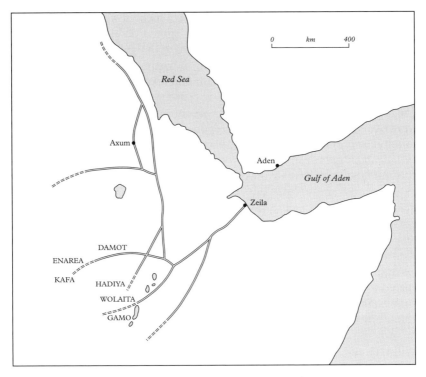

Map 3   Major trade routes in Ethiopia

Lying just a little way off one of the major trade routes, the Gamo Highlands were involved in this slave trade. Unfortunately there are no data
about the local organisation of slave trading at this time, although Marc
Abélès notes how a slave trader in late-nineteenth-century Ochollo was a
very influential man (Abélès 1981:63). Oral histories collected by himself
and Judith Olmstead show clearly that slaves, known as *ayle*, were an important part of Gamo life in the nineteenth century (Olmstead 1973:226–
7; Abélès 1981:42). All Gamo communities were made up of three different categories of people: citizens (*mala*), artisans (*ts'omma*) and slaves
(*ayle*). Only *mala* could own land and only they could become community sacrificers or initiates. *Ts'omma* consisted of marginalised groups of
mana, who worked as potters, and *degala*, who worked as tanners.[3] *Ayle*
were at the bottom of the hierarchy and spent most of their time working
for their *mala* masters.

Older people remember that many farmers used slave labour to farm
large areas of land and wars were fought between different Gamo communities in order to capture slaves. Nineteenth-century Gamo warfare

was highly regulated and there were certain allocated war grounds where the two communities would meet on an agreed date for battle, before going home in the evening and then returning to fight again the next day. Men who succeeded in killing an enemy in battle, and bringing home his penis as proof, were given great honour and took the title of 'killer'.

Once one community succeeded in gaining the upper hand, the defeated community became its vassal. According to Judy Olmstead there were two kinds of vassal community: one kind owed the dominant community support in future wars, and was known as either 'child community' (*yelo dere*) or 'spear community' (*tora dere*), while the other kind owed agricultural labour, and was known as either 'wife community' (*mach'o dere*) or 'slave community' (*ayle dere*). Citizens of 'slave communities' remained living at home, but had to work for specific individuals in the dominant community as well. Olmstead writes that 'the victorious warriors would race through the conquered *dere*, pillaging and claiming households as their own' (Olmstead 1973:227). The defeated community would then become a district of the dominant community and its *kawo* would be relegated to the status of district sacrificer, while the *kawo* of the dominant community exerted his power over the whole federation. The defeated community would maintain its own assemblies, and continue to make its own initiates. When the defeated community felt strong enough, it could try and win back its autonomy by going back to war with the dominating community. In some cases the dominant community would grant rebellious communities equal status rather than see the break up of a large political unit and in this way large federations could become stable (Abélès 1981:42–5).

Thus we can see that the process of inter-*dere* warfare, driven by the desire to capture slaves, led to a constant flux in the organisation of Gamo *deres*. Throughout the nineteenth century, federations of *deres* were expanding and fragmenting as small *deres* were conquered and then regained their independence, and then were conquered by other *deres*. When a *dere* that had previously been autonomous became part of a larger *dere*, its internal structure was essentially unchanged, and thus *deres* developed a multi-scalar nature whereby both large polities and the smaller districts that constituted them were called by the same term and had the same internal structure.

Towards the end of the nineteenth century, while the communities of the Gamo Highlands were fighting each other, the northern Abyssinian empire came out of a period of decline, and began to nurture expansionist ideas. Under Emperor Menelik II the northern empire started a series of campaigns to expand its influence southwards. Starting with the defeat of Gurage in 1875, Menelik's troops moved southwards, conquering the local peoples and incorporating them into what was to become the nation state of Ethiopia. Some groups submitted peacefully and quickly agreed to pay tribute, while others resisted and were subsequently conquered and pillaged (Donham 1985:32).

In 1894 Menelik's troops reached the kingdom of Wolaita, just north of the Gamo Highlands. The Wolaita king, *kawo* Tona, was determined to resist Menelik, and there followed one of the bloodiest battles in the whole of this period. An eye witness reports, 'One had the feeling of watching some kind of infernal hunting where human beings rather than animals served as game' (Vanderheym 1896:181, cited in Bahru 1991:65). Witnessing such a massacre, the peoples of the Gamo Highlands submitted quickly to Menelik's advances in 1897. Thus began a period of dramatic change in the Gamo Highlands.

The Imperial era, 1897–1973

Changing power relations

Menelik's administration of the south-west relied on a network of garrison towns, manned by northern soldiers (Donham 1985:33), and in the Gamo Highlands the small town of Chencha was built on land taken from the communities of Dorze, Doko and Chencha to serve as the administrative centre in that area, while smaller towns, such as Ezzo, Gulta, Gerese, Baza and Kamba, were founded as local administrative outposts elsewhere in the highlands. For the most part the Amhara[4] northerners stayed in the town and the Gamo villagers stayed in the countryside. Initially there was little mixing of the people, and the Gamo avoided the Amhara markets, their court and their Orthodox church rituals (Bureau 1981:34).

The northern governors had to rely on indirect rule through local leaders, whom they appointed to the position of *balabbat*. In the southern Ethiopian communities that had submitted peacefully to Menelik, the kings were made *balabbat*, while in those that had resisted, such as Wolaita, the highest ranks of the indigenous political hierarchy were eliminated and lower-level offices were incorporated into the administrative hierarchy (Donham 1985:34). The communities of the Gamo Highlands had submitted peacefully, and thus the *dere kawos* were appointed as *balabbats*, intermediaries between their people and the state, whose tasks included collecting tribute and settling disputes. The appointment of *kawos* as *balabbats* had two major consequences. On the one hand it confirmed the traditional legitimacy of the *kawo*, and on the other it transformed the role of the *kawo* so that he took on certain responsibilities and privileges associated with the national government (Bureau 1978:279). The *kawo* was awarded quasi-ownership of all *dere* land, and he could exact corvée labour from his *dere* 'subjects' (Bureau 1978:282; Abélès 1981:61). He also became a juridical official and was in charge of the local police. All criminal cases were to be brought to the new courts, but first they were heard by the *balabbat*. The Ochollo *balabbat* even had a local jail built next to his house (Abélès 1981:62). Many *balabbats* enjoyed their new privileges, and they started to copy Amhara dress and language as they made the most of their transformed political role.

The system of *balabbat* landowners and peasant tenants was a northern Ethiopian system, and it required massive reorientation of traditional systems throughout southern Ethiopia (Donham 1986:39). The role of the Gamo *kawo* was radically altered from senior sacrificer to political leader, and the role of the average Gamo man was transformed from landowner to tenant farmer. Such a system was not accepted easily, and had to be imposed by force. Amhara soldiers settled in the highlands and, armed with rifles, enforced the new administration. These soldier-settlers were known as *neftenya*, and they had to be fed and supported by the local farmers (Donham 1985:36). Each *neftenya* was appointed a number of Gamo families as his *gebbar*, who had to provide him with food and services while he was stationed in the area. This system was extremely exploitative, and this was not an easy time for the Gamo people.

This period came to an end in 1936 when the Italians occupied the country. The Italians abolished the *gebbar* system and gave much more freedom to the people of southern Ethiopia (Donham 1985:37; Bureau 1981:35). During their few years of occupation they set about building some infrastructure in the south, most importantly a network of roads. In the Gamo Highlands one or two basic mud roads were cleared, and the Italians made themselves popular by paying for local labour, rather than demanding it corvée-style (Bureau 1981:36). Although their presence was relatively brief, and the development they planned did not reach fruition, the simple roads built at this time are still used today.

In 1941 the Italian occupation came to an end, and Emperor Haile-Selassie returned to the throne. For the next thirty years or so he ruled Ethiopia with a firm hand, becoming increasingly autocratic as the years went by. With a strong, centralised government, the provincial governors lost considerable power, and, with their immediate superiors relatively uninfluential, the *balabbats* gained more control during this time (Donham 1985:39). This was even though the administrative system was modernised and bureaucratised in these years, and the official role of the *balabbats* was substantially reduced (Bureau 1978:283). The *gebbar* system was not reintroduced, and tribute and corvée labour were replaced by taxes that went to the central administration. The *balabbat* had the job of collecting taxes, and this was a period characterised by corruption and exploitation, as many *balabbats* took bribes, appropriated land, and generally abused their power (Bureau 1978:283; Abélès 1981:62).

The powerful and exploitative character of the *balabbat* contrasted strongly with the previous role of the *kawo*. Tensions mounted as the people of the highlands could see that their *kawos* were not behaving as they ought to. During this period a solution was found by separating the role of *balabbat* from that of *kawo*. In most *deres* the role of *kawo* continued to be inherited agnatically, while the role of *balabbat* was often given to younger brothers, to uterine kin or to wives. In Bonke, for example, the roles of *kawo* and *balabbat* were dissociated after only one generation, as the eldest son of the *kawo-balabbat* became *kawo* and the second son became *balabbat*. In Ganta the dissociation took place after two generations of *kawo-balabbats*, when the sister of the *kawo* was made *balabbat* (Bureau 1978:285). In other *deres* the dissociation took place after three or more generations, and it was not unusual for a woman to take on the role of *balabbat*. These women were often strong characters, and despite the contradictions surrounding women leaders in the predominantly male arena of Gamo politics, they frequently managed to exert considerable influence (Olmstead 1997). Doko was perhaps a little unusual in that it was one of the few *deres* where the roles of *kawo* and *balabbat* were not dissociated, and where in fact the *kawo-balabbat* was not too exploitative and was much respected. This, though, was the exception that proved the rule, and by the 1970s most Gamo highlanders were extremely resentful of their *balabbats*.

Religious alternatives

The Imperial period was thus marked by much turbulent change in the lives of the people of the Gamo Highlands. The new political reality meant that there was a massive decrease in their freedom and autonomy and a degree of exploitation that had been unknown in their recent past. In this difficult situation people tried to improve their lives and alleviate their ills through the medium of religion. And with the opening of the area to new peoples and its connection with the broader Ethiopian state, there were a number of external influences and new religions that were important during this time.

Orthodox Christianity First of all, the Amhara settlers brought with them Orthodox Christianity. Although not entirely new to the area, as attested by the fifteenth-century churches in the northern highlands,

Orthodox practice was fairly negligible in the nineteenth century, except perhaps in the immediate vicinity of the old churches. But with the arrival of the *neftenya*, the Orthodox religion took on new life in the highlands. Although there was much initial hostility to the Amhara and their religion, the images and the ceremony of the church soon began to attract attention (Abélès n.d.:193). And it also became clear that involvement in the Orthodox church was a good way to gain influence with the Amhara. Since Orthodoxy did not interfere too much with traditional practices, many people nominally became Orthodox while continuing to participate in sacrifices and initiations. During the latter part of this period many new Orthodox churches were built, including one in Dambo in Doko Masho.

Essa Woga At the turn of the century, soon after the Amhara had arrived, an indigenous religious movement started up. Its leader was a man from the *dere* of Zad'a, called Essa Ditha (Abélès n.d.:189; Olmstead 1973:229; Sperber 1973:218). Essa walked over the highlands preaching his new tradition, to become known as *Essa Woga*, in contrast to the old tradition, or *beni woga*. The central point of Essa's teaching was the abolition of sacrifices and sacrificers. He taught that offerings should not be made to the spirits, and that only God should be honoured. Instead of the hierarchical arrangement by which seniors sacrificed for their juniors on all levels of society, each man should, on his own, make offerings of honey directly to God. Essa exhorted the Gamo people to stop respecting their *kawos* and to treat them as regular people. In Doko I was told that Essa had also instigated a number of fast days, and that he told people to slaughter and eat animals, because more animals would magically come. Thus Essa's revisionary movement can be seen as a kind of cult of resistance against the Amhara and the new powers of the *kawo-balabbat*. And like many such cults it had a messianic element to it. Essa promised that soon a new *kawo* would come from the earth, accompanied by a goat, and bring about a new and fair social order (Abélès n.d.:189).

It is worth noting that while Essa strongly attacked the sacrificial system, he actually encouraged the initiatory system. People in Ochollo recall him saying 'Next to the house of God are those of the *halak'as*' (Abélès n.d.:189). And the rest of Gamo tradition was taken as given; thus the form of marriages, singing, dancing, funerals and so on were unaffected by *Essa Woga*.

Essa's teaching was remarkably popular at first, and seems to have been adopted all over the Gamo Highlands. In Dorze it was popular in peripheral areas, although it was avoided in the area of Amara where the *kawo* lived (Sperber 1973:218). It was unanimously adopted in Ochollo, and contemporary elders in Doko recall that the whole community followed

Essa, with the exception of just one man. For three years Doko did not perform any sacrifices, and juniors slaughtered animals without the permission of their seniors. People fasted on Fridays, and made offerings of honey in their own homes. However, a few years of bad harvest followed, and people began to doubt the efficacy of Essa's *woga*. The new *kawo* had not come, and the *dere* had problems. Essa had been arrested, and was in prison in Addis Abeba (Abélès n.d.:189). The people of Doko sent an assignment of *halak'as* to an important diviner in Dorze Amara and asked what they should do. The diviner told them to return to *beni woga*, and most people in Doko did as he said. The sacrificial system was reintroduced, and the *kawos* returned to their former positions. The same happened in Ochollo, and in most of the Gamo communities. This turnaround seems to have been remarkably smooth, and as Abélès writes, 'the ritual organisation had definitely been shaken up, but its foundation remained solid' (n.d.:190).

Not everyone, though, returned to the practices exactly as they had been done before. A number of people in Doko, and throughout the highlands, continued to refuse to ask their seniors to sacrifice for them. And instead of returning to the traditional offerings of barley porridge to the spirits, they continued with the simple offerings of honey to God. Although these people continued to practice a form of *Essa Woga*, they partook in all aspects of communal life that were not associated with the sacrificial system, and thus were not seen as a terribly disruptive element. Such followers of *Essa Woga* were still going strong in the 1990s.

Protestant Christianity Although Essa's revisionist cult had proven unsustainable, the tensions that it had addressed, particularly the inequality and exploitation that was increasingly felt to be characteristic of the sacrificial system, remained active in Gamo life. In fact they became more and more extreme in the 1920s and 1930s as the number of northerners in the area increased. It was in this situation that the first Protestant missionaries arrived in the highlands.

The first white missionaries came with the Sudan Interior Mission (SIM), an organisation of non-demoninational fundamental Christian evangelists (Fargher 1988), and visited parts of the Gamo Highlands in the 1930s. They went to Ochollo and addressed its inhabitants in the assembly place. According to one story, the missionaries exhorted the assembly to believe in Jesus Christ, and ridiculed traditional practices. Having heard of Essa, the missionaries threw a leaf into the air and let it fall to the ground, and then said, 'If honey falls to the earth like the leaf, how could God consume it? Do you also believe that God drinks the blood of your sacrificial animals?' When the people of Ochollo heard the strangers speak these words they refused to listen to them any longer, and chased them away (Abélès n.d.:191).

The introduction of Protestant Christianity in the neighbouring area of Wolaita went rather more smoothly. Although initially hostile to the attacks on their tradition, the people of Wolaita soon found meaning in the Protestant teachings. Perhaps because their traditional system had long been more hierarchical and exploitative, they quickly embraced the more individualistic and egalitarian teachings of the Protestants. When the foreign missionaries were forced to leave after the Italian occupation, local converts continued evangelising with renewed zest and rigour, and within a few years the vast majority of Wolaita people had become 'believers'. The rapid spread of the Protestant faith in Wolaita surprised even the SIM missionaries when they returned some years later, and was said to be a great miracle (Davis 1966).

The conversion of Wolaita had its repercussions in the Gamo Highlands. In the 1940s a respected man from Ochollo went to Wolaita, and was there converted to Protestantism. This man, *halak'a* Gembo, then returned to Ochollo, accompanied by two Wolaita 'believers', and began to try to evangelise his own people. Much of the 1940s and 1950s in Ochollo was characterised by a religious war between Gembo and the Protestants, and the *balabbat* and the Orthodox. Individuals converted to one religion, and then changed their minds and converted to the other (Abélès n.d.:191–2). While the Orthodox could continue participating in sacrifices and initiations, the Protestants had to give up most aspects of their tradition. Not only could they not participate in sacrifices and initiations, but neither could they have more than one wife, join in the singing and dancing at celebrations, or drink alcohol.

Although this religious struggle was taking place in Ochollo, it did not at this time spread much further into the highlands. An SIM mission was set up in Chencha town, but local government officials were unfriendly and openly antagonistic towards the missionaries (Fargher 1988:512). The people of Dorze were staunchly Orthodox, and were not interested in this foreign religion. The people of Doko were not about to stop initiating *halak'as*, and attempts to introduce them to Protestantism at this time were singularly unsuccessful. It seems that the Protestant message did not filter much further into the highlands during these two decades.

It was only in the 1960s that Protestantism began to be taken up in the Gamo Highlands. Through SIM support, a school was built in Ochollo. The local Ochollo teachers taught the basics, and then sent the students to the mission school in Chencha town to complete their secondary education. In this way, the majority of Ochollo youth were converted (Abélès n.d.:193). By the late 1960s Protestantism was beginning to spread to

Doko, also via people who had been converted during visits to Wolaita. However, the hostility to the Protestant church was still pronounced, and even during this time there were few converts in Doko Masho, although there were more in Doko Gembela. The Gembela community built a church in Shaye, and in 1973 the fledgling Protestant community in Doko Masho built a small church in Yoira. The slower uptake of Protestantism in Doko Masho, compared to Doko Gembela, is still evident today, and, as I shall argue in chapter 8, can be explained in terms of the more hierarchical form of the Doko Gembela initiations. But on the eve of the revolution, Doko Masho had few converts to Protestantism, while Doko Gembela was considerably missionised.

Transport, trade and weaving

Other important changes centred around the increasing integration of the Gamo Highlands into the developing and modernising state of Ethiopia. In the early part of the century Ethiopian currency was introduced, replacing the iron bars (*march'o*) and salt bars (*amole*) that had been used before. First *Marie-Theresa Thallers*, and then the Ethiopian *birr*, were brought into the highlands, and became the predominant means of payment of government tax and for purchases in the local markets.

In the 1960s outside influence became more direct. The town of Arba Minch was founded, and the provincial administration moved there from Chencha. A lowland road connecting Arba Minch to the town of Soddo in Wolaita and on to Addis Abeba was completed, providing a better route than the muddy highland road. This route was soon plied by buses, thus making Addis Abeba only a day's journey from Arba Minch. In the early 1970s some enterprising Dorze men joined with some *neftenya* merchants in Chencha town and formed a transport co-operative that would bring buses and taxis right up into the highlands. By 1971 they owned a bus that travelled the Addis Abeba–Arba Minch route, another bus that went between Addis Abeba and Chencha, and two taxis that linked Chencha to Arba Minch (Olmstead 1973:232).

Many men in the *deres* around Chencha and Dorze had taken up weaving during the early part of the century, and as transport links improved, some of them began to sell their cloth in Addis Abeba and other urban centres. The Dorze men were the trendsetters in this regard, and by the 1970s many of them spent most of their year in Addis Abeba, returning home only for the *Mesqalla* celebrations of the New Year. Some men from other *deres* also went weaving in urban centres, but the number of migrant weavers from *deres* more than a few miles from Dorze or Chencha was considerably less, and for this reason all weavers from the Gamo Highlands came to be known generically as 'Dorze' by other townspeople (e.g. Mesfin in press). By 1971 77 per cent of Dorze men made a living predominantly from weaving[5] (Olmstead 1973:230). The majority of these men maintained a house and a wife in Dorze, and returned home to settle after some years. With only a small percentage of Dorze men working the land at any one time though, agricultural labour needed to be found elsewhere, and for the most part men from other Gamo communities were hired by their wealthier Dorze neighbours. Working for room, board and a cash wage, these men farmed Dorze land, and returned to their communities with cash in their pockets (1973:232).

Other men took advantage of the improved transport links to become merchants and traders. From Addis Abeba they brought second-hand salvage clothes (known as *selbaj*), plastic plates and jugs, pens and notebooks, coloured thread, scrap metal, and so on. These would then be sold in Chencha and Dorze markets, where local traders would buy them and take them further into the highlands. Imports outnumbered exports in the Gamo Highlands, but traders would take spun cotton and woven cloth to markets in various urban centres, and some animal hides were sold to tanneries in the capital.

As more and more men went away weaving and trading, and more and more men worked as hired agricultural labourers, the Gamo Highlands became increasingly integrated into the national economy, and local people became more knowledgeable about life outside of the highlands. People saw the secondary school and hospital in Arba Minch, and demanded schools and clinics up in the highlands where they lived (Bureau 1979a:210). Those who had been to Addis Abeba felt the buzz of vibrant urban life, learned to speak Amharic and talked to people from different cultures and backgrounds, and became more aware of the ins and outs of national politics. When they returned to the highlands, they came as knowledgeable and cosmopolitan individuals who felt very much part of an Ethiopian state.

Revolution and the Derg government, 1974–91

The increasingly autocratic government of emperor Haile-Selassie, and the contradictions between an essentially feudal system and processes of modernisation, set up tensions that eventually erupted into revolution. In 1974 Haile-Selassie was overthrown, and the Imperial throne of Ethiopia came to an end. Some years of confusion, power struggles and violence followed, but by 1978 Mengistu Haile-Mariam had emerged as the totalitarian leader of the new Marxist-Leninist military regime, commonly known as the Derg. For the next fifteen years or so the Derg government ruled Ethiopia and embarked on a process of development and transformation that would affect even the most far-flung of its peoples.

Soon after the revolution all universities and secondary schools were closed, and the students were sent out into the countryside to teach the socialist values of the new government. These young men and women of the Development Through Cooperation campaign became known as *zamach* (Amh: campaigners), and with greater or lesser degrees of sensitivity they gathered together local elders and told them to change their ways. Their role was to nationalise land, build schools, bring basic health education and modernise what Mengistu saw as a backward and superstitious peasantry. This involved the abolition of all religious practices except Orthodox Christianity and Islam, including all traditional practices that were deemed to be exploitative or hierarchical.

In the Gamo Highlands the *zamacha*, as they were locally called, taught that everybody was equal, that the *kawo*, the regular farmer and the artisan were all brothers. Stirred up by the campaigners, most communities expelled their *balabbats* and looted their houses and property. Many *balabbats* were forced to flee the highlands, and they sought sanctuary in Arba Minch or Addis Abeba. The situation in Doko was somewhat unusual. This was one of the few *deres* where the *balabbat* was still the *kawo*, and *kawo-balabbat* Darza had managed to carry out his roles with a degree of honesty and fairness that was unparalleled in other communities. The campaigners who went to Doko also seem by chance to have been rather more flexible and sensitive to cultural values than most. Thus when the other communities were expelling their *balabbats*, Darza stayed put and Doko decided to keep him as their *kawo*.

The campaigners forced the people of the highlands to stop their 'backward traditions'. All sacrifices were banned, and sacrificers were to be treated like other people. Initiations were also banned, and any status differential between farmer-citizens and artisans was rendered illegal. In short, most aspects of traditional Gamo life were banned. Land was nationalised, and there was some redistribution such that land was taken from richer families and given to those who were poorer. The previously landless artisans were all given small plots of land, and told that now they could farm it like everybody else. The extent of land redistribution varied throughout the highlands however, and in Doko it seems to have been fairly minimal.

The words of the campaigners were initially greeted with enthusiasm by most people in Doko. The teachings of equality resonated with the earlier teachings of Essa, and many people embraced them. People in different social positions, of course, reacted differently. Those with most to lose were more resistant, while those with most to gain jumped on the socialist bandwagon with vigour. The artisans, for example, became ardent socialists, and used the backing of the new government to press their case for equality. The campaigners gave them land, and forced *mala* farmers to accept them into their workgroups so they would hoe the land together. They also gave them places on the new local Peasant Associations and exhorted farmers and artisans to eat together. Most farmers considered this to be going too far with equality, and there was some resistance. For example, when an artisan woman died in 1980, the farmers could not bring themselves to bury her in the communal burial ground, traditionally reserved for the farmers but now officially open to all. Instead she was buried in the separate artisan burial place, against the government rules. The artisans however, flushed with the excitement of their increased status and power, protested against this. One of them, a fiery character called Kampo, decided to take the case to the court in Chencha town and demand that she be reburied with the farmers. He returned from town accompanied by police and cadres and set about digging up the corpse. When the corpse was uncovered the stench was so terrible that the farmers begged the police to let them leave it there, and they promised that in the future all the artisans would be buried in the regular farmer burial places. The Peasant Association chairman ran away to Addis, fearing that he would be put in prison for allowing the initial burial to have taken place, and from then on all artisans who died were buried with the farmers. Kampo used to go to each burial to check that they were buried in the right place, walking all over Doko in his mission.

For the most part the campaigners were successful in stopping the practices that they thought were backward, including both the sacrifices and the initiations. After they left, the local administration continued their work and by the late 1970s they had also banned Protestantism, as 'foreign' practices became to be seen to be as bad as 'backward' traditional practices. But it was the attack against traditional practices that affected most people in Doko. During this period people say that no sacrifices were performed. Neither the *kawo* nor any of the local sacrificers carried out their traditional roles, and the elaborate practices of clan seniority, which had previously affected the order in which people starting sowing their land, were given up. The sacrificial system, attacked before by *Essa Woga*, seemed finally to be crumbling under the impact of the Derg. The initiatory system, in contrast, proved remarkably resilient. Its centrality and importance to Doko life were such that people adapted it to the new conditions. *Halak'as* were initiated in secret. People say that there was not one year when there was no *halak'a*. But instead of making many *halak'as* each year, it was honed down to a minimum of one. And elements of the ritual were changed. Instead of erecting large bamboo poles in the *halak'a*'s compound, for example, small bamboo twigs were stuck in the ground so that the local government spies and officials would not notice. Instead of publicly parading in the market place, the new *halak'a* kept out of the public eye, and paraded secretly in a small assembly place high in the mountains. Many of the necessary feasts were scaled down to their bare essentials, and the initiates promised to make up the debt some time in the future. In this way the initiatory system kept going throughout the period of the Derg government. Given that a great many of Doko cultural practices effectively came to a halt in this period, this is a truly remarkable fact.

In 1990 the people of Doko Masho went one step further. The elders got together and decided to ask the administration in Arba Minch for permission to make *halak'as* and follow their customs. They sent a letter, written in the hand of Desta, son of *kawo* Darza, which explained how their traditional practices caused the *dere* to be well and kept away hunger and disease. They ended it with the following request: 'We are asking your office to understand that our customs are useful, and not harmful. We respectfully apply for permission to perform our customs, and to thus alleviate the problems that we are currently facing.' Fifteen men put their thumb prints to this letter, and it was taken to the Department of Culture and Sports in Arba Minch. The head of that office was a local man who had been one of the *zamacha* in Doko Masho. He rather admired Gamo culture, and he tacitly gave his permission. Thus in the final years of the Derg government *halak'as* were being initiated openly in Doko Masho.

For many people in Doko, though, the most significant thing about the Derg period was the wealth that came to the community. One of the original tasks of the campaigners was to set up service co-operatives, and one was set up in both Doko Masho and Doko Gembela, and others were formed in every community throughout the highlands. These co-operatives were supposed to collect contributions from all their members and then to buy materials from Addis Abeba and sell them locally at minimum cost. Thus the service co-operatives provided coloured thread for the weavers, metal for the blacksmiths, exercise books for the school children, and other things such as salt and sugar. After a year or so, however, most of the co-operatives descended into in-fighting and corruption. In many communities one or two people became very rich at the expense of the local populace, and the local experiment in socialism was, by and large, a failure.

Doko, though, was unusual. Both the Doko Masho and the Doko Gembela co-operatives were phenomenally successful. By the late 1980s the Doko Gembela co-operative owned two trucks, while Doko Masho surpassed all other communities and owned four trucks. These trucks took people and produce between Addis Abeba and the highlands, and were frequently rented out by the other co-operatives in the area. Run by astute and yet honest men, the Doko Masho co-operative made such a profit that exercise books could be given, rather than sold, to the school children, and every year free salt was given to each household at the New Year. This period, then, was one of plenty for the people of Doko, and it is often fondly remembered.

People's worst memories of this period, though, are of army conscription. During the mid to late eighties many young men were conscripted into the National Military Service, and went to fight in northern Ethiopia. Those who came back often returned with the glory of a killer, and many of them went through the traditional ritual of ear-piercing that honoured such men. But as the fighting in the north got worse, increasing numbers of men did not return and people began to fear and resent conscription. Mothers worried about their sons fighting wars with unknown people, and young men tried to remain elusive when officials came looking for them. Thus the fighting that would eventually lead to the fall of the Derg also cast a shadow over life in the Gamo Highlands.

The EPRDF government, 1991 onwards

In May 1991, following years of unrest in northern Ethiopia, particularly in the provinces of Tigray and Eritrea, Mengistu's government was in its turn overthrown, and the Ethiopian Peoples' Revolutionary Democratic Front (EPRDF), led by Meles Zenawi, marched into Addis Abeba and took power. A short period of turmoil followed, as the country descended into chaos before a strong rule of law was enforced. Towns were looted, powerful leaders under the last regime were murdered or expelled, and old scores were settled. The Gamo Highlands managed not to descend into this chaos, as despite the efforts of the *zamacha*, much day-to-day life was still managed, overtly or covertly, by local people and institutions, and not by the state. Thus the fall of the state did not leave a political vacuum, and the rioting and looting that swept the country at this time did not impinge much on Gamo Highlands life.

Over the next year the EPRDF formed a transitional government and soon the rule of state law was returned. A few years later the transitional government became the nationally elected government, and Ethiopia entered into yet another new phase of her history. Although continuing the general socialist ethos of the previous government, the EPRDF has reversed many of the trends of the Derg. Religious freedom has been reintroduced, and Protestant churches have been allowed to function again. This has resulted in a massive wave of conversions throughout the Gamo

Highlands. In Doko Gembela the vast majority of young people now belong to the church, and a number of older people have also joined. In Doko Masho the growth has been slower, but there is still a burgeoning community of young believers. The small church built before the Derg period cannot hold the current numbers, and a new building is being constructed. When it is finished it will be by far the largest and most impressive building in Doko Masho. The Protestants turn their back on much of traditional Gamo life, claiming that it is the work of Satan. They do not participate in sacrifices or initiations, and they only participate in weddings, funerals and assemblies in a modified way. All but the lax do not drink or smoke, and they prefer their songs about Jesus to the traditional Gamo songs. The conversion of many of the young people in the Gamo Highlands has thus led to some tension between traditionalists and Protestants, particularly in families split by belief.

The EPRDF has also reversed the Derg's policies about traditional practices. In reaction to the Derg's attempts to create a nation of modern 'Ethiopians', the new government is trying to organise the state into a federation of mini-states according to ethnicity. The internal map of Ethiopia has been redrawn along ethnic lines, and a federal state structure that theoretically guarantees the unrestricted right of nations and nationalities to self-determination up to secession has been adopted. Local languages are now being used in schools instead of Amharic, and the process of writing down these previously oral languages is well under way. In this context traditional practices are actively encouraged as an expression of ethnic and cultural identity, and thus those who have not converted to Protestantism are going through something of a cultural revival.

In many parts of the Gamo Highlands this has been expressed by a return to the traditional practices banned by the Derg. In the early 1990s in Doko Masho, for example, the elders called an assembly to discuss the problems of the *dere*. There had been a few years of bad harvest, and, as in the time of Essa, the elders decided that this had been caused because they had not been following *woga* properly. They argued that treating the artisans the same as farmers was a serious infringement of taboo, or *gome*, and that their former low status should be reinstated. The land that had been given to them was forcibly taken back, and they were removed from the Peasant Association council. A few days later an artisan man died and, despite Kampo's protests, he was buried in the separate artisan burial place. Furthermore, while the artisans were mourning, the farmers went and dug up the bones of all the artisans who had been buried in the farmer burial place and threw them into the same grave. When the artisans found out they were furious, but now that their state backing had gone, they were powerless. Kampo came with his spear and threatened to kill someone for this atrocity, but the farmers outnumbered him and his neighbours held him back and took away his spear. In this rather dramatic way the 'traditional' distinction between farmers and artisans was revived.

Not all traditional practices were revived however. Different communities in the highlands made different decisions – few other communities, for example, have taken back land from the artisans – and it is not the case that all old practices were simply reproduced as they had been before the Derg came to power. Certain practices have been tacitly allowed to drop by the wayside, while the reintroduction of others is being heatedly debated in series of assemblies that span months or years. Other practices, by contrast, were quickly reinstated straight after the fall of the Derg, and have continued since then in seeming stability around all the debates. A simple generalisation that can be made from this complex process of discussion and debate is that, on the whole, the sacrificial system is fading in importance, while the initiatory system is the locus of most cultural efflorescence. The reasons for this disparity will be one of the main themes of this book, but it is worth noting here that this pattern is a continuation of a process that has been unfolding in different contexts throughout the whole of the twentieth century: sacrificers are on the decline, initiates are on the ascent.

Doko, 1995–7

When I first passed through Doko in 1995, during the New Year festival of *Mesqalla*, *halak'as* were visible in the market place in full ceremonial attire and people were stopping on the path to wish each other the traditional New Year's greeting, '*yo-ho-o!*' The excitement of the celebration was palpable, and traditional practice seemed to be in full swing. When I returned there to live in 1996 my opinion was not much changed. Doko was a place with a vibrant cultural life and traditional practices were an important part of most people's lives. *Kawo* Darza had died a few years ago, and his son Desta was about to be installed as the new *kawo*. *Halak'as* were being initiated with flourish, and assemblies were taking place at least once a week.

There was perhaps a special buzz to cultural life at this time though, as people were still celebrating their ability to follow their customs as they liked. More importantly, people were still in the process of deciding what practices should be reinstated post-Derg, and what should be allowed to fade into the past. Clan assemblies discussed the possibility of performing clan sacrifices that had not been performed for twenty years; community assemblies discussed holding the women's *maraʔe* ceremony that had not been held for a similar period; and inter-community assemblies discussed how and whether they should renew their peace treaties. In these assemblies, then, cultural life was actively being re-created.

At the same time people in Doko were actively engaged in making the most of many of the non-cultural opportunities that were now open to them. The junior school in Masho, founded in the late 1960s and taught by local teachers trained in Arba Minch, was full of children attending half the day and working on the farm or at home for the rest of the day. Once they had finished the six grades, some of them went on to the secondary school in Chencha town, walking an hour there and back daily. As the number of children making this trek had grown, the community had decided that their school should be extended to grades 7 and 8. On their own initiative they have collected contributions from everybody, and have started to build a new school block to house the extra classrooms. The construction was well under way during my stay.

Other people prefer to gain experience outside of the highlands, and the number of migrant weavers from Doko has steadily increased. Nowadays most families have at least one member who has spent some time weaving in Addis Abeba, Wolaita or elsewhere. Still others have become traders, and the elite few have made it to university or college in one of the major urban centres in the country. Doko continues to be an enterprising community, and during the time of my fieldwork they were trying to set up a generator in the market place in Doko Masho, so that there would be electric light in the bars during the evening. The scheme worked for a number of months, making Doko Masho market the only place in the whole of the highlands that had electricity, surpassing even Chencha town.

The past two centuries, then, have been a time of great change in the Gamo Highlands and in the community of Doko. External events in Ethiopia and beyond have impacted on the Gamo Highlands, causing change in most areas of life, religious and secular. In this chapter we have seen some of the ways that life in Doko changed over this time and how people have accommodated to new situations, resisted unwelcome impositions and taken advantage of new opportunities. In the rest of this book we will focus on a more narrow range of activities and seek to understand in detail how they have changed over the past two centuries and how the external events discussed here have *caused* that change.

The activities we will focus on are the performance of sacrifices and initiations. These activities are the backbone of cultural life in the highlands and are part of a broader politico-ritual system that sets up various types of hierarchical relations between men. Throughout this century there have been changes in the meaning of these rituals and in the way that they have been performed. In order to understand the nature of these changes and the causal relations that brought them about we must first provide some background sociological information and then look at the contemporary organisation of both the sacrifices and the initiations.

3   Production and reproduction

Communities

The people of the Gamo Highlands live in communities called *dere*. These communities are small, autonomous political units and there is no overall Gamo polity that unites all the people of the highlands. As a result of the patterns of conquest and rebellion in the nineteenth century, most *deres* have a fractal-like internal structure so that large *deres* are made up of several smaller *deres*, which are in turn made up of yet smaller *deres*. Now that warfare has ceased, these federations are reasonably stable. And because even the smallest unit of *dere* governs its own matters to a very large extent, large federations can today remain nominally intact while the constituent *deres* look after most of their own affairs. The large federation of the K'ogota, just north of Doko, for example, includes the *deres* of Chencha, Doina, Birbira, Ezzo and several others. Each of these is about the size of Doko, and thus the K'ogota is one of the largest federations in the highlands. Although representatives from each *dere* meet every week or so at an assembly in Chencha, where they discuss certain ritual matters which unite the federation, for the most part these *deres* are fairly autonomous and there is a great deal of variation in their internal cultural practices.

The *dere* of Doko is itself a reasonably large *dere* in the present context of the Gamo Highlands, and has a population of about 20,000 people (Population and Housing Census 1994:314–15). It is made up of two medium-sized *deres*, called Doko Masho and Doko Gembela, each with a population of approximately 10,000 people. And each of these medium-sized *deres* further sub-divides into even smaller *deres*, each with a population between 1,000 and 2,500. There are eight small *deres* within Doko Masho, and these are Shale, Woits'o, Masho, Ch'ento, Yoira, Dambo, Gedeno and Eleze. And in Doko Gembela there are nine – Kale, Shaye, Dalo, Ts'ida, Zad'a, Upper Losh, Lower Losh, Zolo and Elo. Figure 1 shows their respective locations.

There are three essential factors that define a typical *dere*. Every *dere* should have a senior sacrificer who sacrifices for the well-being of the *dere*

Figure 1   The *deres* of Doko

and symbolises the unity of the community. Every *dere* should also make its own initiates. And finally, every *dere* should have its own assembly place where men meet to discuss communal matters. Thus there is a senior sacrificer, called *kawo*, for Doko as a whole, and, with one or two exceptions, also senior sacrificers, known by the generic term *ek'k'a* (lit: sacrificer), for all the constituent *deres*. Likewise, the *dere* of Doko makes its own initiates, called *dana*, while Doko Masho and Doko Gembela both initiate their own *hudhughas*, and all of the smaller *deres* initiate their own *halak'as*. And each *dere*, at whichever scale, has its own assembly place.

The term *dere* is used to refer to both the people and the land and it is common to hear people say things like 'the *dere* decided to perform the sacrifice on Thursday' or 'the *dere* really needs some rain now'. And when arriving home from travels it would be natural to ask how the *dere* is. Groupings smaller than a *dere*, in contrast, are rarely spoken about in this way. Within *deres* there are neighbourhoods, called *guta*, consisting of between approximately forty and sixty households. These neighbourhoods have no formal structure, no sacrificer, initiate or assembly place, and are mainly significant in defining work group membership and in day-to-day affairs. People in Doko spend a lot of time with their closest neighbours, the three or four houses that are within a hundred yards, helping them out with problems, keeping an eye on their children and chatting around the fire in the evening. In most cases, many neighbours will be kin, because brothers tend to build houses next to each other and over time this results in little clusters of patrilineally related men and their families. Not all neighbours, though, will be kin, and in many respects your day-to-day relationship with your neighbours is much more important than your relationship with more distant kin.

People in Doko belong to exogamous patrilineal clans. Clans are divided into two categories, called Mala and Dogala, but this distinction does not play any role in contemporary Doko life. Many of the Mala clans, such as Gaomala, are found throughout the Gamo Highlands, and also amongst other neighbouring Ometo peoples such as Wolaita, Dawro and Gofa, while the Dogala clans tend to be more localised and in some instances are only present in one *dere*. The clan of Gutara, for example, is only found in Dambo.

Each neighbourhood is made up of predominantly two or three clans. Thus in Masho the neighbourhood of Decha is 49 per cent K'ogomala and 36 per cent Michamala, while the neighbourhood of Afa Masho is 50 per cent Yell?amala and 31 per cent Gezemala. The other clans which are present in smaller numbers have often moved there from other neighbourhoods, or are those that stayed behind when family members moved away. Thus the few K'ogomala families that make up 3 per cent of Afa Masho originally came from Decha and only moved there within the last generation or two. This moving is possible because most families will own land in several different locations and thus can easily transfer their house from one plot to another.

Houses

Perhaps the most important unit in Gamo life is the household. The household is the basic unit of production and consumption, and all its members work and eat together. A typical household will consist of a household head and his wife, their unmarried children, and their married sons with their own wives and children. Thus three generations are commonly present in one household, although households with two or four generations are also found. The male household head is the boss of the household and his status in the house is analogous to that of the *kawo* in the *dere*. Indeed there is a saying that every man is *kawo* in his own house. The authority of the household head is derived from the fact that he owns the house, its contents and the land on which it is built. Sons cannot own land while their father is alive, and women are never able to achieve landownership. In this way women and young men have been rendered dependent on older men. It is only in the last fifty years or so, with the increase in trade and weaving, that such people have been able to achieve some limited independence through activities in the cash economy.

None the less, agriculture is still the mainstay of most people living in Doko, and the household remains the basic unit of production and consumption. All Doko households have a layout that, despite variation in details, is topologically the same, and we can learn much about the Doko worldview from a consideration of this domestic organisation of space. Houses in Doko are made from split bamboo, woven like an upside-down basket, and then thatched (see also Olmstead 1972). Houses are located in compounds, and Figure 2 shows a typical Doko house and compound.

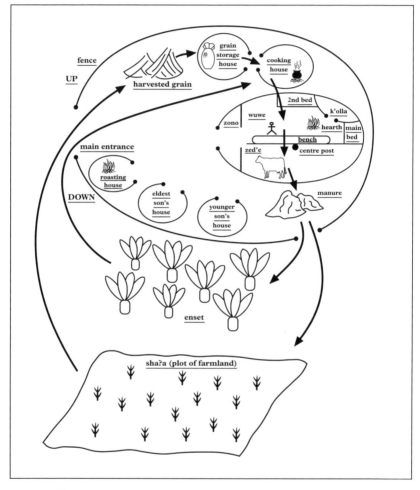

Figure 2   The house and compound, showing cycles of production and consumption

Just inside the entrance to the house is a porch-like area called *zono*, which is an area both 'inside' and 'not inside'. Running along the length of the house is a partition which separates the house into upper and lower parts. Doko is a mountainous area and all houses are built on sloping hillside to some extent. While the base of the house is obviously levelled, the division into upper and lower is a key part of local conceptual ordering. The lower part of the house is called *zed'e*, and this is where cattle are kept, along with horses and smallstock. It is thus also important as the place where manure is produced, for later use in agriculture. The centre-post of the house, symbolic of the male household head, stands in the *zed'e*, just by the central partition.

The upper part of the house is known as the *wuwe*, and is the main living area where people eat, talk and sleep. A bench runs alongside the central partition and small puff-like seats (*shid'a*) are generally spread around for people to sit on. A three-stone hearth, located towards the far end of the *wuwe*, is used for brewing coffee, providing embers for the bubble pipes that men smoke, and occasionally for cooking. At the very far end of the *wuwe*, perpendicular to the central partition, is the main bed, where the senior couple sleep. If the household head dies before his wife, then his eldest son will become the new household head and will move into the main house and sleep in the second bed, located along the upper wall, while his mother continues to sleep in the main bed.

The heads of both the beds come up against a partitioned-off area called the *k'olla*. This is the most private part of the house, and is where valuable possessions are stored. This is primarily milk, but also includes grain, spears, ceremonial staffs and so on. Outsiders do not enter another person's *k'olla*.

This house, with this formal structure, is called *kets*. In most cases such a *kets* will be located in a compound with other buildings used for cooking, or housing a married son and his wife, and so on. None of these other buildings is called *kets*; they are instead referred to as 'huts', or *embere*. None of them has any internal structure, and in particular they have no centre-post. It is thus possible to consider the whole compound as a magnification of the main house, with these additional huts serving as extensions of particular parts of the house.

On the lower side of the compound are the huts of any married sons and their wives. When the eldest son marries he will build a hut near the *zed'e* of his father's house and live there with this wife. When the next son marries, the hut of the elder brother will be lifted up and moved a little way towards the compound gate and a new hut for the younger son will be built next to the father's house. In this way the huts of the married sons are arranged in order of seniority, with the most senior closest to the compound gate and the most junior closest to the *zed'e* of the main house.

These huts have no internal structure and are just for sleeping in. A few Protestant sons have built modern-style rectangular wattle-and-daub houses in recent years, and since the internal structure of sons' houses is conceptually unimportant, this innovation has not provoked any reaction from the traditionalists. As long as they are built in the right place, on the lower side of the compound, then everyone is satisfied. I lived in such a modern son's house in a traditionally headed compound, and Shagire, the household head, would often admire the new house but say that it was impossible to live a traditional life in it. To my knowledge there were no modern-style main houses in existence in Doko. When the Protestant sons become household heads in their own right this may change.

On the upper side of the compound there is an area that is used to store harvested grain before it is threshed. Beyond that, further into the compound there are two huts facing each other, often hidden behind a fence. The first of these is the grain storage hut, and the second is the cooking hut. Once grain has been harvested, dried and threshed, it is stored in bamboo containers inside the grain storage hut. This hut is also used for cooking, along with the cooking house next to it. Here the high-status foods made from barley and *itima* (part of the *enset* plant) are prepared, and wheat beer is brewed. Other cooking is carried out in a small hut located by the compound gate. Tasks such as roasting and grinding are often performed here, and foods which have no symbolic value, such as potatoes, cabbage and *kolts'o*,[6] are cooked here.

Below each compound there is a plot of farmland known as the *sha?a*. Even the houses of otherwise landless people have a *sha?a*. Part of this plot is generally used for *enset*, and the tall leaves of the plant hide the compound from view and provide shade on sunny days. Because *enset* requires lots of fertiliser, the *enset* plot is also the general toilet area of the compound. The rest of the *sha?a* will usually be planted with barley or wheat, or the lower-status peas, beans, potatoes or cabbage. The rest of the household's farmland will be scattered around the *dere*, sometimes an hour or two's walk away.

Agricultural production

Because of the clay soils in the highlands, agriculture is incredibly labour-intensive. In order that the aerobic bacteria necessary for successful plant growth can grow on the exposed surfaces, fields must be turned over several times before planting can begin, manure must be added to the soil to increase its permeability and nutrient content, and terraces must

Plate 3   Men farming with a work group.

be built on steep slopes (Olmstead 1973:228). Labour, then, is a critical factor in production.

There are two harvests a year. The main harvest is around January, of the crop sown in July or August. And there is a much smaller crop sown in February that is harvested in August, just before the New Year festival of *Mesqalla*. Figure 2 shows the cycle of production and consumption of grain in a Doko household. We can follow this cycle round, and by doing so uncover the tacit model of production–consumption inherent in this schema.

To start at the *zed'e* then. Here household waste, excrement and cow dung is converted into manure, one of the key elements of production. Before the main farming season starts women carry manure from the *zed'e* out into the fields. Men spread it over the fields and mix it into the earth as they turn over the land before sowing. Men also sow the seed and hoe the soil again. Subsequent work in the fields, such as weeding and harvesting, can then be done by either men or women.

Once harvested, the grain is carried into the compound and piled up on the upper side. When it is dry it is threshed by men and women, and placed in the storage containers in the grain storage hut. From here the grain progresses into the cooking hut where it is cooked by women, over fire made with wood chopped by men. The completed meal is brought into the *wuwe* where it is eaten together by men and women. Waste

Plate 4   Woman grinding grain.

and excrement pass into the *zed'e*, and the whole cycle begins once again.

The lower side of the compound is thus associated predominantly with production, while the upper side is associated predominantly with consumption. Other sets of symbolic oppositions also map onto the upper–lower dichotomy. The most significant ones are damp/dry, cool/hot and fertile/sterile. The lower side of the compound is cool, damp and fertile. Water flows downhill such that moisture from the upper side drains into the lower side. The tall leaves of the *enset* in the *shaʔa* provide shade from the hot sun. The *zed'e* and the *shaʔa* are damp with excrement and manure. The land is fertile from this dampness and brings forth crops. Cattle in the *zed'e* are fertile as they give birth and produce milk. In contrast, the upper side of the compound is hot, dry and sterile. Moisture flows away downhill, and grain is left to dry in the sun. The fires in the cooking house and the *wuwe* produce heat and further dryness. Nothing fertile is found here.

This cycle contains within it the seeds of gender inequality. The status of Gamo women is rather high, compared to women in other communities in Ethiopia, but there is indeed a status differential between men and women. The ownership of land and houses by male household heads is the most obvious basis of this inequality, and also of the inequality between these men and their sons, but the symbolic organisation of production also subtly subverts women's input and allows their labour to be devalued.

If we look at the cycle of production and consumption we see that it is formed of units in which gendered labour culminates in non-gendered labour. Women carry manure to the land, men sow and hoe the land, and then both men and women harvest. Men chop firewood, women cook food, and then both men and women eat. In each case the gendered activities are considered to be productive, whereas the non-gendered activities are considered to be consumptive. This oscillation between gendered and non-gendered labour can be considered as the most basic model of production and consumption. Productive activities are valued more than non-productive activities, and since both male and female labour is necessary for production, both are valued. We have the pattern:

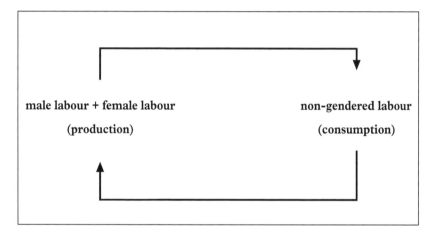

However, when the cycle is taken as a whole as it is mapped onto the compound we find that a slightly different picture has been created and that male and female labour becomes differentially valued. The different parts of the cycle become positioned in different parts of the compound, and since these parts of the compound have their own symbolic associations, the activities that take place in them become reinterpreted to be congruent with this symbolic system. Gender is not significant in the layout of the compound, and production and consumption simply form alternating parts of a cycle. Thus the gendered production–consumption units described above fall into either the production or the consumption part of the cycle. One type of labour is emphasised over the other, as carrying manure is eclipsed in one part, and chopping wood in the other. Men play the dominant role in the production of grain, and women play the dominant role in its consumption. This allows the illusion that:

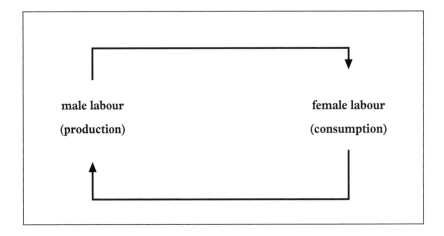

male labour   female labour

(production)   (consumption)

This is thus the second model of production that can be discerned here. Whereas the first model is based on the notion that production can only be accomplished by the combination of male and female efforts, the second model is based on the notion that production is a purely male activity. The two different models of production interact in such a way that women's labour is both acknowledged and valued (as integral to production), and yet devalued (as non-productive) at the same time. Men's labour is always deemed to be productive, and is therefore more highly valued. The basis of gender hierarchy is thus evident through the tacit views about production that can be discerned from the organisation of domestic space and some of the mundane phenomena of everyday life.

Although households are the basic unit of agricultural production and consumption in terms of ownership of land and grain, it is not the case that all agricultural labour is carried out solely by household groups. As noted above, labour is a critical factor in agricultural production and several households will own more land than they can farm themselves. In the nineteenth century oral histories relate that there were great differentials in landownership such that wealthy men owned huge areas of land while others owned barely enough to live off. During this time, systems that allowed wealthy landowners to exploit the labour of their less well-off countrymen were common.

Most easily, rich landowners could maximise the exploitation of the labour of their wives and children by practising polygamy. Many rich household heads in the nineteenth and early twentieth centuries had two wives, living in two different houses. The first wife would live in the main house, while the second wife would live in a second house, known as *motsa*, which would be located close to more distant fields. Cattle would also be kept in the *motsa*, so that manure could be produced near to the land on which it would be used, and the household head would stay there when he was working on the land in that area. In this way large landowners managed approximately to double their labour force and locate them usefully around their land.

During the nineteenth century many landowners were also slave owners. Captured through war, these slaves, or *ayle*, had to work on their master's land. Oral histories relate that many of the richest people at this time rarely farmed their land themselves, but engaged in trade and local politics while their slaves sweated away in the fields. This most exploitative form of labour transfer was widespread and it underpinned Gamo relations of production at this time.

Another form of labour transfer was share-cropping (*t'e?o*). This somewhat less exploitative set-up allowed men with little land to work the fields of large landowners in return for half the crop. This form of labour transfer seems to have become most popular in the early twentieth century, when warfare and slavery were banned by the national government.

Another way in which large landowners accessed extra labour was through work groups. Communal work groups are common in southern Ethiopia (e.g. Donham 1985) and there were several that were active in Doko in the nineteenth and early twentieth centuries. The most important type of work group was the *ts'ire*. There were *ts'ires* for men, which hoed the land and harvested the crop, and *ts'ires* for women, which carried manure to the fields. A typcial male *ts'ire* would consist of thirty or forty men from one of the small *deres*, and one artisan who would blow a horn while the men worked the land. Anyone could ask the *ts'ire* to work on their land and would pay a set fee. These payments were generally made in the form of barley, and after harvest the *ts'ire* organiser would go round the *dere* and collect up all the barley payments. Each *ts'ire*, however, had two members who did not have to pay the group directly for each day it worked their land. These members, generally the large landowners, were known as the *ts'ire kawo* and *dana*, and instead they put on a big feast for the group after the fields had been harvested. More importantly, these two men were the only members of the *ts'ire* who did not work on other people's land.

After harvest the *ts'ire* organisers would collect up all the barley payments from the *ts'ire* members and take half to the house of the *ts'ire kawo* and half to the house of the *ts'ire dana*. More work days would be organised to thresh, roast and grind this grain and to make it into simple dough balls called *kurch'aka*. The *ts'ire kawo* and *dana* were also expected to use their own grain, along with milk, to make better-quality foods like *gabula* (barley and milk paste) and *gordo* (barley and butter porridge). Then would follow a long period of feasting. First there would be two days at the *kawo*'s house, feasting on the food that he had provided, and then several more days feasting on the *kurch'aka* that the group had prepared. Then everyone would move to the *dana*'s house and the pattern would be repeated. In good years this feasting could last for several weeks, and on Sundays the *ts'ire* would parade in the market place and spend the day drinking and dancing. *Ts'ire kawos* and *danas* that put on a good feast and led a successful *ts'ire* gained a good name and became highly respected men in the *dere*. None the less it seems that the organisation of labour in the *ts'ire* was skewed in their favour and enabled them to farm large areas of land with little exertion and relatively little cost.

If someone owned more land than he could manage to farm, whether through his own labour or that of others, then there was one more option open to him. This was the 'reversible sale' or *aitsa*. Land could be exchanged for grain, cloth, cattle, and later cash, in what would look like a commodity transaction. However, *aitsa* differed from a straightforward sale because the initial owner could at any point return the original payment and claim back his land. *Aitsa* was popular with people who needed to raise large amounts of wealth quickly, and appears to have been most common at the end of the nineteenth century and at the beginning of the twentieth.

Nowadays, however, few people have really large landholdings. Increasing population density and an inheritance system whereby land is divided amongst sons has led to more people owning smaller amounts of land. The land redistribution during the Derg years further led to a break up of any really large landholdings, and even though there are still significant inequalities between farmers, these do not compare to the wealth differentials that existed in the nineteenth and early twentieth centuries. Because of this, many of the systems of labour transfer that flourished in the nineteenth and early twentieth centuries are now no longer functioning. Some less exploitative forms, however, are currently in practice.

Because people enjoy working together and because it helps keep morale high during the hard agricultural season, some work groups still function in Doko. The most common work group while I was in the field was the *zurra*, a neighbourhood work group in which one man from each household must participate. During the heavy agricultural season the *zurra* will usually work together one day a week. Any member of the neighbourhood who wants the *zurra* to work on his land must arrange it with the *zurra* organiser and pay a set fee, and any household that fails to send a man to work with the *zurra* is fined for each work day that is missed. At the end of the season the money is divided among the men. Like the *ts'ire*, each *zurra* has a *kawo* and a *dana* who do not pay for each day the *zurra* works their land, but instead each feasts the *zurra* members for two days after the harvest. Unlike the *ts'ire*, though, these men do contribute their labour to the group and they work as equals alongside the other men. The feasts given by the *zurra kawo* and *dana* are a much-enjoyed feature of harvest time. These feasts cost a lot in grain and milk and it is unlikely that they are cheaper than the cost of the group's labour-days on the land of either the *zurra kawo* or the *dana*.

While I was in Doko one family set up a new kind of work group that worked rather like a *zurra*, but was composed of kinsmen rather than neighbours. A group of patrilineally related second cousins got together and formed the new work group to work on each other's land. The member with the largest amount of land became the *kawo*, and feasted the group after harvest instead of paying directly for the labour on his land. Several people in the *dere* heard about this new group and many seem to think that it is a good idea, so it may be that this type of work group becomes more popular in the future.

Nowadays men with large landholdings must either pay the *zurra* to farm it or hire wage labourers from their own or other *deres*. Many households in the *deres* around Chencha town, including Doko, Dorze and Ochollo, have at least one member who has a cash income, usually from either weaving or trading. Men in these wealthy *deres* will often hire wage labourers from the poorer *deres* on the other side of the highlands, who will live and work with the family during the agricultural season. Labour, then, is still an important factor in agricultural production. But nowadays it is bought and sold in the cash economy.

In many households it is a son who has got involved in the cash economy. In this way he can avoid the gruelling physical exertion of farming for his father, and can instead supply the money that will pay a wage labourer. Rights over the rest of the son's earnings in this situation are frequently contested, as fathers try to maintain control over their sons' productivity while sons look to the cash economy as a way to forge their independence. This tension will form a central theme throughout the rest of this book.

Ownership in the Gamo Highlands, though, is rarely a matter of purely private property. Clans have certain rights over land that clan members nominally own. While individuals have use-rights over the land and the right to dispose of the produce as they choose, they do not have the right to sell or otherwise transfer the land outside the clan. If an individual wants to sell a piece of land, he must first discuss the matter with the clan. Clan members will usually offer to buy the land themselves, and only in very unusual circumstances will they give permission for land to be sold to other people. None the less, now that the power of the clans has decreased, land transactions do take place in the Gamo Highlands, although these transactions invariably lead to disputes between close kin and clan members.

Kinship and marriage

In the Gamo Highlands kin are referred to as *dabo*. This term is extremely vague and can also be used to refer to close friends and neighbours. People will often refer to *asho dabo*, or 'flesh relations', in order to indicate an actual biological relationship. The Gamo language does not have a wide vocabulary of kinship terms, and beyond mother/father, brother/sister, husband/wife, child and in-laws, most relatives are simply referred to as *dabo*. One reason for this is that most people are related to each other by many different routes. This is a consequence of a preference for close marriage, in both genealogical and geographical terms.

Although the potential choice of marriage partner is very wide, as there are few rules restricting marriage between particular clans or between particular categories of people, most people will marry someone from the same *dere* or even from the same neighbourhood. Moreover, many people marry distant relations in such a way that over time clans tend to marry in a circle. The marriage patterns in Figure 3 illustrates some examples from Doko.

Marrying in a circle in this way ensures that no permanent hierarchy develops between the different clans. The movement of women between households at marriage sets up hierarchical relations between the houses such that wife-givers become senior, or *baira*, to wife-takers. In a society where labour is one of the most critical factors in production, this seniority is expressed in demands for help in the fields, and sons-in-law must work for their fathers-in-law for a number of days each year. The number of days decreases as the years go by, but in contrast to societies that give bridewealth, the debt to one's in-laws continues throughout most of a man's life. It can only be finally paid off once his wife has reached menopause and he has taken a series of gifts to his in-laws.

Marriage in Doko consists of the transfer of a woman from the house of her father to the house of her husband's father. There is no separate verb meaning 'to marry' in the Gamo language. A man simply 'takes' a wife (*macha ekkes*), and a woman simply 'enters' a husband (*azina gelaus*). Although she indeed physically enters his house at marriage, her symbolic incorporation into the household is a long process which takes

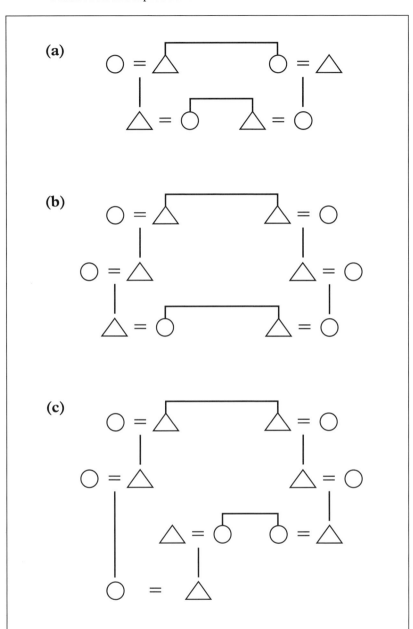

Figure 3   Marriage patterns in Doko

place over the next few years and cannot be fully completed until she has reached menopause and her husband has taken the required gifts to her parents. Until this time she cannot partake in the household offerings to the spirits which, until recently, were a central part of Doko life.

There are three different ways that a marriage can take place. One possibility is known as *mak'o*. This involves the bride willingly leaving her father's house for that of a man she likes, without the knowledge or permission of her father. When the deed is done an intermediary, known as a *lazantsa*, makes peace between the two households. This type of marriage is quite common now as it bypasses the often lengthy waiting period that a girl's parents might impose before they lose the labour of their daughter. Another possibility is kidnap, or *dafa*. The groom or his father, having decided whom they want as the new wife, may get together with other family or clan members and go out and kidnap the girl on the road, or at a market, or in the fields. The girl will scream for help, and it is unlikely that a successful kidnap will take place without the prior permission of the girl's father. He may give such permission if the girl continually turns down offers of marriage from suitable young men. Such marriage by kidnap is very rare now, but it was extremely common in the 1970s, and many couples now in their thirties and forties were married this way. The most common, and most proper, form of marriage is that known as *sorro*, which refers to the feast that is central to this standard type of marriage. Because the symbolism of the marriage ritual is central to many other aspects of Doko culture, I will describe the whole marriage process here in some detail.

The marriage ritual deals with the transferal of the bride and her initial incorporation into her husband's house, although at this stage her incorporation is far from complete. After a full day feasting at the houses of both bride and groom, the groom and a party of friends and relatives set off for the house of the bride. The groom's party is led by a man known as a *lazantsa*. His role is to be the intermediary between the two households and he would have been the person who carried out all the pre-nuptial negotiations between the fathers of the bride and groom. When the groom's party reaches the bride's house they are greeted by the bride's friends and relatives. Amidst much singing and dancing the two groups sit down and eat together.

Later, after nightfall, the groom and his party try to take the bride and leave. This is not a simple process, though, and the bride's clan sisters generally resist and try to block the exit so that she cannot be taken away. They will only relent if they are given sufficient gifts, traditionally butter and nowadays money. Once these gifts have been given, they stand aside and watch their sister depart with the men.

Along the route to the groom's house the party is supposed to stop on some land that belongs to the clan of neither the bride nor the groom. Here the groom unties the cloth belt from around her waist, showing his ownership of her sexuality and fecundity, and then walks on ahead of the party towards his father's house. When the *lazantsa* arrives at the house with the bride and the rest of the party, the groom is waiting inside the main house with his mother and father. The *lazantsa* takes the bride up to the entrance of the house and tells her to put her right foot through the doorway and into the house. After she does this the groom, from inside the house, places his right foot above hers. His mother places her foot above his, and the father places his foot above them all. He then pours a mixture of *uts'uma* grass[7] and water over the hierarchy of legs and blesses the bride to live in peace with them and to bear many children. The bride then enters the house.

Inside, the process of her incorporation continues. The father takes a bowl of barley porridge and eats three mouthfuls. He then feeds three mouthfuls to his wife, then to his son and then to the new bride. He next takes a full gourd of wheat beer and drinks three times from it, together with his wife, cheek to cheek. The groom and his bride then also drink together three times. The food and drink that the father feeds in this context is called *kacha*. While the tower of feet makes clear the order of the household hierarchy, feeding *kacha* shows that it is the father who provides for this household and thus justifies his position as head of the house. The *lazantsa* then takes the young couple to the groom's hut where the marriage will be consummated.

Nowadays many of the young people getting married are Protestants. Although they keep to the general format of the marriage ritual, they make a number of small but significant changes. Most importantly, in a Protestant wedding the bride and groom do not enter the groom's father's house and they do not perform the foot-over-foot ritual or the feeding of *kacha*. Instead they stand outside in the house compound and a preacher from the church conducts a short marriage ceremony in which they both assent to the marriage and the groom is asked to kiss the bride. The father of the groom has no role in this ceremony, and his authority is further challenged when the couple enter directly into their own hut without first entering the main house where he resides. The Protestant version of the marriage ritual thus subtly challenges the authority of the father and symbolically asserts that the groom is an autonomous individual acting independently.

After the day of the marriage, whether traditional or Protestant, the process of incorporating the bride into her new house continues. The marriage marks the beginning of a period where members of the house of the bride and the house of the groom should remain distanced. Most importantly, they should not enter each other's houses or eat together. The groom in particular must avoid his father-in-law, to the extent of hiding his face and running away if they accidentally meet. The fiction of complete incorporation of the bride and complete separation of the houses is maintained for some time.

During this period the bride's incorporation into her new house continues. For a month or two after the marriage she is considered to be in a liminal state known as *gach'ino*. In this state she must stay inside her husband's hut and do no work. On no account should she enter the main house or see her father-in-law during this time. Instead she should be well fed with all the best Gamo food, and kept warm and content as she gets to know her husband a little better.

After a month or so, for non-Protestant marriages, the father summons the *lazantsa* and tells him that he is ready to accept the couple into his house. The *lazantsa* then comes at night and leads the couple out of their hut and into the father's house. Here they kiss the feet of the father and mother and receive blessings to be prosperous and fertile. Then, for the first time since the wedding, they all eat together. This reconciliation between the parents and the young couple ends the period of *gach'ino*, and now the bride is expected to commence work as a household member. The next market day the couple and the groom's parents will *sofe* in the market place. This involves each couple drinking wheat beer together three times and then parading around the market place, thus publicly marking the new status of the young couple as married. Later on, at the New Year festival of *Mesqalla*, the couple will *sofe* again with all the other couples married throughout that year.

After this the bride can pop over to see her parents, whom she will not have seen since the day of her marriage. She must not enter her father's house, but instead she can sit in one of the other huts in the compound or in the porch-like *zono* at the front of his house. While the other members of her new household must still entirely avoid her father, she is allowed to come and eat with him. This suggests that her incorporation into her new household is not as complete as would otherwise appear.

Some time later, a few months or years, the bride's father will decide to activate the relation which everyone has so far pretended does not exist. He summons the *lazantsa* and tells him to bring the young couple to his house for *guyhatets*. *Guyhatets* literally means 'togetherness' and it marks the reconciliation of the two houses and the formal establishment of a relation between them. On the arranged day, the *lazantsa* leads the couple to the house of the bride's father. This time they enter on their knees and approach the father and mother who are sitting inside. After kissing the feet of the father and mother, they are blessed to be fertile and prosperous, and the groom then gives a full pot of wheat beer to his father-in-law. This is the first gift of *kumets*, literally meaning 'fullness' or 'wholeness', to pass from wife-taker to wife-giver. They all then spend the day eating together, and food is also sent to the groom's house for his parents to eat. The *guyhatets* marks the end of the avoidance between the two households, including the exclusion of the bride from her father's house. When she comes to visit now she may fully enter the main house.

The *guyhatets* also marks the establishment of a formal and hierarchical relation between the wife-giver and the wife-taker. From now on the bride's father can demand labour, help and money from his son-in-law. In the first year the groom will be expected to bring ten or twenty friends and come and work the land of his father-in-law for a few days. In subsequent years he may be asked to hoe the land a day or two per season, or to help with some other work. The birth of a child further adds to the indebtedness of the groom, and for each child he must take his father-in-law another gift of *kumets*. Like the *guyhatets* ceremony, taking *kumets* is said to reconcile the two houses. If the child is a girl he must take a full pot of wheat beer and some barley, and if the child is a boy he must give a sheep as well. Until these gifts are taken, there is some slight avoidance behaviour between the two houses, manifested again in the restriction on the bride from entering her father's house.

This hierarchical relation continues between the two houses throughout the bride's fertile period, the birth of each child further indebting the son-in-law to his father-in-law. But when the bride reaches menopause the situation changes. At this stage, if all the *kumets* gifts have been taken, the groom can take a final gift, known as *guʔa*, to his father-in-law. This again is a full pot of wheat beer, and this gift marks the end of the groom's indebtedness to his father-in-law and the termination of the hierarchical relation between the two houses.[8] Only now is the bride considered fully to have left her father's house and to have been completely incorporated into her husband's house. Now she should slaughter a sheep in the *enset* plot by the house, and after that she can partake in the regular household offerings to the spirits.

We have seen that people in Doko go to great lengths in their agricultural production and that those with large amounts of land do their best to exploit the labour of their neighbours, and sons-in-laws, in order to produce large amounts of grain. This raises the question of what it is that people do with their surplus grain. While some clearly is brewed into wheat beer and taken to in-laws as *kumets* payments, the next two chapters show that there are other competing uses to which this surplus wealth can be put.

4 The sacrificial system

In the last chapter we saw how labour has been a critical factor in agricultural production and we saw some of the ways in which large landowners gained access to extra labour throughout the nineteenth and twentieth centuries. In this chapter we will now turn to consider Gamo ideas about productivity, about what has to be done so that the land will be fertile and bear many crops, and we will explore the ways in which these ideas underlie a hierarchical set of relations of production within clans and communities.

Spirits, seniority and the flow of fertility

Gamo ideas about productivity centre around a belief in spirits known as *ts'ala?e*. These spirits, a combination of ancestral spirits and nature spirits, are thought to live in the ground and in water and they are considered to have great powers over agricultural production and human well-being. Local thought holds that, if fed through offerings and sacrifices known as *maggana*, the spirits will cause the crops to grow, the cows to give milk and women to have babies. In short they will cause the people who feed them to become fertile and prosperous. However, if these spirits are ignored and the requisite offerings are not made, then they can cause crop failure, sickness and conflicts. Feeding the spirits, then, is considered to be crucial to successful productivity.

According to Gamo tradition, however, not everyone can make offerings to the spirits for themselves. Only certain people can make offerings to the spirits, for themselves and on behalf of their juniors. These people thus mediate the rather important productive relation between their juniors and the spirits. The fact that seniors mediate this relation means that the productive relation effectively becomes that between seniors and their juniors, and it appears that seniors control the fertility of their juniors (see also Todd 1978:316; Donham 1990:104–13). This is the ideological basis by which hierarchy is constructed according to the set of beliefs and practices that I will call the sacrificial system.

These hierarchical relations can be considered to be like a set of channels down which fertility flows, from senior to junior. By behaving in the appropriate way to one's seniors, the social gradient is set up that enables the downward flow of fertility. Conversely, if one does not follow the rules or behave appropriately, it is as if either the gradient has been flattened or there is a blockage in the channel. In either case the flow of fertility is hampered and those downstream of the obstruction would be expected to experience agricultural failures, illness or other misfortune. This state of blockage in the system of flow is known as *gome*, a term which refers to both the initial transgression and the misfortune that follows (cf. Sperber 1980:207–8). Thus when a person experiences some misfortune they will immediately try to work out what rule they have broken or to which senior they have behaved inappropriately, and will then seek to make amends. In most cases the *gome* can only be cleared once the junior has given the senior a sheep to sacrifice, thus re-establishing the social gradient.

Seniority in Doko is figured according to primogeniture. So fathers are senior to their sons, elder brothers are senior to younger brothers, and the descendants of an elder brother are senior to descendants of younger brothers, irrespective of age. Within this general framework of genealogical seniority there are particular seniors who can make offerings to the spirits on behalf of their juniors. These seniors are the clan head, or *korofine*, who can make offerings for the whole clan; the lineage head,[9] or *angisa*, who can make offerings for his lineage; the segment head, or *bekesha baira*, who can make offerings for his segment down to four generations; and the household head, or *kets ade*, who can make offerings for his household. Beyond the clan the same idea is extended outwards into the *dere* and an easy elision is made from genealogical senior to community senior. Community seniors are known as sacrificers, or *ek'k'a*, and they make offerings to the spirits on behalf of the *dere* as a whole. There are sacrificers for all different sizes of *dere*, and at the top of the hierarchy is the most senior sacrificer, who makes sacrifices for the whole of Doko, and is known as *kawo*.

Succession to all these positions is by primogeniture. So the eldest son of the *kawo*, for example, will become *kawo* when his father dies. The eldest son of a segment head will likewise become segment head, but after four generations of succession in this manner the group will divide, as shown in Figure 4, and other men in his generation will also become segment heads even though their fathers did not have this position. In each case the succession is not entirely automatic, and it is generally necessary for the son first to sacrifice a number of animals of his own before he can sacrifice animals donated by community or kin group for which he is now senior.

Each of these seniors, then, has a group of people who are dependent on him to make the important offerings to the spirits. Linked to this ritual dependence are various forms of material dependence, and the two combine to form the hierarchical relations of production that characterised Doko agriculture in the past, and to some extent continue into the present. The dependency relation between seniors and their juniors is modelled on the relation between father and son, and men often refer to these seniors as 'father' or *ade*. In the Gamo language the words for senior, *baira*, and father, *ade*, can be used more or less interchangeably. In order to understand further the workings of the sacrificial system, then, a good place to start will be the father–son relationship.

Fathers and sons

As mentioned in chapter 3, fathers and sons usually live together in the same compound throughout their lives. Only in cases of continual fighting between household members will a father allocate his son a plot of land nearby and let him build his own house. Even then this house may not have a centre-post, and the son remains dependent on his father and is not considered to be a true household head. More usually though, fathers and sons, along with their wives, form one combined unit of production and consumption as they work and eat together.

As household heads, fathers own the house, the animals, and the land and its produce. This renders sons extremely dependent on their fathers, as up until recently they had no independent way of making a living. It is fathers who have the prerogative to make decisions about who will do what work, and when. In most cases such decisions are made in consultation with sons and wives, but the overall position of the father as 'boss' is clear. If a father decides to send his son to work with the neighbourhood work group while he himself attends to other business, it is rather difficult for a son to refuse. And if a father thinks it is more sensible to sow a particular field with wheat, then it is unlikely that his son will convince him to sow it with barley. Thus in daily life sons must continually defer to their fathers and do as they are told. This situation can continue well into middle age, and can be a source of considerable frustration as sons increasingly resent their junior status. This only changes when the father becomes incapable or dies, and thus the tensions between fathers and sons are felt throughout the duration of most men's lives and are a general theme in Gamo social and cultural life.

The hierarchical relation of dependency between father and son is also elaborated in the ritual practices of the sacrificial system. Only household heads can make the crucial offerings to the spirits and thus all household members, including adult sons, are dependent on him, as through these offerings he is thought to ensure their fertility and well-being. Sons cannot slaughter an animal or make offerings of barley porridge while their father is alive. In this way the authority of the household head is sacralised through his apparent control of the productive ability of his dependants.

The offerings that a household head makes to the spirits are quite a simple affair. Before and after all major productive events, such as sowing the land, harvesting, childbirth or the birth of a calf, a household head will pour some wheat beer onto the ground and then put a dollop of barley porridge on the tip of an *enset* leaf and flick some of it up into the air three times, calling out 'eat this!' (*haissa ma!*). This will be repeated at particular places around the house, notably at the centre-post, the doorway and the *k'olla*. Once the spirits have been fed in this way, the remainder of the food and drink can be consumed by the household members. On other occasions, if a member of the household falls ill for example, the household head will slaughter a sheep, and offer the blood to the spirits, in order to clear the *gome* for them.

The importance of being a household head is mirrored in the greater respect that is shown to him by the community at large. One way in which this is manifested is through the use of teknonyms. Most household heads, in most contexts of daily life, are referred to not by their own names, but as 'father of X', where X is the name of their first-born child. Thus I rarely referred to Shagire as 'Shagire', but addressed him instead as Assani Ade (Assani's father), and indeed there are many people whom I only know by their teknonym. Their status as fathers, as men with dependants, was made known and emphasised in all social contexts. Sons who are still living with their father, however, are not addressed using the teknonym, no matter how many children they might have. Only in light-hearted jest might friends refer to each other in this manner, but for the most part personal names continue to be used. Thus Wale, despite being in his late thirties and the father of three young children, was always addressed simply as Wale. In this way the teknonym is used in daily life to draw attention continually to the differential status between household heads and their sons.[10]

So we can see that the principal elements of the father–son relationship are an economic dependence in which fathers own the means of production, and a ritual dependence such that sons are dependent on their fathers to make the offerings to the spirits that ensure productivity and keep away misfortune. In one form or another, these principal elements are found in all the senior–junior relations elaborated in the sacrificial system. This is because all relations between senior and junior kin are seen as extensions of the father–son relation, stretched over generations and between households. To see why this is so, let us consider what happens when a father dies.

After the death of a father his sons will not continue living together in the same compound and the household will split. In the nineteenth century the eldest son would be given half of his father's land and the rest would be divided equally among the younger brothers. Throughout the twentieth century this inequality in inheritance patterns has progressively diminished, and nowadays land is generally distributed equally between the sons. None the less, it is always the eldest son who will move into his father's house and become the new household head. The other sons will move out and build new houses of their own nearby. The original house is referred to as *gole*, and is thus distinguished from the other houses which are its derivatives. Each of these new houses will have its own centre-post and will be located in a full compound, and each son will finally become the head of his own household. In many respects, though, the new houses are still considered to be 'sons' of the original house, and the eldest brother inherits the role of being 'father' to the other brothers.

This is seen when it comes to making the offerings to the spirits. Every time a younger brother wants to offer to the spirits, for example before sowing his land, he must first ask his eldest brother, now conceptually his 'father', to come to his house and make some of the offerings for him. Thus the relation of dependency that exists between fathers and sons in one house is extended to eldest and younger brothers in different houses. In other words, the brother–brother relationship is restructured into one of father–son. Although these separate houses could act as autonomous productive units, they are organised in such a way that they appear to be part of the greater productive unit of the original house from which they derive.

After some time the eldest brother will in turn die and his eldest son will take his place and the other brothers will move out and form more subsidiary houses. Likewise the fathers of the first generation of subsidiary houses will die and their eldest sons will take their places while the other brothers move out and form more subsidiary houses. All of these second-generation subsidiary houses relate directly to the original house, not through the mediation of the house of their immediate father, and they must ask the man who now heads the original house to help them make the offerings to the spirits whenever such an offering is necessary. This process continues uninterrupted for four generations. After that the houses split so that new 'original houses', or *goles*, are formed and new 'fathers' are brought into being. These fathers, down to four generations, are the segment heads, or *bekesha bairas*.

This process, by which houses derive from other houses and patrilineal kin continue to look back to their 'original house' as the source of their fertility and well-being, extends right back, via the houses of the lineage heads, to the house of the clan head. This is considered to be the 'original house' from which all the clan descended, and thus the relation between the clan head and any of his clan members is analogous to the relation between the head of an original house and the head of any of its subsidiaries. And that relation is ultimately analogous to the relation between father and son.

So the relation between any senior and his juniors is ultimately analogous to that between father and son, and is based on an economic and ritual dependence tied up with agricultural production and the fertility imparted by the spirits. None the less, the form and degree of both the economic and the ritual dependence that exist in the different senior–junior relations vary considerably. It is also the case that the precise nature of these relations, within the general logic outlined, changes over time, and there have been some fairly significant changes throughout the twentieth century. To start with then, let us look at the way the sacrificial system functioned in the 1960s, just before the revolution, and after that we will consider how this had changed by the 1990s when I was in the field.

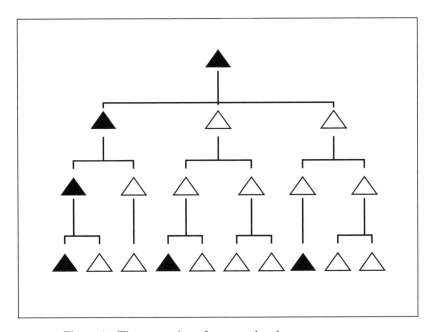

Figure 4   The succession of segment heads

The sacrificial system in the 1960s

Segment heads

In the 1960s the relation between a segment head and his juniors was extremely important. There were a number of practical consequences of this relation that rendered the juniors very much dependent on their senior. The most important of these was that at this time the vast majority of people, excepting the followers of *Essa Woga* and the few Protestants, considered it very important to make the offerings to the spirits before they started sowing or harvesting their land. To do this they needed to call their segment head to make some of the offerings for them. If the segment head refused to come, or chose to delay, then his junior had little choice but to wait for him before he could start to sow his crops. To do otherwise would anger the spirits and thus risk almost certain crop failure and disaster. Effectively then, the junior needed his segment head's permission before he could sow or harvest his own land. The segment head thus had certain rights over the land that his juniors nominally owned. While these rights were markedly fewer than those that a father had over the land that he and his son farmed, they were nevertheless important enough to invoke a degree of economic dependency between the segment head and his juniors.

During the 1960s, then, agricultural production was ordered so that within lineage segments men started sowing the land in order of strict genealogical seniority. First the segment head would make the offerings in his own house and start to sow his own land. Then one by one, in order of genealogical seniority, his juniors could start to call him to make the offerings in their houses so that they could commence sowing. They would each go to his house in turn and take a gift of raw barley, a pot of wheat beer and a male sheep, known collectively as *hinguts'ats'o*. As Sando, a Masho elder and segment head, remembers it:

We are approaching the farming season. It approaches. I have a junior, a junior, a junior, four or five juniors. They bring *hinguts'ats'o* barley to my house wrapped in *enset* leaves. Carrying it and bringing it they come to my house. I put a mat by the *k'olla* and they put it there saying, 'Come and make the offerings for me! I'm pouring it here. It's full.' If they don't complete this, then I don't make the offerings for them. It's known as 'calling', it's like saying 'come to my house'.

The segment head would then kill the sheep by the *k'olla*, putting some blood on his forehead, and then bless for fertility and prosperity for himself and his junior. Afterwards he and his wife and children would cook and eat the meat and enjoy a meal at the expense of his junior.

The next day or so he would go to his junior's house and kill another male sheep, provided again by the junior. This time he would kill it at the junior's centre-post, and again bless for fertility and prosperity for them both. After putting some blood on his own forehead, this time he also put some on his junior's forehead. He would be given the heart and the front right leg of this sheep to take home, and then he would sit down with the junior and his family and enjoy a good meal from the rest of the meat. After the meal the segment head would then take some barley porridge and wheat beer prepared in the junior's house and make offerings to the spirits at the centre-post, at the upper side of the doorway, and at various other places around the house and compound. After this the junior could then make offerings at the *k'olla* and on the lower side of the doorway. When all these offerings had been completed, the segment head would then go to the plot of land by the junior's house and hoe a little area of land and sow a small amount of grain. No manure would be used on this occasion, and only after all this could the junior begin to sow his land.

A segment head with several juniors could amass a fair amount of barley and wheat bear through this process, and would get to eat a great deal more meat than the average person. Juniors, in contrast, had to ensure that they had sufficient surplus wealth to give the *hinguts'ats'o* gifts to their segment head at sowing time. And of course there were political implications in this relationship. Because of the junior's dependence on his segment head, there was considerable pressure not to anger him throughout the year. As with fathers and sons, one man's apparent control of another's fertility created a relation of authority and obedience between them.

Lineage heads and clan heads

Although a similar logic underpinned the relation between lineage heads and their juniors and between clan heads and their juniors, the economic aspects of these relations were considerably less important than that between segment heads and their juniors. Although both of them made offerings for their juniors, these offerings were carried out for the juniors as a group, not for each individual junior in turn, and they were not linked directly to each year's agricultural production. Sowing was not ordered according to genealogical seniority above the level of the segment head, and thus segment heads did not have to wait for their lineage head to sow their land before they could start their own agricultural work. This meant that although juniors were collectively dependent on their lineage and clan heads to make offerings to the spirits on behalf of the lineage or clan, they were not individually dependent on them for these offerings or for permission to start agricultural work on their own land.

Rather, every four or five years or so, or when there were problems in the clan, the members of one lineage would get together and ask their lineage head to offer to the spirits for them. They would all contribute money and one of them would buy a bull or a male sheep. On the specified day all the juniors would gather at the lineage head's 'spear house' (*tora kets*), where the lineage head would kill the animal and make blessings for the fertility and prosperity of himself and all his juniors. He would put some blood on his own forehead, and then on the foreheads of all his juniors in order of seniority. Everyone would then go back to the lineage head's house for a feast. The lineage head did not have to contribute to the cost of the bull or sheep, and he kept the heart and the front right leg for himself, but he did have to provide ground barley (*kurch'aka*) for all his juniors to eat. They, in turn, would each come with a gourd of wheat beer. The lineage head would offer some of the wheat beer to the spirits and again bless for fertility. The meat from the animal would then be cut up into little pieces and spread out on some *enset* leaves and everyone would sit in a line and feast on it with the ground barley and wheat beer.

Every eight or nine years, or even more infrequently if all was well in the clan, all the clan members would similarly get together and ask the clan head to offer to the spirits for them. The event was more or less the same as when the lineage head made his offerings, only in this case the clan head would only kill a bull, and not a sheep. The second most senior man in the clan would collect contributions from all the clan members to buy the bull, and the clan head would then slaughter it at the clan assembly place. He would put blood on his own forehead, and then dip a leaf in the blood and flick it over the assembled crowd. Again the clan head took the heart and front right leg, and there was a similar feast on raw meat, with ground barley supplied by the clan head and wheat beer provided by each participant.

So we can see that although there was a conceptual logic whereby everybody in a clan derived from the house of the clan head, and thus that the clan head was the source of all fertility for his clan members, down through the lineage heads and the segment heads, in actual fact this logic, in the 1960s, did not create much dependency or inequality above the level of the segment heads. The same was true for the relation between community sacrificers and their juniors.

Sacrificers

Sacrificers, or *ek'k'as*, are community seniors whose seniority is modelled on that of genealogical seniors. They can make offerings to the spirits for the well-being of the community which they head. There is a sacrificer for most of the *deres* within Doko, although not for the medium-sized *deres* of Doko Masho or Doko Gembela, and not for one or two of the smaller *deres*. As with genealogical seniors, sacrificers are considered to be like fathers to their juniors. The importance of their position as controllers of fertility, though, is further marked by their long hair, which they must not cut or cover, and which makes them easily recognisable as people with some ritual importance. Most sacrificers are also heads, or owners, of community assembly places, known as *dubusha*. During assemblies they sit in the prime position and must be accorded special respect and on other occasions they often carry out sacrifices at these assembly places. One man described the role of the *ek'k'a* as follows:

An *ek'k'a* takes from the *dere* and sacrifices and makes offerings so that the *dere* will grow well; so that the boys and the girls of the *dere* will grow up; so that the cows will produce milk; so that the sheep will give birth. That's what he does, the *ek'k'a*. When he slaughters cows produce milk, sheep give birth, people give birth, and children that have been born grow up.

In the 1960s sacrificers made offerings to the spirits in much the same way as did lineage and clan heads. All the men in the community contributed money and one of them bought a bull and took it to the sacrificer. The sacrificer would slaughter it, and then put some blood on his forehead and sprinkle blood over the rest of the crowd that was present. He would keep the heart and the front right leg for himself, while the rest of the meat was cut up into little pieces and eaten with ground barley and wheat beer by all the men of the community.

Over and above this, however, the sacrificers for the small *deres* of Masho and Kale performed sacrifices at the beginning of the agricultural season that bore some similarity to the offerings made by the segment heads on behalf of their juniors. Nobody in Masho or Kale could start sowing their land until the sacrificer had first made the offerings to the spirits and started agricultural work on his own land. What would happen was that all the men in the *dere* would contribute money and buy a sheep to give to the sacrificer. On the day of the sacrifice these men would go to the sacrificer's house and spend the day feasting on ground barley and wheat beer that community members had provided. The sacrificer would slaughter the sheep and put some blood on his forehead. Then he would go to the plot of land by his house and hoe a little area for the first time that year. Then he would take the stomach fat of the sheep that he had just slaughtered and bury it in the earth, before sowing the first seeds of barley. In Kale the sacrificer did this accompanied by another type of sacrificer, known as a *maaka*, and the initiate for the *dere* of Doko Gembela, known as a *hudhugha*. The three of them together hoed the land, buried the stomach fat, and sowed the seeds. In either case, once this ritual had been performed community members were free to start agricultural work on their land.

So the sacrificers for Masho and Kale had some limited control over agricultural production in the 1960s, and could choose to delay the start of agricultural work if they wished. None the less, the dependence between these sacrificers and their juniors was still far less significant than that between segment heads and their juniors, although the similarity of the logic is clear. The sacrificers in the other *deres* did not perform these sacrifices though, and segment heads could start sowing when they pleased.

The most senior sacrificer was the *kawo*, who made offerings to the spirits for the whole of Doko. Rather unusually, the Doko *kawo* did not make sacrifices in the senior assembly place for the whole of Doko, but rather he made separate sacrifices in two different assembly places, one in Ch'ento in Doko Masho and one in Kale in Doko Gembela. I will return to the significance of this in chapter 6, but for now let us focus on the form of these sacrifices. As might be expected, they were essentially the same as the sacrifices made by clan heads. The *kawo* would slaughter a bull that had been contributed by the *dere*, put blood on his forehead and sprinkle some on everybody else, keep the heart and the front right leg for himself, and then feast on the rest with barley and wheat beer along with all the *dere* men. The sacrifices of the *kawo* had no direct link to the agricultural calendar, and there was no rule that said that the *kawo* had to be the first person in the *dere* to hoe the land or sow seeds.

So we can see that the beliefs and practices of the sacrificial system led to a hierarchical arrangement of people within clans and communities. Seniors gained some degree of economic advantage, while juniors had to find the necessary surplus wealth to take the *hinguts'ats'o* gifts to their segment heads and to contribute to the cost of the animals sacrificed on their behalf by other seniors.

Only the followers of *Essa Woga* and a handful of Protestant converts did not participate in this ritual system. Those that followed *Essa Woga* made offerings of honey in their own houses. These offerings were considered to be directly to God, and did not need to go through the mediation of a hierarchy of genealogical and community seniors. None the less, it was only household heads that could make these offerings, and sons and women were thus still rendered dependent on their senior men. The Protestants went that extra final step and declared that anybody and everybody could pray directly to God in their own right. But in 1960s Doko few people had heard these Protestant teachings.

This outline of how things worked in the 1960s thus gives us a general picture of the ideas that influenced agricultural production in Doko before the 1974 revolution. In the aftermath of the revolution, though, *zamacha* campaigners from schools and universities across the country came to Doko and told the people to stop worrying about such backward nonsense. Offerings to the spirits were banned, sacrificers were forced to cut their hair, and people were told over and over that everybody was equal. People say that throughout the years of the Derg government no sacrifices or large-scale offerings to the spirits took place. People just farmed. And the crops just grew. Then in 1991 the government changed again, and suddenly all the restrictions on traditional practices were lifted. At the same time Protestant missionaries from Wolaita flooded into the area.

The sacrificial system in the 1990s

With the new religious and cultural freedom of the 1990s, people in Doko faced a choice. They could either return to the practices of the sacrificial system or they could join the Protestant church and continue to farm without making the offerings to the spirits. Many people chose the second option and large numbers joined the church. The majority of these were young people who had grown up during the Derg time, poor people and genealogical juniors who had nothing to gain from engaging in the hierarchy of the sacrificial system. But some sacrificers and genealogical seniors also joined the church, mostly those who had spent some time away from the Gamo Highlands, weaving in Addis Abeba or other towns. The Protestant teaching claimed that the spirits were the devil and that all the offerings and sacrifices of the sacrificial system were thus devil worship. Instead people should pray directly to God and join in with the communal prayers in the church on Sundays. It is clear why this would sound an appealing option to many people.

Those who did not join the church had a more complicated time. Returning to the practices of the sacrificial system, having not performed them for over fifteen years, was not a simple matter. Life had moved on in that time. Production patterns had changed as increasing numbers of men had taken up weaving, and even the traditionalists were not immune to the new ideas that had come to the highlands with the *zamacha* campaigners and the Protestants. Quite how things should be done, and indeed whether they really needed to be done, had to be discussed and debated at length, and offerings and sacrifices could only be performed if there was a consensus from everybody involved. So what took place in the early 1990s was not so much a reproduction of the sacrificial system as it had existed in the 1960s, but rather an explicit re-creation of that system in the new context of the 1990s.

Some practices were quickly reinstated in the years immediately following the fall of the Derg. Thus in many *deres* people asked their community sacrificer to slaughter a bull on their behalf and they carried out the ritual much as it was done in the 1960s. In Masho the sacrificer also started to make the annual sheep sacrifice before the agricultural season and this was being performed in 1995–7, while I was living in Doko, although its equivalent practice was not being performed in Kale. Some practices seemed to have been allowed simply to fade away. No one asked their lineage head to make sacrifices for them and very few people waited for their segment heads to make offerings for them before they started to sow their land. Other practices were the subject of protracted assembly discussions that were still going on while I was in Doko. Many clans, for example, had suggested that their clan head sacrifice a bull for the good of the clan, but no clan had actually performed this sacrifice by 1997. In some cases the clan head had joined the church, in other cases he was living in Addis Abeba and only returned home at *Mesqalla*, while in other cases intricate discussions about exactly how the sacrifice should be performed divided the clan, so that no consensus could be reached.

In general, the practices of the sacrificial system that were taking place in Doko in the 1990s were a somewhat weaker and looser version of those in the 1960s. Practices that had created severe economic dependencies, such as the offerings by the segment head, were dropped and the seniority of these seniors was retained in only a symbolic sense. The sacrificial system as a whole was re-created as a predominantly symbolic system, stripped of any practical or economic implications.

Few men in 1990s Doko, for example, asked their segment head to make offerings on their behalf. There were one or two who did, generally small groups of brothers, amongst whom the eldest was the segment head. For the most part, though, the segment head was accorded special respect, was allowed to talk first in discussions and was given the best seat by the fire, but otherwise had little special role with regard to his juniors.

Shagire's segment had just divided in the last generation, and thus, with no brothers in Doko, he was a segment head with only his son as his junior. His cousin, Anjulo, had also become a segment head this way, but with three brothers and many sons and nephews, Anjulo already had a number of juniors. Of his three brothers, the elder two, Maaga and Dola, asked Anjulo to make offerings for them. The youngest brother, Abeyneh, chose not to ask him and instead made the offerings on his own.

Even Maaga and Dola's relationship with their segment head was their own creation, only loosely based on the previous practices. Whenever they wanted to make the offerings to the spirits they would prepare the barley porridge and wheat beer and then call Anjulo to their house to offer at the centre-post, before they made the offerings at the *k'olla* and doorway. Anjulo would generally then stay and join his brother's family in eating the porridge. Before sowing, however, they did not take him the *hinguts'ats'o* gifts and they did not give him sheep to sacrifice on their behalf. Thus the extent of the dependency between Anjulo and his brothers was minimal. And when Abeyneh decided not to call him to make the offerings at all, there was nothing he could do.

Much the same was true of the relationship with lineage and clan heads. Shagire's lineage head was a pleasant man called Meresho. He lived nearby, just ten or fifteen minutes' walk uphill from Shagire's house, and the two of them would often bump into each other in the market or at assemblies or just walking around. When I first moved into Shagire's house he was a frequent and curious visitor, and I could tell from the respect that was accorded to him that he must be somebody fairly important. He was always offered the first cup of coffee, the first bite of food, and the best seat near the fire. However, beyond these shows of respect, Meresho did not seem to play any particular role in Shagire's life, or in the lives of any of his other juniors. Shagire's clan head was an even more distant figure. He lived in Doko Gembela and he was the senior of all the Michamala clan members in the whole of Doko. While Shagire spoke about him with great respect, the fact that he lived some way away, and was part of the Doko Gembela community while Shagire lived in Doko Masho, meant that there was little day-to-day contact between them. He never visited our house during my stay, and the only time he and Shagire met, to my knowledge, was at the special Michamala clan assemblies that took place at the clan assembly place outside his house.

The role of the sacrificers was a little more prominent. Most of the sacrificers carried out sacrifices for the *dere* on various occasions and as the heads of assembly places they continued to sit in the prime position during discussions. As the most senior men in the *dere* they continued to be involved in communal affairs and to be present at most of the important happenings in the *dere*. Some sacrificers were more important than others, depending on their personalities and their ability to lead. The Yoira sacrificer, for example, was held in high regard and people tended to listen attentively when he talked. When I witnessed him talking at *dere* assemblies I could see that his calm manner and his good judgement were taken very seriously by the members of the assembly. He spoke with the air of a leader, and was treated as the head of the assembly, even though he was only a relatively young man. People said he was good for the *dere* and thus the *dere* listened to him. In contrast, the sacrificer of another *dere* was shown respect in public but often derided by people in private. This particular *ek'k'a* was considered to be rather selfish and arrogant, and many people felt that he did not carry himself with the dignity that was required. When a man in his *dere* overheard him telling me that he was like the *dere*'s father and that everyone else was like his children, he waited until the sacrificer was safely out of earshot and then spluttered angrily, 'I am not his son and he is not my father. He just has the tradition to be *ek'k'a*, that's all.'

For all the community sacrificers, though, their most important role in the 1990s was their involvement in initiating *halak'as*. This involvement was not something new and, as we shall see in the next chapter, sacrificers carried out many crucial functions in the initiation process. While their importance in other spheres of life had diminished, their involvement in the initiations had continued to be important, and for many young people in 1990s Doko an *ek'k'a* was 'someone who makes *halak'as*'.

The senior sacrificer in Doko, the *kawo*, was not involved in the initiation of *halak'as*, and his position during the time that I was living there was somewhat ambiguous. The last Doko *kawo* had died a few years before I arrived in Doko, and while I was there his son, Desta, was part way through his installation to become the new *kawo*. The first part of the ceremony had been performed before I arrived, and had been a huge event in which Desta had sacrificed a bull for the *dere* and there had been much feasting and celebrating. However, the completion of his installation was being held up for a number of reasons, both traditional and modern. A heated debate was going on between the communities of Doko Masho and Doko Gembela as to how and where Desta's installation should be performed. The argument hinged around seniority, not of Desta, but of the two communities, who both claimed that he should be installed in their territory as there was no central place that would encompass both *deres* at once. In a rather different vein, Desta's installation was also being held up because one of the Protestant converts in Doko Masho was bringing a serious court case against him and the date of the hearings in Arba Minch was still pending. Desta's position as *kawo* was therefore somewhat ambiguous, and he did not appear to play a central part in *dere* affairs.

Thus the sacrificial system in Doko in the 1990s seems to be of relatively little importance. Although people still believe in the spirits and are aware who their respective segment, lineage and clan heads are, relations between these seniors and their juniors are rather unimportant. For the most part they do not affect political or economic life, and are merely ones of respect. The relation between a household head and his sons, though, is still one of authority and dependence because it is still the case that only they can own land, slaughter animals and make offerings to the spirits.

Trends of change

The sacrificial system has changed a fair amount in the last half of the twentieth century. Increasing numbers of people have opted out of it altogether, and those who have continued with some form of the practices have changed them so that their economic importance has been eroded and only the symbolic system has been left. It is perhaps interesting that there has been no real *transformation* of the system though, only a general weakening of it that can better be described as *devolution*. The system is rather less elaborated in the 1990s than it was in the 1960s, but its general structure is still pretty much the same. As we will see in the next few chapters, this is in stark contrast to the *halak'a* initiations, which have changed in such a way that their overall structure has radically transformed.

Furthermore, there is some reason to think that the devolution of the sacrificial system is not something that was 'caused' solely by the banning of its practices under the Derg government, but is rather a process that has been going on in the highlands for some time. It was already being attacked by the local prophet Essa at the very beginning of the twentieth century, and his teachings have provided a way out of the practices of the sacrificial system for many people since then. The changing pattern of land inheritance between fathers and sons throughout the twentieth century also seems to be a clear case of the lessening of the economic importance of genealogical seniors. While they had a great economic advantage in the nineteenth century, owning much more land than their juniors, this advantage had been greatly eroded by the move towards more equal inheritance patterns well before the Derg came to power. Oral histories also claim that in the nineteenth century sacrificers were far more important than they are now, or were in the 1960s. The strength of a *dere* was known by its *kawo*. Stories abound of strong *kawos* whose sacrifices led to their *deres* being rich in milk and crops and whose power led the *dere* to triumph against its neighbours in war. The curse of the *kawo* was greatly feared and in some *deres* he was even isolated from the public by a piece of material so that his strong supernatural power, or *tema*, would not harm them (Abélès 1981:48). It was not uncommon for people to prostrate themselves in front of the *kawo*, and many *kawos* wore insignia of power, such as rings and bracelets made of silver or gold.

Looking at the form of the sacrificial system in the late twentieth century, this does not really come as a surprise. Even the 1960s version looks very much like a system on the wane. The logic of the system suggests a neat hierarchy of conical domains, with the *kawo* at the top, stretching down through the community sacrificers, the clan, lineage and segment heads to the household head and his sons. But the actuality in the 1960s suggests a fragmented and devolved version. Conceptually, for example, we might have expected that first the *kawo* would sow the land, then the *ek'k'a*, then the clan head, then the lineage head, then the segment head, and finally the household head. But instead, some levels of the system worked like that while other levels did not. And by the 1990s another level, that of the segment head, had stopped working in that manner, leaving the only significant relation that between a household head and his son.

The potential of the sacrificial system to exist as a 'neater' hierarchy of conical domains is not a matter of purely abstract speculation. Abélès reports that in the nineteenth century *kawos* indeed used to have rights to the first crops (1981:48), and in Balta, one of the *deres* in the southern part of the Gamo Highlands where I lived for a few months in 1995, early-twentieth-century agriculture was organised so that first the *kawo* sowed, then the community sacrificers and then the ordinary people. And in Maale, over in the Gofa Highlands, the system was taken to its logical extreme such that first the *kati* received tribute and sowed the land, followed by the chiefs and then the sub-chiefs, and so on right down to the lineage and segment heads (Donham 1990:104). So while we cannot say for sure how fully elaborated the Doko sacrificial system ever was, the combination of comparative ethnography and oral history certainly suggests that the system has been devolving since well before the Derg came to power. Why this should be the case will be discussed in chapter 6, but first we must take a look at the other cultural system that exists in Doko, namely the *halak'a* initiations.

5   The initiatory system

In the last two chapters we have caught a glimpse of how agricultural production was organised in the nineteenth and twentieth centuries and we have seen the lengths that some people went to in order to produce huge amounts of surplus crops. This rather leads us to ask, what exactly did people do with this surplus? The short answer is that they used it to buy status by getting initiated.

Initiates in Doko

There are currently three types of initiates in Doko, known as *halak'a*, *hudhugha* and *dana*. Initiation to any of these positions requires the sponsorship of huge feasts and participation in a series of rituals that can span between two months and two years. The main difference between the three positions is one of scale. Small *deres* such as Masho or Kale initiate *halak'as* and require the sponsorship of large feasts. Medium-sized *deres* such as Doko Masho and Doko Gembela initiate *hudhughas* and require the sponsorship of much greater feasts, while the large *dere* of Doko initiates *danas* and requires that the initiate sponsor feasts of almost potlatch proportions. The status that one gains by taking these titles is correspondingly ranked, so that *danas* command far more respect than mere *halak'as*.

By the 1990s the cost of being initiated to the positions of *hudhugha* or *dana* in Doko had become almost prohibitively expensive. In Doko Masho there were fewer than twenty men alive who had become *hudhugha*, less that 1 per cent of all household heads. And in the whole of Doko there were only two men still alive who had taken the title of *dana*. In the late nineteenth and early twentieth centuries, however, people report that it was not unusual for two or three *hudhughas* to be initiated in a year, although even then it was still quite a rare achievement to take the title of *dana*. Nowadays most energy is devoted to becoming *halak'a*, and the positions of *hudhugha* and *dana* have become less central in Doko life.

Plate 5   The author sitting with local men at a meeting.

Halak'as are said to 'herd' the *dere* (*dere hemo*). A *halak'a* who does this well is thought to cause the *dere* to be fertile. If he has 'good shoulders', the crops will grow, cows will calve, women will give birth, and the *dere* will live in peace and prosperity. In some *deres* there is only one *halak'a* at a time, while in other *deres* several *halak'as* are initated together in batches, although *hudhughas* and *danas* are only ever initiated singly. After herding the *dere* for a certain period of time, between one day and several years, *halak'as* leave office and become 'community fathers' or *dere ades*. As *dere ades* they are highly respected and they generally participate more actively in *dere* discussions and events. Non-initiated men, or *k'ach'ina*, tend to be less vocal in community affairs.

Halak'as are easily recognisable by the special clothes that they wear and the ceremonial staff that they carry. A *halak'a* must wear his cloth shawl wrapped to the right, whereas other men wear it wrapped to the left. In the first half of the twentieth century Doko *halak'as* wore a black sheep-skin around their shoulders, but nowadays people prefer cotton to skins and the sheepskin has been replaced by a striped cotton cloth, known as *k'ole*. Instead of trousers, *halak'as* wear a special wrap-around loin-cloth, called *assara*, tied with a cloth belt around their waists. They rub butter into their long hair, and the resulting hairstyle, known as *dishko*, further marks them out from other men. And *halak'as* also carry a ceremonial staff, known as *horoso*. This distinctive staff, made with a wooden handle above an iron base and with brass twirls at the join and on the top, is usually presented to the *halak'a* during the lengthy initiation process.

While in office, *halak'as* herd the *dere* not by ruling or by imposing orders, but rather by observing a number of prohibitions themselves and by carrying out the will of the communal assembly. The precise list of prohibitions on the *halak'a* varies from community to community, but in general these prohibitions serve to distance the *halak'a* symbolically from death and weakness and to associate him with success and fertility. Thus in 1990s Doko *halak'as* were prohibited from cutting their hair, falling over or entering a burial place. They should not beat their wives or argue with other people, and they should remain calm and well behaved at all times. When sitting with people they should sit in the middle rather than at the end. And so on. There were some prohibitions that had been allowed to drop, however, and were now no longer in force. The most significant of these was that in the past *halak'as* were not allowed to spend a night outside their *dere*. Nowadays many young *halak'as* are weavers or traders and they spend much of their time away from the *dere*, and the community has decided that this is acceptable.

The infringement of current prohibitions is, however, a serious issue. It is considered to be *gome*, and the cause of possible drought, crop failure or other calamity in the *dere*. In 1994 one of the Masho *halak'as* was found taking a shortcut through a burial ground. The community was shocked and took the matter to the assembly. After a long discussion it was decided that the *gome* was so serious that this man could not continue to be *halak'a*. The *gome* had to be cleared by the sacrifice of a sheep and the *halak'a* was dismissed from office. In Masho there is a rule that if one *halak'a* is expelled, all the *halak'as* must leave office together. This caused a great deal of anger among the other *halak'as*, but they were all removed from office, and a man who had been *halak'a* the previous year was put in their place to herd the *dere* until next *Mesqalla*, when the next batch of *halak'as* could take over.

Halak'as also have a political role and they are active in the communal assemblies that take place in each *dere*. These assemblies are a central feature of Doko life and will be discussed in detail in chapter 7. Nowadays many of the former roles of the assemblies have been taken over by the state judicial system, but they none the less continue to be an arena where communal matters are discussed and interpersonal conflicts are resolved. *Halak'as* do not rule over these assemblies or have any rights to impose their views on others. They have no authority to make decisions, and their role is to carry out the decisions of the assembly. They bless the assembled people before the proceedings start, and they may be sent to represent their community at the assembly of another *dere* or to fetch a defendant who has not arrived. In 1990s Doko the role of the *halak'a* was very much to be the messenger of the assembly.

In the nineteenth century, however, before the incorporation of the Gamo Highlands into the nation state of Ethiopia, the assemblies had a much more important role. They formed the central locus of legal and political life in each *dere*, and they passed laws, dealt with litigation and made decisions about whether or not to go to war. People who refused to abide by the decisions of the assembly were liable to fines, and, in extreme cases, expatriation (Abélès 1981:52). At this time, although the *halak'a* was in no way the leader of the assembly, his role in the preparation and the proceedings often allowed him to exert some influence on the outcomes of discussions. In some *deres halak'as* introduced the issues for consideration and then summed up at the end of lengthy debates. In Ochollo it was *halak'as* and *dere ades* who decided whether or not an issue was worthy of being brought to the communal assembly at all. If a man wished to bring a matter before the assembly he first had to speak to the *halak'a*, who would then convene a special restricted assembly for all the *dere ades*, who in turn would decide whether or not the motion should be brought before the communal assembly (Abélès 1981:51).

Halak'as and *dere ades* thus had important political roles, and they often became very influential in running the *dere*. Their power, though, was always checked by the communal assembly, and *halak'as* who tried to become autocratic were always stopped. Abélès reports a case in Ochollo at the end of the nineteenth century where a wealthy *halak'a*, whose opinions were often acted upon by the assembly, tried to order people to farm specific lands. The community decided that this was taking his power too far and he ended up being exiled from Ochollo altogether (Abélès 1981:57). Although this example illustrates what happened if a *halak'a* tried to impose his authority beyond certain limits, the fact that this *halak'a* thought that he would be able to get people to do as he wished gives us some indication of the influence that *halak'as* wielded at that time.

The importance of the *halak'a* in local politics has thus clearly diminished throughout the twentieth century. But rather than simply fade away in terms of cultural importance, *halak'a* initiations have transformed and taken on new meaning in several Gamo *deres*. The status change that once marked the uptake of political office has transformed into a status change that marks the passage from community junior to community senior. This was always part of the package of becoming *halak'a*, but the ability to buy seniority *alone* has proved important enough to the people of Doko that they continue to be initiated in great numbers.

This can most obviously be understood against the backdrop of the sacrificial system, where seniority is immutable and fixed at birth. In contrast, the initiatory system offers men the opportunity to achieve seniority through their own personal success. If they can find the wealth necessary to sponsor the feasts, genealogical juniors can become *halak'as* and then *dere ades*. And like genealogical or sacrificial seniors, initiatory seniors are indeed spoken of as 'fathers' or *ades*. However, while the logic of the sacrificial system sees 'fathers' and 'sons' as two components of a hierarchical relation, the logic of the initiatory system considers them to be two separate categories, so that 'fathers' are simply 'fathers', without having to be 'father' to any particular 'son'. As a categorical status, then, all initiatory 'fathers' are equal. So, for example, if both a lineage head and his junior have become *halak'a*, then the logic of the initiatory system would regard them as equals, even though the logic of the sacrificial system would consider them to be senior and junior. Being initiated thus offers men the possibility of improving their status and in the 1990s it was not unusual for genealogical juniors to try to assert some kind of equality with their seniors by emphasising their status as *ades*.

In theory any man can become *halak'a*. This does not however include slaves and artisans, or *degala*, who are not considered to be true citizens of the *dere*. Women also cannot become *halak'a* in their own right, but they do get initiated along with their husbands or sons. In fact it would probably be more strictly accurate to talk of couples getting initiated, rather than men, because a man cannot be initiated without the involvement of either his wife or mother. None the less, the wife/mother of the *halak'a* has no special role in the assemblies like her husband/son and her status change is considered far less important. She is subject to certain rules and prohibitions, such as not cutting her hair, not falling over and not arguing with people, but otherwise her role is mainly one of 'completing the *halak'a*', in the sense that a couple is more complete than a single person. If the wife of the *halak'a* dies while in office, the *halak'a* will be dismissed unless he speedily remarries.

There is one further rule that affects the eligibility of men to become *halak'a*, and that is that a man cannot become *halak'a* before his father or elder brothers. Within any family then, first the father will get initiated, then the eldest son, then the next son, and so on. In this way initiatory seniority cannot invert genealogical seniority, even though it can allow a junior to compete for equality. Depending on the wealth of the family, the differential wealth between eldest and younger brothers, and the cost of the initiation feasts, this rule can sometimes make it difficult for younger brothers and their descendants to get together the necessary wealth to sponsor the initiation feasts. In some *deres* this rule thus has the effect of restricting *halak'a* to senior brothers and senior lines (Sperber 1973:215), while in other *deres* it only orders priority and does not unduly hold back younger brothers.

Trends of change

Throughout the twentieth century there have been considerable changes in the initiatory system. As well as the political changes discussed above, it is clear that changes in agricultural production and inheritance patterns will have affected the way that the initiations took place and indeed who was initiated. In the nineteenth century the positions of *halak'a*, *hudhugha* and *dana* were generally taken by men who owned large areas of land and controlled a great deal of slave labour. Owing to the unequal inheritance system at the time, most of these would have been genealogical seniors and the descendants of senior lines. The only other people who would have been able to amass enough wealth to take the titles would have been successful traders, mainly those involved in the slave trade. While the initiatory system opened up the way for these traders to buy seniority and improve their status in the *dere*, for the most part it seems that initiatory seniority would have been accorded to more or less the same people who already held genealogical seniority. The ability of initiatory seniority actually to challenge genealogical seniority would only have become significant as trade became more important and greater numbers of people found the ability to generate wealth in ways other than through agriculture.

In the next chapter we will consider in more detail how the economic changes of the past two centuries have impacted on the initiatory system, but for now we can note one very important fact. While there has been some change that we could call devolution, for example in the declining importance of the larger-scale initiates such as *hudhughas* and *danas*, the initiatory system does not seem to be universally on the wane. On the contrary, we have already noted that people in Doko Masho considered initiating *halak'as* so important that they continued to perform these initiations throughout the years of the Derg government when they were officially banned. And even though Protestant converts will not get initiated, as many as 60 per cent of all men in Doko Masho had become *halak'a* by 1997. In the two years that I lived there another seventy or so men were initiated. Initiations are clearly still going strong in Doko Masho.

In other *deres*, however, the initiatory system does indeed seem to be on the wane. Even within Doko, the people of Doko Gembela seem considerably less enthusiastic about the initiations than their neighbours in Doko Masho. Most *deres* in Doko Gembela did not initiate new *halak'as* during the Derg period, and in the 1990s the percentage of men who had become *halak'a* was only about 9 per cent (Cartledge 1995:80, 121, 171). While I was in Doko only two new *halak'as* were initiated throughout the whole of Doko Gembela.

This raises two important questions. First, why are *halak'as* on the wane in Doko Gembela and not in Doko Masho? And second, what type of change has taken place in the Doko Masho initiations if it has not been one of devolution? The answer to both these questions, I believe, is that the *halak'a* initiations in Doko Masho have undergone a structural transformation. What exactly this means and quite how it has been achieved will be the subject of the next few chapters. The possibility, at least, that such a transformation has taken place is evident from the fact that the *halak'a* initiations in Doko Masho are carried out rather differently from those in Doko Gembela. It is also noteworthy that no other initiations in Doko are carried out like the Doko Masho *halak'a* initiations, while both the *hudhugha* and *dana* initiations are carried out according to more or less the same format as the Doko Gembela *halak'a* initiations. But before we get into a discussion about structural change, it is first necessary to take a look at the contemporary structures themselves.

The form of the initiations

Although the *halak'a* initiations in the *deres* of Doko Masho and Doko Gembela both elaborate the transition from *k'ach'ina* to *ade*, there are significant practical and symbolic differences in the contemporary form of the initiations in each set of *deres*. In Doko Gembela, for example, only married men can be initiated, while in most of the *deres* of Doko Masho single men and even young boys are initiated. And in Doko Gembela only one *halak'a* is initiated at a time, whereas in Doko Masho many *halak'as* are initiated together in batches. On a symbolic level *halak'as* in Doko Gembela are thought to be like warriors and the initiations involve much male symbolism, while in Doko Masho *halak'as* are considered to be like the *dere*'s bride, and the initiations draw on symbolism from the marriage ritual.

In what follows I will present an outline of the *halak'a* initiations in Doko Gembela and Doko Masho. Because many of the rituals that make up these initiations were taking place at the same time in different *deres*, and because some *deres* did not initiate new *halak'as* at all while I was in Doko, my ethnography is more detailed for some *deres* than for others. The reader is thus forewarned that the accounts of initiations in Doko

Gembela are presented in a 'this is how it was done' type of way, and asked to be patient for the more lively ethnography that depicts the initiations in Doko Masho.

Doko Gembela halak'a *initiations*

The following is an account of how *halak'as* are initiated in the small *dere* of Upper Losh in Doko Gembela. Upper Losh did not initiate any *halak'as* while I was living in Doko, and the last time they initiated a *halak'a* was in 1992. This was how they did it.

Arrangement and announcement First the community sacrificer and the *dere ades* went to the main community assembly place and discussed who should be made *halak'a*. In Upper Losh, as in most of Doko Gembela, only one *halak'a* can be initiated at a time and he must be a household head who is married and of fairly advanced age. When they had chosen the potential *halak'a*, in this case a man whom we shall call Sando, they sent a messenger, known as an *u?e*, to tell him. An *u?e*, incidentally, is also the name of the little fly that buzzes around piles of cow dung, indicating how the lowly messenger is seen in comparison to the prosperous *halak'a*.

The *u?e* then went to Sando's house and called out three times, 'Losh *halak'a* Sando!' and Sando responded '*yeh*' to each call. Then the *u?e* called out three times 'Woman of Losh Tsaltamo!', and Tsaltamo, his wife, also replied '*yeh*' to each call. In this way they accepted the decision that they had been chosen to be initiated. The *u?e* then entered their house and told them to wrap their cloth shawls to the right from now on. He then spent the rest of the day at their house, eating and drinking with a few neighbourhood people. On this day the initiate is said to be a like a newborn baby. He enters the state of *gach'ino*, and stops work.

Seclusion For the next seven days Sando and his wife remained in seclusion and did not leave their house.

Uts'uma On the seventh day the community sacrificer went to Sando's house, and did '*uts'uma*'. Sando and Tsaltamo sat on the bench by the centre-post of their house and the sacrificer put some *uts'uma* grass mixed in butter on their heads. From then on they were forbidden to cut their hair. He then fed them each three mouthfuls of barley and milk paste, and then asked them to drink three mouthfuls of wheat beer together from the same gourd. This feeding is known as *kacha*. Finally the sacrificer presented Sando with his ceremonial staff, and then the rest of the day was spent eating and drinking with kin and neighbours.

Presentation of lashuma A few days later Sando took some butter, barley and wheat beer and gave it to the sacrificer. Then he went to join the *dere ades* at the main community assembly place, where the sacrificer presented him with a stick, known here as *lashuma*. A man with the title of *dorane* then picked some grass and handed it to Sando. Holding the *lashuma*, Sando threw the grass on the ground and blessed the assembly for the first time.

Work days Even now, though, Sando had still not started to herd the *dere*. He would not take on that role until the Naming Day, and from now on he worked on preparing for the feast that he would throw on that day. First he prepared food for a small feast, and invited people to come and eat and to pledge *woito* gifts. Friends, neighbours and kin came to this little feast, and each pledged a donation, such as a pot of beer or a sack of barley, that they would contribute to his Naming Day feast. One of the literate men in the neighbourhood wrote down a record of all these pledges, some of which were returns of contributions that Sando had made to other people's Naming Day feasts and others of which were new debts that Sando would have to repay when these people became *halak'a* themselves.

During the next week or two Sando then organised a couple of work days, during which kin and neighbours came to his house and spent the day chopping firewood, grinding grain and generally preparing for the feast. Sando provided food and drink for everybody on these work days, and would also be expected to help out on other people's work days in the future. Eventually, after several weeks of hard work, everything was ready and a date was set for the Naming Day.

Naming Day In Upper Losh the Naming Day is always on a Saturday. On the day, early in the morning, *k'ach'ina* boys from the neighbourhood got up at dawn and went to cut bamboo. They took the bamboo poles, known as *gazo*, back to Sando's compound and waited for the sacrificer to arrive. When the sacrificer came he took one of the poles and stuck it in the ground by the side of the compound entrance. Then the boys erected the rest of the poles around Sando's compound, including one on the other side of the compound entrance and a few others dotted around in different places. These poles are an acknowledged symbol of maleness and maturity and, like the centre-post, they represent the father of the house.

After that there was a small feast in Sando's house, and kin, in-laws and neighbours came to eat. In the early afternoon the men got up and paraded Sando to Gad'a assembly place. When they got there all the *dere ades* were sitting inside, and the exiting *halak'a* was sitting on the special *halak'a* stone at the front of the assembly place. Sando waited outside while a close kinsman of his went into the assembly place and held up a large lump of butter that Sando wanted to present to the *dere*. This prestation was an obligatory one, and the *dere ades* studied the lump for a while to decide if it was big enough. Eventually they agreed that it was sufficient, and it was then unwrapped and divided between all those present. After that Sando was finally brought into the asembly place and blessed by the *ades*. Close kinsmen held him on each side to ensure that he did not fall over as he bent down to kiss the ground and accept the authority of the *ades*.

Sando then went over to the exiting *halak'a*, who was still sitting on the *halak'a* stone, and together they drank three mouthfuls of wheat beer from the same gourd. After this show of unity, the exiting *halak'a* got up from the *halak'a* stone, and Sando sat down. Now he had officially started to herd the *dere*.

The rest of the day was then spent drinking the wheat beer that Sando had spent so many weeks preparing. This Beer Feast took place in the assembly place, and all the men in the *dere* were invited. The *dere ades* drank together in one part of the assembly place, while the *k'ach'ina* drank together in another. Large amounts of beer were consumed, approximately seven pots for the *dere ades* and seven pots for the *k'ach'ina*.

Sofe   The following day, Sunday, was the *sofe*. In the morning there was more feasting in Sando's house and then in the afternoon Sando and Tsaltamo got ready to *sofe* in the two main assembly places of Doko Gembela. Neighbourhood women arranged Tsaltamo's hair into the special quiff-like style called *ante*, and a generous amount of butter was rubbed over it. Some red and white feathers were fixed onto two small sticks and tied on either side of her head. She then put on lots of necklaces and a new white shawl, wrapped to the right. Sando also rubbed some butter into his hair and put on a new white shawl, wrapped to the right. He also put on the striped *k'ole* cloth over his shoulders, and the *assara* loin-cloth, tied round his waist with a cloth belt. The sacrificer then tied a large white ostrich feather to the back of Sando's head, and a metal phallus, known as *kallacha*, on his forehead. Sando completed this array of male symbols by taking his spear and carrying it with him.

Thus decked out, he and his wife paraded to Alipango assembly place, accompanied by their neighbours and relatives. At the assembly place the whole crowd paraded around, singing and chanting, while the *degala* blew their horns. Then Sando and Tsaltamo sat down at a designated place and drank wheat beer together three times from the same gourd. After more singing and dancing, the crowd then moved on to Indota assembly place, where they did much the same thing and the festivities continued until dusk.

This day marked the end of Sando's period of being *gach'ino*, and he could now resume work. This also was the day that he started to herd the *dere*. He was symbolically a warrior, the ideal brave man protecting his community. I was told that his maleness is shown by the *kallacha*, his maturity by the ostrich feather, and his bravery by the spear.

Sacrifices Over the next few months both the sacrificer and Sando had to perform a number of animal sacrifices. The sacrificer slaughtered a bull and two male sheep at the main community assembly place, and Sando killed a number of male sheep at various places around the *dere*. Most importantly he slaughtered sheep at the borders with other *deres*, such as Lower Losh, Shaye and Chencha.

During this period the *halak'a*'s wife should also have slaughtered a sheep, although this practice was not followed during Sando and Tsaltamo's initiation. In the past the *halak'a*'s wife would slaughter a female sheep in the *enset* plot outside her home. Only women could eat meat from this sheep, and neither the meat nor the knife that is used in the slaughter could be brought into the house. Afterwards she would give her husband a male sheep, and he would slaughter it inside the compound.

Seniors' Feast Some time later the *halak'a* must throw the Seniors' Feast. This is a large feast that really tests the *halak'a*'s resources. It involves the preparation of huge quantities of the best Gamo food – roasted barley, barley and milk paste, barley and butter porridge, and wheat beer. In order to provide such great quantities of food and drink the *halak'a* must again rely on *woito* gifts from kin and neighbours. In Upper Losh both the *dere ades* and the *k'ach'ina* are feasted, although the *k'ach'ina* will only be feasted for two days, while the *dere ades* will be feasted for several days more. Sando threw this feast two years after he first became *halak'a*.

Exit The Upper Losh *halak'a* can stay in office for any period of time. He continues to herd the *dere* until the *dere ades* decide to choose a new *halak'a*, either because some problems have befallen the *dere*, or

Table 1. Halak'a *initiates in Kale and Shaye*

Kale	Shaye
One *halak'a* at a time.	One *halak'a* at a time.
Halak'a must be married.	*Halak'a* must be married.
Cannot be initiated while father still alive.	Can be initiated while father is still alive.

Announcement: *Dere ades* choose an initiate and send a messenger called **u?e** to tell him. The *u?e* must be a *k'ach'ina*. He goes to the initiate's house and calls out '*gondale atuma* X' and 'Woman of the *gondale* Y' three times. They reply '*yeh*'. Enters and puts their shawls to the right. Spend day eating.

Seclusion: The initiate and his wife stay in their house for seven days. Have entered the state of *gach'ino*.

Uts'uma: Three sacrificers come to house and put *uts'uma* grass on heads of initiate and wife. Feed *kacha*. Presents the *halak'a* with **horoso**.

Work days: Kin and neighbours work and pledge *woito* at small feasts.

Naming Day: On a Saturday. **Bamboo poles** cut by *k'ach'ina* and erected in initiate's compound in the afternoon. First one is erected by one of the sacrificers. One is placed on either side of the compound entrance. Later in the day, initiate gives a female sheep and some butter to the community sacrificer, and then goes to the assembly place. **Butter distribution** to the *dere ades*, and blessed by them. Drinks beer with exiting *halak'a* and then **takes his place on the *halak'a* stone**. An unmarried boy presents him with the special *halak'a* shield. **Beer Feast** for *dere ades* and *k'ach'ina*.

Sofe: With ostrich feather, *kallacha* and spear.

Announcement: *Dere ades* choose an initiate and send a messenger called '**ek'k'a**' to tell him. The '*ek'k'a*' must be a *k'ach'ina*. He goes to the initiate's house and calls out 'Shaye *halak'a* X' and 'Woman of Shaye Y' three times. They reply '*yeh*'. Enters and puts their shawls to the right. Then the '*ek'k'a*' takes the initiate back to the assembly place and the community sacrificer puts **uts'uma** on his head and presents him with the **lashuma**. Then the sacrificer goes home with the initiate and they spend the day eating.

Work days: Kin and neighbours work and pledge *woito* at small feasts.

Initiate gives a female sheep to the sacrificer, and is presented with the **horoso**.

Naming Day: On a Saturday. The sacrificer puts *uts'uma* on heads of initiate and wife. **Bamboo poles** cut by *k'ach'ina* and erected in initiate's compound in the afternoon. First one must be erected by a *k'ach'ina* from a particular neighbourhood. One is placed on either side of the compound entrance. Later in the day, the initiate goes to the assembly place. **Butter distribution** to the *dere ades*, and blessed by them. **Beer Feast** for *dere ades* and *k'ach'ina*, although *k'ach'ina* sit in a different assembly place. (Initiate does not sit on *halak'a* stone.)

Sofe: With ostrich feather, *kallacha* and spear. (*Kallacha* is tied on by a certain *degala* man, whose ancestors were brave in war.)

Table 1 (*cont.*)

Kale	Shaye
Sacrifices: Many animal sacrifices by the initiate and the community sacrificer, including one where they hold the knife jointly and slaughter together. The **initiate's wife** kills a female sheep in the *enset* plot.	**Sacrifices:** Many animal sacrifices by the initiate and the community sacrificer, including the initiate killing sheep at the *dere* borders.
Seniors' Feast: Only the *dere ades* are fed. Afterwards the initiate goes to the assembly place and makes his **first blessing**. Now he starts to herd the *dere*.	**Seniors' Feast:** Only for the *ades*. Afterwards the initiate goes to the assembly place and drinks beer with exiting *halak'a* and **takes his place on the *halak'a* stone**. Makes his **first blessing**. Now he starts to herd the *dere*.

simply because there is another man ready to be initiated. Sando was still herding the *dere* of Upper Losh in 1997. If and when a new *halak'a* is chosen, Sando will exit office on the Naming Day of the new *halak'a*, when he gets up from the *halak'a*'s stone and lets the new *halak'a* sit down. After that he will cut his hair, put his shawl back to the left, and resume normal life as a *dere ade*.

This general form of the initiation process is much the same for all the small *deres* of Doko Gembela. None the less, there are a number of variations in the details such that each *dere* carries out its initiations in very slightly different ways. Some of these variations give us clues about how the initiations have transformed over time, and it is necessary to take quite a careful look at this comparative ethnography. Outlines of the form of the initiations in two other *deres*, Kale and Shaye, are presented in Table 1. A new *halak'a* was initiated in Kale in 1997, while the last Shaye *halak'a* was initiated in 1974, just before the revolution.

There are a number of quite significant differences in the way these two *deres* carry out their initiations. To point out just a few, it is noteworthy that Kale is one of the few *deres* in the whole of Doko where a man cannot become *halak'a* while his father is still alive. It is also unusual in that the Kale *halak'a* is referred to as *gondale atuma*, and is given a special shield, or *gondale*, that he keeps at home while he is herding the *dere*. Both Kale and Shaye differ from Upper Losh, and the rest of the *deres* of Doko Gembela, in that the *halak'a* does not start herding the *dere* until after the Seniors' Feast. In all the other *deres* he starts herding on the Naming Day. And while only *dere ades* are fed at the Seniors' Feast in Kale and Shaye, *k'ach'ina* are also fed in most of the other *deres*. We will return to the significance of these variations in chapter 8.

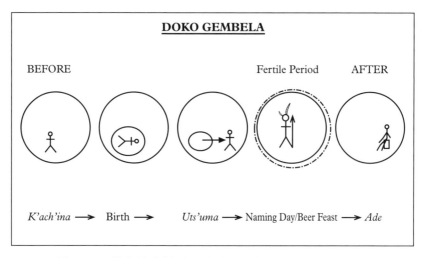

Figure 5   *Halak'a* initiations in Doko Gembela

Despite these myriad small variations, the symbolism of all the Doko Gembela *halak'a* initiations tells the same story about the transition from *k'ach'ina* to *ade*. As a *k'ach'ina*, a man is considered as a junior in the *dere*. He still gets to partake in the *dere* feasts, such as the Beer Feast and the Seniors' Feast of new *halak'as*, but only in a limited way. Then, when the *uʔe* comes to his house, he is suddenly 'reborn'. After the first seven days he has symbolically grown into a young boy, and on the Naming Day he matures into a young man, obedient now to the whole community. And the next day this change of state is marked socially by his *sofe* in the main assembly places of Doko Gembela. He has now symbolically become the ideal man, mature, virile and brave. Thus he herds the community for a period of time. At some point he gives the Seniors' Feast, proving that he too is worthy of becoming a senior, a provider, an *ade*. And then, when he hands over to a new *halak'a* and cuts his hair, he fully becomes a *dere ade*, a respected elder in the community. This process is shown schematically in Figure 5.

Doko Masho halak'a *initiations*

The *halak'a* initiations in the *deres* of Doko Masho take place in a rather different manner. Although many of the same elements are present, they are arranged in a different way so that the overall form and meaning of the initiations is quite different. There were several new *halak'as* initiated in all of the *deres* of Doko Masho while I was living there. The following is an account of how they were initiated in Masho.

Arrangement and announcement In all the *deres* of Doko Masho the initiation of *halak'as* takes place according to an annual cycle, and each year a whole batch of *halak'as* are initiated together. In Masho in 1996 fifteen new *halak'as* were initiated. Once the *dere ades* have decided who will become *halak'a* in a certain year, they will announce the names at Gad'a *dubusha* on the Naming Day of the previous *halak'as*, generally in October or November. Thus as one batch of *halak'as* start to herd the *dere*, the names of next year's *halak'as* are announced. The community sacrificer announces the names of each *halak'a*-to-be in turn, calling out 'tie *bullus* for Goba!' or 'Yesa says tie *bullus* for his son!' In Doko Masho it is currently very common for men to become *halak'a* while their fathers are still alive, and in such instances the father becomes *halak'a* along with his son. One of my neighbours, a young man called Abera, became *halak'a* along with his father, Yesa, in 1996–7.

Bullus is the name of the germinated wheat that is used as the agent of fermentation when brewing wheat beer. It is tied above the hearth to dry and then it is ground into a powder. Thus telling someone to tie *bullus* is equivalent to telling them to brew beer, and this is exactly what is necessary for the next stage of the initiation.

Beer Feast There is no change to a man's status after his name has been announced as a potential *halak'a*. He carries on with his life as normal until the following March or April, after the wheat has been harvested and threshed. Then he must sponsor a huge beer feast. He must provide enough beer for all the *dere ades* to drink well for a whole day. This requires twenty-five to thirty pots of beer (about 750–900 litres). When Shagire became *halak'a*, about thirty years ago, each *halak'a* had to produce this amount of beer by himself, but nowadays the neighbourhood helps by giving *woito* gifts. Thus Abera produced seven pots of beer himself and received another eighteen pots as *woito*.

On the day, the *halak'a*-to-be will sponsor two feasts, one in his house and one in the communal beer assembly place. Friends and neighbours, men and women, will come to the feast of beer and barley in his house, while only *dere ades* can attend the more extravagant Beer Feast in the assembly place. The *halak'a*-to-be hosts the feast in his house, while the community sacrificer leads the feast in the assembly place. No one can drink in the assembly place until he opens the pots and flicks some beer on the ground for the spirits. Then the close kin of the *halak'a*-to-be pour the beer into gourds and pass it round to everyone. Just as on the day of a marriage, two separate feasts are going on in two separate houses. And just as the focal point of the marriage day is the transfer of the bride from one house to the other, so the focal point of the day of the Beer Feast is the transfer of the *halak'a*-to-be from his own house to the assembly place, the symbolic house of the *dere*.

This is how it happened when Abera and Yesa gave the Beer Feast in Masho in 1997. A few days before the feast a sacrificer known as the Surra *ek'k'a* came round to Yesa's house to put *uts'uma* grass and butter on the heads of all the family members, marking the beginning of the period in which they were forbidden to cut their hair. Abera was the first of the *halak'as* to give the Beer Feast this year, because he, or rather his father Yesa, was the oldest of the year's initiates. Thus there was a great feeling of excitement and celebration on the day of the feast. I arrived at Yesa's compound early in the morning of a bright Saturday in April and found a group of some twelve neighbourhood men already sitting inside the main house eating ground barley and drinking wheat beer. The Surra *ek'k'a* had come by before anyone else had arrived and had eaten a little bit of the food and drunk some of the beer, because there is a rule that he must eat some food before anyone else can start. He had then dashed off to another engagement. The men were now discussing the case of a stolen horse and trying to bring two disputing parties to terms. A few women were sitting in one of the other huts also eating and drinking. Abera, Yesa and Mome, Yesa's elder brother, were running around greeting people as they arrived and serving up more barley and more gourds of beer.

More neighbourhood men and women continued to arrive throughout the morning, and soon the main house and two other huts were full of people eating and drinking, talking and laughing. By about 11 a.m. the men who were *dere ades* started to leave and go to the beer assembly place. Some women were chosen to carry pots of beer there, and a few of the younger men were designated to distribute tobacco during the feast. A discussion ensued as to whether or not I should be allowed to enter the beer assembly place, as women are generally not allowed in. Some men said that I should stay here in Yesa's house, while others said there was no problem with me coming to the assembly place. Another person suggested that I could come to the assembly place but not drink there, and his suggestion was finally agreed upon.

Soon most of the men had gone, and more and more women and children started to arrive, many bringing beer or barley as *woito*. The older women had now taken the positions in the main house, and most of the other huts in the compound were full of the happy sound of people eating and laughing. Yesa, Mome and Abera continued running around serving people, and their wives bustled away dishing out the barley and beer behind the scenes.

Meanwhile all the *dere ades* had gone to the beer assembly place and were seated in rows facing twenty-five pots of beer lined up invitingly in front of them. The head of the assembly place blessed the gathering,

May the blessing of the assembly place reach us!
May the blessing of the sacrificer reach us!
May what you have brought here cause us to burp and pee!

The community sacrificer then opened the first pot and spilled some on the ground for the spirits. After he had drunk the first mouthful, close kin of Abera got up and started to pour out the beer into gourds and pass them around the expectant men. Everyone drank heartily and the spirit of intoxication soon filled the air. The men chatted and joked amongst themselves, while Abera's cousins ran around filling and refilling the gourds and putting more tobacco on the bubble pipes. A little while later someone walked down to the front of the assembly place and presented a case to the gathering, as if it was a community assembly, which in a way it was. Men continued to call out for more beer, and others periodically shushed them because they could not hear the case. And thus it went on for most of the day – drinking, joking and bringing reconciliation to the *dere*.

Back at Yesa's house, the women and *k'ach'ina* continued feasting, and by about 2 p.m. the women started to sing. After about an hour of this singing, Yesa, Abera and their wives went off to get dressed. The men put on the *assara* loin-cloths and they all wore clean white shawls, wrapped to the right. The women started to sing a special song about good strong beer and how it should be plentiful in the future. Yesa took some butter and put a dollop on his head and on the heads of his wife, son and daughter-in-law. As the women sang the song about the beer, the four of them left Yesa's compound and walked as two couples towards the beer assembly place.

As they neared the assembly place the sound of men talking and laughing could be heard. They had finished resolving a number of disputes while drinking huge amounts of beer, and now they were joking and laughing and were clearly rather drunk. Some of the women who had helped carry pots to the assembly place were sitting outside the fence and also drinking. As the two couples approached the assembly place it started to rain and soon it was pouring. This rather disrupted events and men started to run out of the assembly place and seek shelter. Other men protested that no one should leave until the *halak'a* had entered. Amidst the chaos Yesa and his wife entered the assembly place, followed by Abera and his wife. Both couples fought their way across the assembly place and sat in a certain designated spot at the front. The sacrificer brought them a gourd of beer and Yesa and his wife drank three mouthfuls out of it together, followed by Abera and his wife. This feeding is called *kacha*, like the food fed by the groom's father during the marriage ritual. In other circumstances the two women would then have returned home and Yesa and Abera would have stayed drinking with the men. Because of the pouring rain, they all joined the chaotic exodus out of the assembly place and rushed to nearby houses for shelter. When the rain finally stopped it was beginning to get dark. Most of the men stumbled home, happily drunk, while close neighbours and friends went back to Yesa's house and managed to continue drinking well into the evening.

When Abera and Yesa had entered the assembly place they had symbolically entered the house of the community, like a bride entering her husband's house on her wedding day. This is the conceptual focus of the event, and the similarity with the marriage ritual is explicitly noted by the participants. In fact, throughout Doko Masho the *halak'a* is often referred to as the *dere*'s wife.

The next day close neighbours and those who had helped the day before went back to Yesa's house for more eating and drinking. On this occasion seven artisans, or *degala*, came. They were not invited into any of the houses, but were seated outside in the compound. While everyone agreed it was right for them to come on this day, nobody made any effort to talk to them or to be nice. They ate separately outside, while everybody else ate in the main house or one of the other huts in the compound. This little feast carried on until around midday, when the *dere ades* went off to the assembly place to drink at the Beer Feast of the next *halak'a* out of this year's batch. Since today's Beer Feast was given by someone who lived quite far away, these men did not go to the neighbourhood feast in the *halak'a*'s house, but only joined in the *dere* feast in the assembly place. With fifteen *halak'as* to get through, most of the *dere ades* spent the best part of the next two weeks in a state of pleasant intoxication.

Despite throwing the Beer Feast, the *halak'as* were still not yet ready to start herding the *dere*. Their status had not ritually changed and in the following few months they continued to wear their shawls wrapped to the left. Other than not cutting their hair, they were not yet subject to any prohibitions.

Mesqalla   *Mesqalla* is the Gamo New Year and is the most celebrated day in the year. It takes place in September and it is at this time that the *halak'as* are symbolically considered both to give birth and to be born. They wear a special red feather on their heads as they participate in the day's festivities, and this feather is said to be their *che?o*, the first cry of a newborn baby. *Halak'as* do not wear this feather in Doko Gembela. For the next few months after this the *halak'as* are considered to be in the state of *gach'ino*, and they must do no work.

Naming Day A week or so after *Mesqalla* the new *halak'a* must take gifts called *ifate* to certain people in the *dere*. The most important one is the gift of a young female sheep that has not yet given birth, which must be taken to the man in the *dere* who became *halak'a* the longest time ago. This man is known as the *halak'a baira*, or the senior of the *halak'as*. Each *halak'a* must give him a sheep before he can proceed to the Naming Day.

The Naming Day is the day that the *halak'a* finally starts herding the *dere*. On this day *k'ach'ina* boys of the neighbourhood get up before dawn and creep out and cut bamboo from other men's land. Every man must allow one bamboo to be taken from his land, but in contrast to the more restrained affair in Doko Gembela, the Doko Masho boys try to cut as many bamboos as they can. It is possible for a man to lose as many as fourteen or fifteen trees if he does not go and guard his bamboo. Consequently this is the morning when everyone crawls out of bed in the cold pre-dawn hours and stands on guard in the bamboo groves.

Once the boys have cut the bamboo, they take the poles to the *halak'a*'s house and stand them against the fence, awaiting the arrival of the *lazantsa*, the messenger who acts as intermediary between the *dere* and the *halak'a*. This is what happened at Dola's house, one of the 1995–6 Masho *halak'as*. When the *lazantsa* arrived all the boys were served good food and were feasted until they were full. Many of the boys were going off to school at midday, so some of them ate earlier and left. When the *lazantsa* was ready, he went out and cut one bamboo himself. Then he erected it on the upper side of the entrance to Dola's main house. As he did this two men came and blew a special horn called *p'o?ets*. They ate some food and then went off to the houses of other *halak'as*. After that some *degala* came and blew their horns, called *zahe*, as the boys erected the rest of the bamboo poles around Dola's compound. One was placed on the other side of the house entrance, but none was placed by the compound entrance, as they are in Doko Gembela.

The *lazantsa* then took a small piece of bamboo and combed it through Dola's hair, which was by now quite long. He then placed it above Dola's bed, on the wall of the *k'olla*, and some kin and neighbours who had come round to watch started to sing *basse*, a chant of praise to brave ancestors. Then, for the first time, Dola tied an ostrich feather on the

Plate 6   Doko Masho men parading during the *Mesqalla* celebrations.

Plate 7   Erecting bamboo poles in the *halak'a*'s compound.

back of his head. Like the *gazo*, this is also a symbol of maturity, showing that the *halak'a*-as-baby that was born at *Mesqalla* has now grown into *halak'a*-as-boy.

Shortly afterwards everyone was ready and the crowd of neighbours and kin escorted Dola to Gad'a assembly place, wearing the *assara* loin-cloth, an ostrich feather on his head, and with his shawl wrapped to the right. He did not wear the phallus-like *kallacha* and he did not carry his spear. His wife and the other women stayed at home. All the new *halak'as* from all over Masho paraded to this assembly place on this day. As they reached the assembly place the *dere ades* entered and sat down, while the new *halak'as* waited outside. The *degala* sat outside and below the assembly place, and blew their horns at the appropriate points. By about 5 p.m. all the *halak'as* had arrived, and the proceedings started.

First of all the sacrificer called out the names of next year's *halak'as*, as I described above. When this was over a close relative of each of the new *halak'as*, who were still sitting outside the assembly place, stood in front of the *dere ades* and held up a lump of butter that each *halak'a* was presenting to the *dere*. The *degala* blew their horns and the *ades* looked at the lumps of butter carefully and discussed whether they were big enough. Dola's was praised for being the largest, and eventually it was decided that all of them were of a satisfactory size. The sacrificer then began distributing the butter to all the *dere ades*. He walked around the crowd of men and placed a dollop of butter on each man's head. This soon descended into apparent chaos as the men argued that the division was not equal and that they had not been given enough and so on. Eventually all the butter was distributed and everyone was satisfied that they had received a more or less equal share.

Then the new *halak'as* were brought into the assembly place and they stood in an arc before the seated *dere ades*. Their shawls were arranged in a special way so that they hung over both shoulders. Then, supported by their kin so that they would not fall down, the *halak'as* bowed down in front of the *dere ades* and kissed the ground. Everyone cried out 'Yo-ho-ho-ho!' and the *degala* blew their horns. The *halak'as* stood up again, and all went quiet. The sacrificer stood up and blessed:

May the blessing of Gad'a reach us!
May the sacrificer's blessing reach us!
May the shoulders of the *halak'as* be good!
May the shepherd boys herd well!
We will celebrate *Mesqalla* as equals!

After each sentence everyone responded '*amen*', and at the end everyone called out '*yo-ho-ho-ho!*' and the *halak'as* bowed to the ground and the

Plate 8 *Halak'a* being helped with his ostrich feather.

Plate 9   Presenting butter to the *ades*.

degala blew their horns. Some of the elders then blessed in the same way, and the *halak'as* again bowed to the ground while everyone '*yo*-ed'. On this day the *halak'as* accepted the authority of the *dere*, and agreed that they would do what the *dere* asked of them.

Sofe   Some twelve to fourteen days later it is the day of the *sofe*, the public show of a change of status. In the morning there is a small feast at the *halak'a*'s house, to which it is particularly important to invite the wife's kin. They come and eat at their son-in-law's house and present their daughter with a new shawl, cloth belt and necklace for her to wear at the *sofe*. On this day her hair will be done in the quiff-like style called *ante*.

Later on in the afternoon the *halak'a* again ties an ostrich feather to his head, and this time his wife wears a few small white feathers on her head, known collectively as *zazanto*. Both of them put butter on their heads, and then the kin and neighbours parade them to Pango, the market place and assembly place for the whole of Doko Masho. *Degala* follow behind the crowd blowing their horns. In the crowd of people heading towards the *dubusha*, kin are careful to support the *halak'a* couple so that they do not fall down, which would be a serious *gome*. All the *deres* of Doko Masho *sofe* on the same day, so crowds of people can be seen approaching the central assembly place from all over the area.

It is the rule that Masho must enter the assembly place before the other *deres*. They sit at their designated place, and wait until the other *deres* enter. When the *dere* of Shale enters, everyone rushes across the assembly place and the *halak'as* and their wives are supposed to touch the hands of Shale people. After that all the *deres* mix up and they all parade around the assembly place together. After that all the new *halak'as* and their wives go and sit on their own clan stone in the assembly place and drink beer together three times from the same gourd. Then they go and join in the singing and dancing that lasts until sunset.

Sacrifices A few days later the *halak'as* and their wives go to the sacrificer's compound, where the sacrificer presents each *halak'a* with a ceremonial staff, known as *horoso*, and tells them to wear the striped *k'ole* over their shoulders from now on. Then the women go home and the new *halak'as* go with the community sacrificer, and another sacrificer known as *maaka*, to Haile assembly place. The *halak'as* stand in a line and the *maaka* passes a male sheep over their shoulders from left to right. He then slaughters this sheep for the spirits and puts blood on his forehead. This sacrifice is not done in many of the other *deres*, and has the purpose of binding the *halak'as* together into one unit, such that if one *halak'a* is dismissed from office then they all must leave. After this the community sacrificer kills two male sheep, and in the next few weeks there are various other sacrifices that take place throughout the *dere*. In contrast to the initiations in Doko Gembela, there is no tradition that the wife of the *halak'a* sacrifices a female sheep during this time.

When the sacrifices have been completed the new *halak'as* go with the *dere ades* to Bulogars assembly place. For the first time the *halak'as* bless the assembly. A man with the title of *dortane* picks some grass and hands it to each new *halak'a*. Holding his *horoso*, the *halak'a* throws the grass and blesses the assembly. On this day the *halak'as* end their period of being *gach'ino*, and can start to work again. From now on they go about their day-to-day life and perform the duties of the *halak'a*.

Seniors' Feast Many months later, in May or June, the *halak'a* has to provide the Seniors' Feast. As in Doko Gembela, this involves the preparation of huge quantities of the best Gamo food. And in order to provide such great quantities of food and drink the *halak'a* must again rely on *woito* from kin and neighbours. Even when Shagire gave the Senior's Feast it was necessary to ask for *woito*, although he says that in his day *woito* was given predominantly by kin, and not by neighbours.

Plate 10   Eating at the Seniors' Feast.

All the *dere ades* in the community are divided up equally between the new *halak'as*, and they spend four days feasting at the house of one of the *halak'as*. Women who help in the preparation of the food, or in carrying it to the house, are fed in one of the other huts, but only the *ades* can enter the main house. In contrast to Doko Gembela, *k'ach'ina* cannot participate in these feasts at all. For the *dere ades* these are pleasant days, spent eating and chatting with friends. Currently the *halak'as* must also give some money to the *dere ades*, about £20 each. This is because the feasts of today are said to be much smaller than those of yesteryear, and the *halak'as* must make up the shortfall in cash terms. Once the *halak'as* have provided the Seniors' Feast, they are themselves considered to be seniors or *ades*. They have now earned the right to eat at any *dere* feast, including the Beer Feasts and Seniors' Feasts of other *halak'as*.

Exit On the day of *Mesqalla* the herding *halak'as* each wear an ostrich feather on their heads, while the new *halak'as* wear the small red feather. Then on the Naming Day, when the new *halak'as* enter Gad'a assembly place and bow down before the *dere ades*, the old *halak'as* leave office. They can now cut their hair and must put their shawl back to the left. They have now fully become *dere ades*.

This then is how the initiations are carried out in Masho. The pattern is clearly quite different from the pattern of the initiations in Upper Losh, or in any of the *deres* in Doko Gembela. Other *deres* in Doko Masho carry out the initiations in approximately the same way, although again there are numerous small variations. The outline of how the initiations are performed in Dambo and Shale is presented in Table 2. Most of the same elements are present, although in some cases they are in a slightly different order. Some of the more notable differences are as follows: the scale of the Beer Feast is rather different in Shale, and it is referred to as '*Uts'uma*', rather than as a Beer Feast. Both Dambo and Shale contrast with Masho in that the *halak'a* is given a special stick, known as *gatuma*, as well as the *horoso*. And Dambo, along with the five other *deres* of Doko Masho, differs from Masho and Shale in that their *halak'as* do not have to be married and even young boys can take the title. Likewise, Masho and Shale are the only two *deres* where the sheep-over-the-shoulders ritual is done, and correspondingly, they are the only two *deres* where all the *halak'as* must leave office together if one of them is expelled.

Even though there are many small variations, we can see that the overall form of the initiations remains much the same. It tells quite a different story about the transition from *k'ach'ina* to *ade* from that of the Doko Gembela initiations. In short, the story is that before the process starts a man is a social child, not yet a full member of the *dere*, and unable to

Table 2. *Halak'a initiates in Dambo and Shale*

Dambo	Shale
Many *halak'as* initiated at a time. If one *halak'a* is expelled from office, the others can remain. *Halak'as* do not have to be married.	Many *halak'as* initiated at a time. If one *halak'a* is expelled from office, the others are expelled with him. *Halak'as* must be married.
Announcement: *Dere* sends *lazantsa* to tell initiate. Sacrificer announces names of initiates at his house, on the day of the butter distribution.	**Announcement:** *Dere* sends *lazantsa* to tell initiate. Sacrificer announces names of initiates at the assembly place, on *Mesqalla*.
Beer Feast: *Lazantsa* puts **uts'uma** grass on initiate's head, then initiate provides small feast at home for neighbours, and big Beer Feast in the assembly place for *dere ades* only. At the end of the day the initiate enters the assembly place, and is fed *kacha*.	**Uts'uma:** Sacrificer puts **uts'uma** grass on the initiate's head, then the initiate provides a feast in his compound. Only *dere ades* can enter the main house, while neighbours feast in the other huts. At the end of the day the initiate enters the main house, and is fed *kacha*.
Mesqalla: Initiate wears red feather on his head and is symbolically born.	**Mesqalla:** Initiate wears red feather on his head and is symbolically born.
Butter distribution to *dere ades*, at the sacrificer's house. *Lazantsa* combs initiate's hair with small piece of bamboo.	Initiates each take a sheep to sacrificer.
Bamboo poles erected in initiate's compound by *k'ach'ina* boys (but no ostrich feather).	**Bamboo poles** erected in initiate's compound by *k'ach'ina* boys. Initiate kills a sheep, and uses intestines to tie **ostrich feather** on his head. Then initiates go to the assembly place and there is a **butter distribution** to the *dere ades*.
Initiates each take a sheep to *halak'a baira*.	Initiates go to five different assembly places in Shale, and drink a little beer in each. Then they go to Zurgo assembly place, in Zolo where they meet with initiates from Elo, Zolo and Kale (in Doko Gembela). In the evening they return to an assembly place in Masho, where they meet with initiates from Masho.
Initiates go to assembly place, and a certain man ties an **ostrich feather** on their heads. Then they enter a special fenced part of the assembly place, and stand in a line and are blessed. (No kneeling or kissing the ground.)	
Sofe: *Dortane* gives the initiates a stick, known as **gatuma**. After this the initiate can simply take his **horoso** from home. The initiate makes his **first blessing**.	**Sofe:** *Dortane* gives the initiates a stick, known as **gatuma**.
Sacrifice: The sacrificer slaughters a bull and a female sheep.	**Sacrifice:** The *maaka* passes a sheep over the shoulders of the initiates and slaughters it. Then the sacrificer slaughters a bull. After that the *dortane* gives the initiates their **horoso**, and the initiate makes his **first blessing**.
Seniors' Feast	**Seniors' Feast**

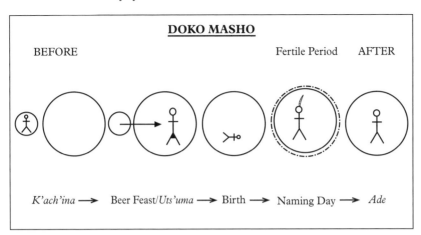

Figure 6   *Halak'a* initiations in Doko Masho

eat at most *dere* feasts. The *lazantsa* tells him of the *dere*'s intention, and on the day of the Beer Feast he enters the house of the *dere*, as a bride enters her husband's house at marriage. Some months later, at the next *Mesqalla*, he symbolically gives birth and is reborn. He has now entered the *dere* as a baby. The erection of *gazo* in his compound later marks his maturity as a youth, and he then kisses the ground in front of the *dere* to show his obedience to them. His new status as *halak'a* is then marked by his *sofe* in the market place. He is presented with the *horoso*, and herds the community, as a son herds his father's cattle. Later he gives the Seniors' Feast, proving that he is a provider, and thus he becomes an *ade*. At the next *Mesqalla* he exits his ritual state, and becomes a *dere ade*, a full member of the *dere*, able to partake in all the feasts. This is shown schematically in Figure 6.

Devolution versus transformation

This outline of *halak'a* initiations in 1990s Doko reveals a number of things. First, in sharp contrast to the practices of the sacrificial system, there is phenomenal variation in the way that the initiations are carried out in the different *deres* that make up Doko. Not only is there a marked structural difference between the general Doko Gembela and Doko Masho forms, but there is also a plethora of variation in the details of the initiations in each of the *deres*. Each *dere*, it seems, makes *halak'as* just a little bit differently.

Furthermore, it is extremely difficult to piece together a historical, or even a diachronic, picture of the initiations throughout the last century. In response to questions about how their *dere* made *halak'as* before the revolution, or in their grandfather's time, people would always say that they have not changed this tradition and that the initiations were carried out just as they are today. This, however, is patently not true. People's accounts of recent *halak'a* initiations frequently mentioned small details that were done differently in the past. An obvious example is Shagire's recollection that when he became *halak'a* in Masho in the 1960s he himself had to provide all the beer for the Beer Feast while nowadays people receive contributions from friends and neighbours in the form of *woito* gifts. Other examples would be the change in the *halak'a*'s garb from the black sheepskin to the striped *k'ole* cloth, or the decline in the sheep sacrifice by the *halak'a*'s wife in Kale. While people would recall all manner of such minor changes, no one could ever give me a full account of how *halak'a* initiations were carried out in the past.

The most plausible understanding of change in the *halak'a* initiations, then, is that over time there have been innumerable minor changes in the details of the initiations in each different *dere*. These little changes are visible synchronically in the variation between the different forms of the initiations in all the *deres* of Doko. As each *dere* changes some small detail or other, they begin to carry out their initiations in a slightly different way from their neighbours.

The overall nature of these small changes, again in contrast to the practices of the sacrificial system, does not appear to be simply devolution. While there is some devolution, particularly in the *deres* of Doko Gembela, it is most definitely not the case that the majority of the small changes are those of people simply discontinuing previous practices. On the contrary, many of the small changes show people modifying previous practices into a new form that is more agreeable to them. As people began to prefer cloth to skins, for example, the *halak'as* stopped wearing the black sheepskin and started to wear the striped *k'ole* cloth instead. Instead of devolution, it is possible to discern a process of transformation.

Transformation is a complicated process that is far more difficult to understand than simple devolution. In some cases little changes will accumulate and result in overall structural transformation, while in other cases little changes will just lead to a high degree of variation in insignificant details. In order to understand the way that transformation takes place, and the effects that it has, it is necessary to understand both the driving forces of change and the way that these forces are experienced in day-to-day and cultural life. These issues have been touched on in chapters 2 and 3 and at the beginning of this chapter, but they will be brought into sharper relief in the next two chapters. Then, in chapter 8, we will bring everything together and try to show how the Doko Masho *halak'a* initiations have in fact undergone an overall structural transformation in the last century or so, while the sacrifices, and to a lesser extent the Doko Gembela *halak'a* initiations, have instead undergone a more linear process of devolution.

6   Experiencing change

This chapter seeks to understand the forces of change in twentieth-century Doko life. The external drivers of this change have already been discussed in chapter 2, where the historical events of this period were described in some detail. The task in front of us now is to consider how these changes were experienced by people in Doko and how they impacted on cultural life, particularly on the two sets of practices that I have called the sacrificial system and the initiatory system.

Changing production patterns

Let us start by considering the situation in the nineteenth century. At this time the inheritance system was heavily skewed in favour of genealogical seniors. The eldest son inherited half his father's land, while younger sons divided the rest equally among themselves. Assuming this pattern of inheritance had been in place for at least a few generations, it would have resulted in a vastly unequal distribution of land amongst people in Doko. Eldest sons of eldest sons would have owned far more land than their more junior cousins, and the descendants of elder brothers and senior lines in general would be favoured over the descendants of younger brothers and junior lines. In a family where each man had three sons, for example, the eldest son of the eldest son of the eldest son would own almost ten times as much land as his most junior cousin, after only four generations.[11] We can begin to imagine, then, the extreme differences in landholdings that must have existed in Doko in the nineteenth century.[12]

Large landowners were thus predominantly the descendants of eldest sons and senior lines. In contrast to their junior cousins, these men often owned more land than they could farm themselves and thus they sought to appropriate the labour of others through work groups, share-cropping or the exploitation of slave labour. Many of them would have been clan, lineage or segment heads and thus they would have gained even further advantage through the practices of the sacrificial system, in which their juniors brought them gifts so that they would make the important offerings to the spirits on their behalf.

These then were the people who could generate enough surplus wealth to be able to sponsor the initiation feasts and take the titles of *halak'a*, *hudhugha* or *dana*. Genealogical juniors tended to own only a little land and they struggled to produce enough grain to feed their families, give the necessary gifts to their seniors and in-laws, and pay for marriage feasts for their children. The initiation to even *halak'a* was well beyond their reach, let alone the more prestigious positions of *hudhugha* and *dana*. Thus in the predominantly agricultural economy of the early nineteenth century, genealogical and initiatory seniors tended to be the same people. In many respects the initiatory system functioned as a way for genealogical seniors to extend their genealogical seniority into community seniority, as they used their wealth to buy political office and the ability to influence community affairs. Community sacrificers, who already had community seniority, could not be initiated to any of these positions and they were generally supposed to act as symbolic figureheads, while real political power fell to the *halak'as* and *dere ades*.

There was, however, one other factor in nineteenth-century Doko that slightly altered this picture. This was the gradually increasing involvement of some men in long-distance trade. This non-agricultural source of wealth opened up opportunities for any man to get rich, and successful traders could also afford the cost of being initiated. Long-distance trade was not new in the nineteenth century, but in the previous two centuries it had been disrupted by the Oromo invasion of what is now central Ethiopia and at that time it seems that very little trade passed along these routes (Abir 1970:123–4). Seventeenth- and eighteenth-century Doko men, it would seem, thus did not have the opportunity to generate much non-agricultural wealth through long-distance trade.

However, by the late eighteenth century many of the Oromo communities had made permanent settlements and gradually merchant caravans began again to push through to the south. It so happens that at around this time British interference in the East African slave trade led to a dramatic increase in the demand for slaves in Arabia. This combination of events meant that long-distance trade began to flourish again in the nineteenth century and that its most lucrative aspect was the trade in slaves (Abir 1970:123). Men in the Gamo Highlands were not slow to get involved in this trade, and as the century progressed more and more men looked to long-distance trade as an alternative source of wealth. Successful traders could accumulate wealth irrespective of the amount of land they owned, and thus as involvement in trade increased throughout the century the pattern whereby only genealogical seniors could afford to take the initiatory titles began to change. Increasingly it became traders who took these titles, and initiatory seniority began to be seen as a type of seniority that anyone, in theory, could achieve. By the end of the nineteenth century the *halak'a* had come to be seen as the 'ultimate tradesman' (Abélès 1981:56).

Even though increasing numbers of men got involved in long-distance trade in the nineteenth century, it was still the case that the vast majority were full-time farmers. Most of these people would never be able to afford to be initiated and were thus stuck with their junior status in the community.

As the nineteenth century turned into the twentieth, and the Gamo Highlands were conquered by Menelik's forces and incorporated into the nation state of Ethiopia, there were a number of important changes in both agricultural and trade patterns. Most importantly, warfare was banned and the slave trade was brought to a halt. The end of warfare meant that wealthy landowners could no longer go to war for local slaves and thus they lost an extremely important source of agricultural labour. Moreover, many 'slave *deres*' took the opportunity to assert their independence and many slaves refused to work for their masters. Under the watchful gaze of the Amhara authorities, there was little that their masters could do.

With little or no slave labour, many large landowners could no longer farm all their land, and during the early part of the twentieth century many men put out their land in sharecropping or 'reversible sale' agreements. Others, it would seem, sold some of their land outright. In this way men who could afford it gained access to more land. Shagire's great grandfather, for example, bought a lot of land at this time and many other moderately wealthy families did likewise. The result was a somewhat more equal land distribution, although significant differentials between rich and poor continued to exist. Another result was that fewer men needed to keep a second house near their more distant fields, and as the years went by the accompanying practice of polygamy also declined. Perhaps the most important result, however, was that large landowners could now no longer produce surplus grain to anywhere near the extent that they had before. The end of the long-distance slave trade dealt a similar blow to those men who had become rich through trading. Quite suddenly this non-agricultural source of wealth was no longer available. On top of all this, most families now had to support a number of Amhara settlers, or *neftenya*, and this imposition was a further drain on the resources of rich and poor alike.

All in all the beginning of the twentieth century marked a big change in production patterns in the Gamo Highlands. The ability to produce huge surpluses diminished dramatically and the unequal land distribution began to even out a little. Even rich men began to find they could not afford to become *danas* and the number who could afford the *hudhugha* feasts also began slowly to decline. As the century progressed and land continued to be divided up amongst sons, people's ability to produce large agricultural surpluses continued to diminish and even the costs of the *halak'a* feasts began to seem prohibitive to many.

At the same time that agricultural production was becoming more and more difficult, however, other forms of non-agricultural wealth production began to become significant. The two most important activities were weaving and trade. Men in the northern part of the highlands, particularly in Dorze, began to take up weaving around the turn of the century, and as the years went by they became known as some of the best weavers in the country. They produced various types of cotton cloth shawls, including *gabis* and *natallas*, that soon came to be worn throughout the country. Some weavers worked from their homes in Dorze, while others moved to Addis Abeba where many of their clients lived. As weaving proved to be increasingly lucrative, more and more men took it up. Those who could produce high-quality cloth with the intricate border designs that were becoming fashionable tended to move to Addis Abeba or other urban centres, while the producers of more standard cloth generally remained in the highlands (Olmstead 1975:91). The majority of those who moved away to urban centres none the less kept a house and a wife back in Dorze, and would return at least once a year for the *Mesqalla* celebrations.

At the same time trading again became important. Twentieth-century trade was centred not on slaves and the market in Arabia, but rather on consumer products. Imported plastic containers, cooking pots, scrap metal and other such things were brought from Addis Abeba down to the markets in the highlands, and cloth shawls were taken for sale in Addis. As the century progressed, traders also brought imported second-hand clothes, known as *selbaj*, manufactured coloured thread for use in weaving, notebooks, padlocks, rat poison and a variety of other things. The main export from the highlands continued to be woven cloth, although a few traders made a living by selling local animal hides to the new tanneries in Addis.

In the early part of the twentieth century both trade and weaving were centred around the *dere* of Dorze in the northern part of the highlands. During the Italian occupation two roads were built from the small town of Chencha down to the lowlands, and one of them went straight through the middle of Dorze. Helped by these favourable transport links, traders from Dorze, Chencha and the immediately surrounding areas would bring goods from Addis Abeba and sell them in the Dorze market, and then local traders would buy these goods and carry them over the highlands for sale in markets in other *deres*. As the century progressed men in other *deres* began to take up weaving and to get more involved with long-distance trade. Several men in Doko took up weaving early on in the century, while those in more distant *deres* have only taken up the craft more recently. By the late 1960s Judith Olmstead reports that approximately 78 per cent of married men in Dorze practised weaving, while in Dita, just 16 km away, the figure was only 9 per cent (Olmstead 1975:91). By this time weaving had become the mainstay of the Dorze economy and several families did not cultivate land at all, while others employed wage labourers from other *deres* to do this work (1975:90).

The number of weavers in Doko was closer to that in Dorze than to that in Dita. Doko Gembela, in particular, bordered both Chencha town and Dorze and was thus very well connected to these important markets and the roads that ran through them. A very great number of men in this part of Doko took up weaving or trading during the twentieth century, and they too hired in agricultural labour from other *deres*. Doko Masho, located just that little bit further away from Chencha and Dorze, was slightly slower in the uptake of weaving and trading. While men in the small *dere* of Masho, situated right next to Doko Gembela and on a small road, increasingly engaged in these endeavours, those in the *deres* on the far side of Doko only took up weaving more slowly and in numbers more comparable to those in Dita.

The significance of this increase in non-agricultural forms of wealth generation in the twentieth century is that, once again, it offered a way for anybody to get rich. While there is scant data about the organisation of long-distance trade in the nineteenth century, it is clear that twentieth-century weaving and trade were open to all. Any man could learn the craft or set up as a trader, and it became increasingly popular with young men. Involvement in the cash economy provided an opportunity for wealth generation that was entirely outside the traditional agricultural system, in which the ability to produce was intimately tied up with hierarchical ideas about genealogical seniority. Trade and weaving gave men independence. Most importantly, it provided young men with the opportunity to assert their independence from their fathers.

Sacrifices and initiations in changing contexts

These changes in production patterns in twentieth-century Doko clearly would have had a great impact on the practices of both the sacrificial and initiatory systems. The decline in the importance of the sacrificial system can most easily be understood in terms of the increasing ability to generate wealth through non-agricultural means. This trend had already started in the nineteenth century and it would seem to be the main driver of change that led to the sacrificial system devolving, as men began to realise that they could produce wealth even without the blessing of their seniors. Even those men who continued to rely entirely on agricultural production, though, would have been influenced by the changing ideas around them. And as their ability to produce large surpluses continued to decrease, because of the increasing population density and the decreasing size of landholdings, they would more and more have come to resent their seniors' control of their production and the gifts that they had to take them.

These same changes would also have led men increasingly to resent the unequal inheritance pattern and push to initiate a change towards the more equal inheritance patterns that now exist. Furthermore, as the national administration and the state courts in Chencha and Arba Minch became the main locus of political power, the practical importance of the clan grouping in matters such as protecting members' land or claiming compensation when a clan member was injured or murdered became less important. All in all, the incentive to partake in the practices of the sacrificial system was clearly diminishing.

The picture with the initiatory system, however, is not so clear. In the early part of the twentieth century getting initiated was still probably the best use you could make of your surplus wealth. Even though the political role of the *halak'a* was becoming less important, *halak'as* still had great status in the *dere*. And status, as will be clear from the preceding chapters, has continued to be a central theme in Doko life throughout the whole of the twentieth century. Genealogical juniors who were increasingly fed up with the power and privileges of their seniors thus had a great incentive to become *halak'a*. In this way they could assert equality with their more senior cousins on the grounds that they were both now *dere ades*.

Furthermore, the more equal distribution of wealth that characterised the twentieth century meant that there were now some men who would be the first in their families who could afford to become *halak'a*. Some of the men who had bought land at the beginning of the century had considerably increased their productive abilities, and those men with little land who had become successful weavers or traders suddenly found themselves in a rather different financial situation from their fathers. These upwardly mobile men would have taken particular pride in becoming *halak'a* and thus enhancing the social status of themselves and their descendants.

Former *halak'as*, or *dere ades*, also had a motive to ensure that men continued to be initiated. They had provided the huge feasts to become *halak'as* themselves, and now they wanted the payback of eating at the feasts that the new *halak'as* would throw. If men now refused to become *halak'a*, then their investment would have been in vain. They wanted to ensure that the new wealth, particularly that from the traders and weavers, was appropriately distributed around the *dere*.

None the less, as the century progressed, the decline in agricultural surpluses made it progressively harder for farmers to generate enough wealth to get initiated. And even men with some income from weaving began to find that there were increasingly all sorts of other things to spend their money on. Consumer goods became more prominent in the markets, government taxes required a cash payment and the new school only accepted pupils on receipt of a cash fee.

Furthermore, trade began to be dominated by young men, as they had the energy and inclination to rush backwards and forwards between Addis Abeba and the highlands, and many of them preferred to spend their wealth on radios or smart clothes rather than on the initiation feasts. Young men whose fathers had yet to become *halak'a* would have little incentive to use their trading money to sponsor their fathers' initiation feasts. And even those traders whose fathers already had become *halak'a*, or who were no longer alive, would have little incentive to become *halak'a* themselves because they spent so much of their time away from Doko.

Marxism and Protestantism in the 'new economy'

As sons began to generate more wealth than their fathers, through either trade or weaving or by becoming school teachers, carpenters or local government workers, the tensions between fathers and sons began to escalate to new proportions. Farming fathers tended to retain the 'traditional' idea that they were the owners of everything produced by their household members, including therefore the money that a son earned from his own labours. Sons who had become involved in the cash economy, on the other hand, bought into the 'modern' idea that they were the owners of the products of their own labour, and thus considered their money to be theirs to do with as they pleased. Many of these sons continued to live with their fathers and to eat from their land, and their wives generally worked with the other household women in agricultural production and food preparation. These sons tended to think it adequate that they pay a wage labourer to work on the land in their place, while the rest of their money belonged to themselves. Their fathers had other ideas, but were increasingly powerless to do anything about it.

We can now see why the Marxist teachings of the *zamacha* campaigners were so readily accepted by the majority of people in 1970s Doko. The economic trends of the previous decades had already taken the people of Doko a long way towards a more equal distribution of wealth and the ideology of the initiatory system emphasised personal success and the irrelevance of hereditary status. The teachings that proclaimed that everybody was equal and the new laws that made the practices of the sacrificial system illegal fitted well with the contemporary situation and, even more importantly, provided a legitimising ideology for those who wanted to stop partaking in these practices.

The same is true of the teachings of the Protestant missionaries. Their claim that everybody was equal under God, and that people could pray directly to God without the mediation of any seniors, hit a similar chord. By deeming both the sacrifices and the initiations to be forms of devil worship, the church provided a way out for those who wanted to avoid those practices. And by challenging even the authority of fathers over their sons, it provided young men with an ideological grounding for their claims to their own wealth and their own autonomy. In short, it legitimised their independence. It is clear, then, why these teachings began to sound appealing to people in Doko Gembela in the 1960s, and later to people in Doko Masho in the 1990s.

Both of these ideologies were used by sons and daughters in 1990s Doko Masho as they struggled to reformulate their relationship with their fathers. In an argument between Protestant Murunesh and her traditional father-in-law, Shata, for example, Murunesh at one point challenged Shata's authority be saying 'it was God that put me here, not a person'. The implication here is that she was created by God, and not by Shata or the spirits to which he makes offerings, and therefore only God had authority over her. Shata replied angrily, 'do you bring God on my land?', thus reminding her that, whatever her beliefs, she still lived on his land and ate his food. She was still materially dependent on him, and thus had better respect his authority and do as he say. At this point Murunesh acquiesced, but the tension between them remained.

In the house where I was living, Wale and his wife Almaz had both become Protestants and there were similar tensions between them and Shagire. Instead of farming with Shagire, Wale spent most of his time working as a carpenter. He paid for Shagire to hire some wage labourers in the heavy agricultural season and he also paid for the *zurra* and other work groups to work the land a number of days per year. Beyond this he considered his money to be his own, and he had bought a radio cassette player, urban-style clothes and other such goods. Arguments and discussions about payment for agricultural labour were a continual part of life in this household and were clearly uncomfortable for both men. Shagire felt that his authority was diminished by him having to ask his son for money, while Wale resented what seemed like a constant drain on his income. Both men, however, made an effort to work things out and the tensions most often became visible through little jokes and jibes. The following is a good example.

One day reasonably early on in my fieldwork I came home and found Shagire and Wale sitting in Wale's house with about twelve of their close patrilineal kin. They were feasting on huge amounts of food, centred around two thigh-high pots of barley and milk paste. When I asked what this feast was for Wale started joking around and said that he was becoming a 'family *halak'a*'. Most of the men fell about laughing and clearly thought this was a great joke. Shagire, however, usually the one with the sharpest sense of humour, got up angrily and walked outside, muttering 'you're not the family *halak'a*'.

The feast was in fact for something entirely different. The group of patrilineal kin had recently started up a work group together, and Shagire had taken the position of *kawo* of the group. As outlined in chapter 3, what this meant was that rather than paying the group each time it farmed his land, he instead feasted the group at the end of the agricultural season. Providing such a feast traditionally enabled rich men to show their generosity and the larger the feast the greater the respect that the work group *kawo* won. Shagire was very much a traditionalist and he wanted to throw a big feast for his group. However, the reality was that it would be Wale who would pay for the feast, and thus the size of the feast had been a considerable source of tension between them over the previous few weeks. For even though Wale would provide the money, Shagire would gain the respect.

In this context Wale's joke about becoming 'family *halak'a*' is revealing. By alluding to the initiation feasts, he was implying that he was throwing this feast to buy status and become 'a father' in the family. Not only did he thus try to claim for himself the respect accorded to the provider of the feast, but he also subtly asserted his equality with Shagire, as both of them would be *ades*. Painfully aware of his lack of control over his son's wealth, and thus his diminished 'fatherhood', Shagire felt the jibe sharply and left the group in anger.

Similar tensions also existed between Almaz and Shagire. An on-going argument simmered between them about the amount of time that she spent trading. Many women engaged in small-scale local trade, buying butter or grain from one market and then carrying it a few hours over the mountains to another market where they would sell it for a few extra pennies. Before she got married Almaz would regularly buy things in the market in Chencha and then sell them in the markets of Wayza or

Anduro, some six or seven hours' walk away. These trips would require an overnight stay, but the profit on the goods would make it worthwhile. When she got married and had children Almaz had stopped making these lengthy trips, and instead tried to trade between Chencha and Doko Masho markets when she had the time. The profit she made from this trade was hers to keep and thus she had a big incentive to spend as much time trading as possible. This meant, however, that she would spend less time involved in household labour and more work would fall to Halimbe, her mother-in-law. Unhappy about this state of affairs and the independence that Almaz tried to assert, Shagire and Halimbe were thus frequently telling her off for not working hard enough and spending too much time at the markets.

These tensions between Protestant sons and daughters-in-law and the traditional parents with whom they lived characterised much of family life in Doko in the 1990s. They can be seen to result from the changing production patterns that rendered 'traditional' agricultural production less and less profitable and 'modern' non-agricultural production more and more profitable, often resulting in sons producing more wealth than their father and thus inverting the basis of his traditional authority. In this situation, the ability to increase one's status in the *dere* by becoming *halak'a* was somewhat irrelevant. Whereas the early part of this century had been characterised by status arguments between *dere* and clan members, by the 1990s the fundamental status argument was taking place in the home, between fathers and sons. Joining the church or moving into town provided a more effective way to assert independence and gain status than getting initiated. The *halak'a* initiations should have been becoming less and less popular as the years went by.

This was certainly true in Doko Gembela, where very few men had become *halak'a* since the 1970s. But it was patently not true in Doko Masho. The ethnographic fact was that over seventy men were initiated there during the two years between 1995 and 1997. While it is extremely likely that this number will decrease in the future, it remains that the Doko Masho *halak'a* initiations are currently much more popular than their Doko Gembela equivalents. This difference in popularity can be explained to some extent by the different degree to which people in Doko Gembela have taken up weaving and trading, so that all the changes and accompanying tensions are slightly more marked there than they are in Doko Masho. But this difference of degrees cannot fully explain the different situation of the *halak'as* in the two groups of *deres*. To understand this fully, we must take another look at the different forms of the initiations in Doko Gembela and Doko Masho.

Doko Gembela and Doko Masho initiations revisited

In the previous chapter we saw that there were some quite significant differences in both the form and the meaning of the initiations in Doko Gembela and Doko Masho. In Doko Gembela the transition from *k'ach'ina* to *ade* is seen as that from community junior to community senior and the symbolism centres around the rebirth of the *halak'a* and his symbolic development into a virile warrior, complete with spear and *kallacha*. Because only one *halak'a* is initiated at a time, and because he must feast the whole community, both *dere ades* and *k'ach'ina*, the cost of being initiated is extremely high. Furthermore, because the *halak'a*'s wife must slaughter a sheep during the initiation process, a man cannot get initiated until after his wife has reached menopause and is able to carry out this act.[13] These features combine to ensure that it is only fairly old men who can become *halak'a* in Doko Gembela, and this fits with the symbolism of *halak'a* as community senior.

In Doko Masho, by contrast, the transition from *k'ach'ina* to *ade* is seen more in terms of that from partial community member to full community member. The initiation symbolism centres around the marriage of the *halak'a* to the *dere*, in which the *halak'a* 'enters' the community as a bride enters her father-in-law's house. The partial community membership of the *k'ach'ina* is evidenced by the fact that they cannot eat at community feasts and, in particular, are excluded from the *halak'a*'s Beer Feast and Seniors' Feast. This results in the scale of these feasts being considerably smaller than their Doko Gembela counterparts. Furthermore, because the *dere ades* are divided out between the group of *halak'as* who get initiated together, the scale of the feasts is even further reduced. In short, it is far cheaper to become *halak'a* in Doko Masho than it is in Doko Gembela. On top of this there is no rule that the *halak'a*'s wife must slaughter a sheep during the proceedings, and thus men can be initiated before their wife has reached menopause. Most *halak'as* are initiated when they are between the ages of twenty and forty, and in some *deres* even young boys can become *halak'a*. Because men are initiated when young, and because many men are initiated together in batches, the result is that a much higher proportion of the community are *dere ades*. This fits with the symbolism of the initiation as a way to join the community fully.

We can see, then, why the Doko Masho initiations are more popular than those in Doko Gembela. They are open to young men and they emphasise community rather than seniority. Most importantly, they are cheaper. Becoming *halak'a* in contemporary Doko Masho is about becoming part of the community, and as such it is seen as something that

all men should do. And since the cost is not too high, it is something that
many men continue to do.

Now it is possible that there have always been differences in the form
of the initiations in Doko Gembela and Doko Masho and that it is just
coincidence that the Doko Masho form is more suited to the contemporary situation in the *dere*. However, there are a number of reasons to think
that this is not the case. Instead it is more likely that the Doko Masho
initiations have changed throughout the last century or two and adapted
to the new conditions.

There are a number of elements in the Doko Masho initiations that
are clearly innovations. For example, it seems that the initiation of young
men must be a relatively recent innovation that only took place during
the middle part of the twentieth century. This can be seen from a number
of contradictions in the system. If a man becomes initiated when he is
in his twenties or thirties, his father will generally still be alive and they
will still be living together in the same compound. In such circumstances
the *halak'a* would not be able to carry out any *dere* sacrifices because he
cannot slaughter an animal while his father is still alive. It would also be
against the whole ethos of Doko life for a son to have a more important
political position than his father. It thus seems extremely unlikely that
young men became *halak'a* in nineteenth-century Doko Masho.

What does seem likely, though, is that the form of the initiations
changed during the twentieth century in order to ensure that men continued to become *halak'a*. As wealth came to be increasingly generated
by the young, the *dere* decided to change a few rules and allowed these
young men to be initiated. They got round the contradictory problems
by deciding that if a man became *halak'a* while his father was still alive,
then his father became *halak'a* with him. It would be the father who carried out the sacrifices, and both men would wear the ceremonial garb,
observe the prohibitions and act as messenger to the assembly. They also
changed the rule whereby a *halak'a* must not spend a night away from
the *dere*, and allowed these young *halak'as* to return to their weaving or
trading activities in other parts of the country while their fathers stayed
in the *dere* and continued to herd the community.

Thus in contemporary Doko Masho it is not unusual for urban-
dwelling weavers to become *halak'a* back in their *deres*. The initiation
of Abera Yesa described in the last chapter was in fact one such case.
Abera was born in Masho to a good farming family and went away weaving with his father's elder brother's sons when he was eight or nine years
old. He grew up in the town in Bale, in south-east Ethiopia, where he
lived with his kin as part of a small group of Masho weavers. He thus
speaks Amharic and is used to town life. Some years ago he joined the

Protestant church, much to the horror of his father. Since then his father and the *dere ades* have insistently asked him to leave the church and join the community by becoming *halak'a* in Masho. He refused a number of times, but eventually they succeeded in persuading him, and in 1994 his name was announced as one of those who would become *halak'a* next year. He returned from Bale a few weeks at a time in order to go through the various stages of the initiation rituals, but managed to spend most of his herding year living in Bale, while his father performed the duties of the *halak'a* in Masho. He now continues to live in Bale with his wife and two young children.

While this situation makes some sense in contemporary Doko, it would have been totally inappropriate in the nineteenth century. The initiation of young men in Doko Masho, we can safely infer, has been a recent change in the system. While we can see the economic forces that would have led to this change, it is another question as to how these forces were actually translated into cultural change by real people. This will be the subject of the next chapter, but for now, remaining on a systemic level, we need to try and work out what the previous form of the Doko Masho initiations would have looked like.

The fragmentation of Doko

There is good reason to believe that in the not-too-distant past, perhaps in the late nineteenth or early twentieth century, men in the *deres* of Doko Masho were initiated in a way rather similar to the initiations in contemporary Doko Gembela. This is because further back in the past these two groupings of *deres* were far less significant, if they existed at all, and instead the whole of Doko was united as one large *dere*.

Oral histories tell of the gradual fragmentation of Doko during the nineteenth century. In the late eighteenth or early nineteenth century Doko was united as one *dere* under a powerful *kawo*. Unlike the present *kawo* who is *kawo* for both Doko Masho and Doko Gembela but who must carry out his sacrifices for them separately, the old *kawo* united the whole of Doko and carried out sacrifices for the whole *dere* in Anka assembly place in Shale. On his installation each of the seventeen smaller *deres* of Doko brought him a bull to slaughter at Anka assembly place and sat there to eat the meat together.

However, six generations ago, sometime around the end of the eighteenth and the beginning of the nineteenth century, one of the brothers of the *kawo* of Shama, a nearby *dere*, left his home and came to Doko. He settled in Yoira, and claimed that he would be good for the *dere* and that they should make him *kawo*. Male, as he was called, was not however made *kawo*, and eventually he died. His oldest son, Dale, moved to Ch'ento, and said that now he should be made *kawo*. However, one of his half-brothers, so the story goes, was so jealous of Dale's wealth and popularity that he killed him. This greatly shocked the community and they decided to make Dale's son, Toito, their new *kawo*. However, just before they could do this, war broke out with the *dere* of Zad'a. Doko was taken by surprise and was not prepared. They fled for protection to the *dere* of Chencha, where they stayed for seven years. Toito was instrumental in making peace and bringing about the return of Doko to their land. Soon afterwards, in the latter part of the nineteenth century, he was made *kawo* and his descendants have held this position since then. Desta, the present *kawo*, is his great great grandson.

The previous *kawo* came to be known as Gamo *kawo*, while Toito became the Doko *kawo*. The descendants of the Gamo *kawo* continued to live in Doko until the early 1970s, when they left because of an argument with the *dere*. Some people attribute the poor state of the *dere* to the Gamo *kawo*'s absence, and people have been sent to Addis Abeba and around the country to find him. None, however, has been successful. The *dere* of Shale retains some prestige because it used to be the *dere* of the *kawo*, and that is why, for example, the new *halak'as* must touch the people of Shale during their *sofe* in the market place.

It was common for *deres* to break up and reconstitute themselves in different groupings during the nineteenth century, as the search for slaves drove incessant warfare between the *deres*, and it seems that the change of *kawo* was a crucial factor in the fragmentation of Doko. As the large *dere* broke up, the smaller *deres* reconstituted themselves into new groupings. The *deres* of Masho, Shale, Woits'o, Gedeno, Dambo, Yoira, Ch'ento and Eleze made an agreement that from now on they would coordinate their *halak'a* initiations and their *halak'as* would all *sofe* together in the market place. The remaining *deres* made a similar agreement, and thus the groupings of Doko Masho and Doko Gembela came into being. The newness of these medium-sized *deres* is further attested to by the fact that there is no community sacrificer, or *ek'k'a*, for either of these *deres*.

There seems to be good evidence, then, that Doko has been fragmenting into two *deres* over the past two centuries. Before this fragmentation started Doko was rather more united and it seems likely that all the small *deres* co-ordinated their *halak'a* initiations to some extent, probably carrying out their *sofes* together, as is common throughout the highlands. In this situation we would expect the variation in the form of the initiations between the *deres* to have been similar to the variation between the *deres* of Doko Gembela (*or* Doko Masho) today. In other words, we would expect a variation in detail, but not in overall form.

What, though, would be the general form of these nineteenth-century initiations? Most likely they changed as the century progressed and the political and economic context altered. What can be said, though, is that until Doko fragmented into Doko Masho and Doko Gembela any significant structural changes in the initiations would have taken place in all the *deres* together, as their initiations would have been coordinated to some extent. Only towards the end of the nineteenth century, when Toito was made *kawo*, would the two groupings of *deres* have been able to make changes to their initiations independently.

The form of the contemporary Doko Gembela initiations seems very well adapted to the late nineteenth century, when wealthy landowners and successful slave traders produced large surpluses and could afford huge feasts. While there have no doubt been some minor changes to these initiations since then, it seems more than probable that their overall form has not changed during the twentieth century. As with the practices of the sacrificial system, people have simply begun to stop partaking in the initiations and have opted for alternatives such as Protestant Christianity. If this is the case, then it follows that in late-nineteenth-century Doko Masho the initiations were performed in a way that was basically similar to the contemporary form of the Doko Gembela initiations. Somehow, throughout the twentieth century, the people of Doko Masho have changed their initiations so that they have adapted to the contemporary situations. This has resulted in their structural transformation from the 'warrior form' to the 'wife form'.

To change or not to change?

Two questions arise from this analysis. First, why did the people of Doko Gembela not change their initiations as well? And second, how exactly did this process of change take place in Doko Masho? We can begin to tackle the first question here, while the second question will be answered in the next two chapters.

Situated just that little bit closer to Chencha and Dorze, the people of Doko Gembela got involved in trade and weaving rather more quickly than their neighbours in Doko Masho. In the early years of the twentieth century large numbers of young men suddenly began to earn money through trade and weaving. The response of the people of Doko Gembela to this rapid change seems to have been rather similar to that of the people of Dorze, where the *dere ades* 'caught' *halak'as* and forced them to be initiated against their will (Halperin and Olmstead 1976). This 'shock reaction' proved unsustainable and it is understandable that when the

Protestant missionaries first reached Doko Gembela in the 1950s many young people saw in their teachings a way out of their predicament.

In Doko Masho the twentieth-century changes took place a little more slowly. The number of men who took up trade and weaving in the early part of the century was fairly small, and it was in this context that the *dere ades* had to decide how to respond to this new occurrence of relatively rich young men. And in this slightly different context they made a slightly different decision. Rather than force men to become *halak'a*, they discussed the possibility of making one or two minor changes to the initiations so that these rich young men would agree to get initiated of their own accord. By the time large numbers of men were involved in the cash economy the form of the initiations had thus already changed slightly, and the issues facing these men were not identical to those facing men in Doko Gembela. Thus, even in the 1960s, men in Doko Masho were not particularly attracted to the teachings of the Protestant missionaries.

While speed of change appears to be a major factor in explaining why the people of Doko Gembela did not alter their initiations while those in Doko Masho did, it does not explain the whole story. Ultimately, room must be left for human idiosyncrasy. Different people come to different decisions about the same things. And when it comes to making communal decisions, the views of those who have the greatest rhetorical skills often prevail. It would be surprising if two communities chose the same response to a new situation, even if the contexts were identical. We are talking here not about major decisions to alter radically the performance of the initiations, but rather about small solutions to the small problems that the changing context presented to real people in early-twentieth-century Doko.

In order to understand fully the mechanisms of change we must move down an analytic level and focus in on real people and on the way in which communal decisions are made. Only in this way can we appreciate why it is not surprising that the people of Doko Masho and Doko Gembela came to different decisions. And only in this way can we understand exactly how change took place in the Doko Masho initiations.

7 Assemblies and incremental cultural change

In the last chapter we saw how the changing patterns of production in the nineteenth and twentieth centuries created new economic realities and new social situations for the people of Doko, and how people responded to these new situations by changing their actions in everyday and cultural life. We saw that these changes were often contested, as certain people stood to lose out by the changing actions of those with whom they interacted, and we also saw how the community would sometimes make decisions to change cultural practices so that they were better suited to the contemporary situation. In this chapter we will look at the process of communal decision-making and consider the ways in which changes in individual circumstances and actions led to communally sanctioned changes in cultural practices.

Strategy and individual change

It is a basic truth that all people want to make the best of their situation and will develop strategies to further their own interests and improve their own lives. These strategies are not necessarily carefully thought out action plans, but are rather sets of strategic decisions that people make as they interact with other people. As changes in the social and economic context alter both personal circumstances and the opportunities that are open to individuals, people begin to make different decisions in what, to the outsider, might look like the same type of interaction. In other words, as the context changes people modify their strategies in order to benefit from the new context.

We have seen that, overall, the strategies of young people and genealogical juniors in Doko in the twentieth century generally involved trying to assert their independence and maintain control over their wealth, while the strategies of older people and genealogical seniors generally involved trying to assert their authority and control the wealth of their juniors. While juniors tried to find ways of avoiding those practices that emphasised their junior status and required unwanted expenditure, seniors stressed the importance of these very same practices and tried to find ways to persuade the juniors to engage in them. Within these overall strategies, people had recourse to a number of 'tactics' that they could use to further their own interests.

The most extreme tactic that a junior could use to avoid having to partake in a cultural practice that he found undesirable was to opt out of the cultural system altogether. While it was difficult to opt out and have no 'religion' or no 'culture' at all, it was possible to opt out of the practices of the traditional cultural system if one took on the practices of an alternative cultural system. Both *Essa Woga* and Protestant Christianity provided such alternatives, and we have seen how many people took on these new practices in order to opt out of various aspects of the traditional system.

A slightly less extreme tactic involved simply stopping doing the practices that one found undesirable. The majority of people have used this tactic at some point throughout the twentieth century. Many men simply stopped calling their segment heads to make offerings for them before they started to sow their land. Other men simply refused to become *halak'a*. A whole collection of other cultural practices that have not been discussed in this book stopped in this way during the twentieth century, as people refused to carry them out because they felt they were unfair and unnecessary.

Another tactic to avoid undesirable practices was to put them off until a later date. This tactic has also proved popular in the twentieth century, as people have increasingly delayed taking the *kumets* payments to their in-laws, and clan members have asked their clan or lineage heads to sacrifice for them less and less frequently. In Doko Masho it is currently very rare for a man to take the *kumets* payments to his in-laws in the first year or two after his wife has given birth. Many men do not take the payments until the child is much older and there are more than a few cases when men have died of old age before they completed all the payments. In such cases the debt is passed on to the next generation and it continues to be something that will be done 'any year now'. It is most easy to put off practices that are not supposed to be performed at a fixed time, such as the *kumets* payments and the clan sacrifices. This tactic would not work for more time-bound practices, such as the pre-sowing offerings of the segment head or the annual *halak'a* initiations in Doko Masho.

While juniors use these types of tactics to avoid the practices they find undesirable, seniors have their own tactics to ensure that the practices they find desirable continue to be performed. Most obviously, seniors can stress the terrible misfortunes that will befall an individual if they do not carry out the cultural practices and instead do *gome*. Whenever someone falls ill, or their cattle die or something else goes wrong, this misfortune is generally interpreted by people in Doko as being the result of some inappropriate thing that that person has done. If a junior has some problem, seniors will very often say that it is the result of them not having followed the traditional practices correctly. Thus if a man falls ill, for example, seniors might interpret his misfortune to be a result of the *gome* because he has acted disrespectfully to his father-in-law by not taking him the *kumets* payments for his child who is now fifteen years old. To regain his health he had better take the payments and then get his father to slaughter a sheep and clear the *gome*. Or if there is poor rainfall in the *dere* and the crops are not growing well, then the *dere ades* might suggest that the current *halak'a* is no longer good for the *dere* and suggest that they really should initiate a new one.

Similar interpretations of illness and diagnoses of *gome* can be used to try to persuade juniors to leave the church. For example, soon after Almaz married Wale she became very ill. At this time she was a Protestant, so she ignored Shagire's views that her illness was due to *gome*, and instead went to the church to be healed. When this failed she went to the clinic in the market place and even to the hospital in Chencha. When all these attempts failed, Almaz slowly began to listen to Shagire.

I was not getting better and I didn't know what to do. Shagire kept begging me to leave the church and return to the *dere woga*. He said I was ill because I had done *gome* by not following the tradition. If I left the church he would take me to a diviner and clear the *gome* and then I would get better. He begged and begged, and eventually I decided I would try. I left the church and started to live according to *dere woga*.

In this instance, however, Shagire's tactics did not work for long and Almaz soon rejoined the church. She completes the story thus:

I lived according to *dere woga* but still I did not get better. I went to diviners in Masho and in other *deres*. One said I had this *gome*, and one said I had that *gome*. I did as they said and Shagire killed many sheep to try to clear the *gome*. But still I didn't get better. One said that I should not work on Fridays, another said I should pray to Maryam. I tried all these things. I even went to the powerful diviner in Ezzo. He said that Wale was sleeping with other women and it was a serious *gome* for me. He said that I would die if I didn't leave him. I didn't know if Wale was sleeping with other women or not, and I was very upset. But I thought I will never find another husband as good as Wale, and so I stayed with him. I tried everything but still I didn't get better. Eventually, after five years, I went back to the church. And then suddenly I got better. I was cured. Over all those years it was my *gome* of leaving the church that was stopping me from getting better. Now I will never leave the church.

Another tactic that seniors use to try to dissuade their juniors from opting out of the traditional system by joining the church is to stress the virtues of 'our culture' versus the 'alien tradition' that the white missionaries have brought from elsewhere. As elders in the community, they still retain a certain moral high ground and sometimes these arguments succeed in making traditionalists of a few young people and genealogical juniors.

As individuals use these tactics to follow their strategies, they gradually change their practice as they choose to do some things and not other things. In this way incremental change in individual practices begins to take place.

Consensus and communal change

Only if the vast majority of individuals choose to make the same incremental changes will these changes become communal changes in a simple and straightforward way. For example, it seems likely that the decision to stop asking one's segment head to make the pre-sowing offerings was a decision that many individuals made at about the same time. The cumulative effect of all these individuals deciding to make this change was that by default it became a communal change. An official policy change, if you like, was never made, and indeed two brothers can decide to carry out this practice in different ways and to different degrees, as was shown in chapter 4. But despite such individual idiosyncrasies, most people stopped calling their segment heads and thus an incremental communal cultural change took place.

In most cases, however, the conflicting strategies of different sectors of society will lead to most individual incremental changes being contested. As juniors and seniors use the various tactics to follow their own strategies, tensions build up and disputes break out. A man whose son-in-law has not brought him any of the *kumets* payments begins to get angry and finds some pretext to start an argument. A rich young man who has refused to become *halak'a* suddenly finds himself embroiled in a number of disputes with various *dere* elders. These arguments and disputes will be taken to an assembly and discussed and debated until a solution can be found. It is in these assemblies, then, that inter-individual disputes become communal issues. And it is through the resolution of these disputes that much incremental communal cultural change takes place.

Even more importantly, it is also possible that certain people, both seniors and juniors, might try to improve their situations by suggesting particular innovations to various cultural practices. People might suggest that the cost of the *halak'a* feasts should be reduced, or that the organisation of a sacrifice be changed. Individuals can only freely innovate on their own personal practices, and any suggestions that deal with community-wide practices will need to be discussed by the community at the communal assembly. This, then, is the second way, again through discussions at an assembly, that incremental communal cultural change takes place. In order to understand how both these changes occur it seems we need look at the organisation and workings of the Doko assemblies.

Resolving conflicts: peace, fertility and reconciliation

Despite all the interpersonal tensions that have been discussed, peaceful living is very highly valued in the Gamo Highlands. It is considered to be a prerequisite to all the other good things in life. Fertility, the life force that energises human, animal and plant reproduction, is considered to flow through the channels of social relations. Harmonious social relations are thus considered necessary not simply to ensure a good atmosphere, but also to make the crops grow, the cattle calve, and people give birth and be healthy. When social relations are not harmonious, when there are arguments and disputes, it is as if there is a blockage in the channel and the fertility cannot flow through. If relations in the community remain in such a state for long then it is considered likely that the *dere* will experience poor harvests or some other form of misfortune. Resolving these disputes and reconciling conflicting parties is thus a very important business, and in the 1990s it was the central task of the communal assemblies.

Keeping peace and reconciliation in the *dere* is an important part of Gamo cultural life, and is seen as a sacred as well as political endeavour. When I asked people why they were going to an assembly, they did not reply that they were going to discuss a case about some stolen sheep, or that they were going to decide what to do about a certain *dere* problem, but instead they would say something like, 'We are going to the assembly to bring reconciliation to the *dere*. For the grain, for the milk, to make the *dere* well.' This is why all *dere* assemblies are preceded by blessings for fertility and most assembly places are sacred spaces where sacrifices and other rituals are also performed.

In Doko, assembly places are known as *dubusha*. They are sometimes also known as *ch'ere*, which literally means 'swamp'. A swamp is a damp place and, as I elaborated in chapter 3, dampness is associated with growth and fertility in the Gamo conceptual worldview. Thus while assembly places are never literally swamps, they are swamp-like in that, by bringing peace and reconciliation to the *dere*, they facilitate growth and fertility.

Assembly places are thus the obvious places to carry out sacrifices and perform other rituals which are considered to stimulate the flow of fertility. Most *dere* sacrifices are carried out in *dubushas*, as are many of the various rituals that make up the *halak'a* initiations. And as we saw in chapter 5, the line between such rituals and *dere* assemblies is itself a blurred one. While the men sat in the beer *dubusha* at the Beer Feast of the new *halak'a*, they spent most of the day discussing *dere* affairs and resolving conflicts between *dere* members. Most rituals, in fact, either include or are preceded by a period of discussion and conflict resolution. There is little point in stimulating the flow of fertility if the channels through which it flows are blocked.

The importance of assemblies for the fertility of the *dere* is further explicated in the blessings that must precede all formal discussions at large community assemblies. These blessings are not for good judgement or calm discussion, but rather for the fertility of the *dere*. Thus before discussing cases of stolen cattle, or disputes about people not turning up to work for a communal work group, or what have you, the following blessings will always be made:

May God's blessing reach us!
May the *dubusha*'s blessing reach us!
May the *ek'k'a*'s blessing reach us!
May the *halak'as* be fat and fertile!
May the *k'ach'ina* have plenty to eat!
May wealth and fatness reach the fathers!
May butter and the *ochi* fruit reach the women!
May the barley sprout!
May the wheat sprout!
May the bamboo grow!
May the *enset* grow!
May the cows give milk!
May the sheep have twins!
May the barren woman give birth!
Give birth to boys and girls!
May the full blessing reach us!
May God and the hoe bless what I have left out!!

These blessings serve to focus everybody's attention on the greater purpose of the assembly and to remind participants that the successful resolution of conflict between *dere* members is to the benefit of the *dere* as a whole. This raises the importance of apparently trivial cases and makes them relevant for everybody. The association between peace and fertility, then, brings a communal aspect into most social relations. Because of this, conflicts and quarrels are never allowed to fester over long periods of time, and there is much communal pressure to bring conflicting parties swiftly to terms. Reconciliation should be final and afterwards there should be no remaining bad feeling.

Since it is thought to be extremely difficult for people to resolve conflicts between themselves, it is common practice to involve a wise and neutral third party as an arbitrator, or *ganna*. People with a reputation for good arbitration are much respected, and may be asked to help resolve conflicts rather frequently. There is little privacy in quarrels and anyone may feel that they have a right, or even a duty, to resolve other people's arguments. I would quite often be walking in the neighbourhood with someone, when we would pass a group of people sitting outside their house discussing a case and my companion would immediately go and join in. Such behaviour was considered to be totally proper and there was no notion that conflicts should be hidden away behind closed doors.

Assemblies

Assemblies take place on all scales and in varying contexts. Small local disputes are handled in small assemblies in someone's house or compound, while larger assemblies are held in proper assembly places, or *dubushas*. There are clan assemblies in clan *dubushas*, and *dere* assemblies in *dere dubushas*. *Dere* assemblies can take place at any scale of *dere*, and there are *dubushas* for small *deres* such as Dambo and Kale, for the medium-sized *deres* of Doko Masho and Doko Gembela, and for the large *dere* of Doko. All these types of assembly share much in common, most importantly that all decisions are made by unanimous agreement.

The general format of all these assemblies is the same. Participants speak one at a time, and if people interrupt they will generally be told to wait their turn. Only if someone repeats himself endlessly, or goes way off the point, will interruptions be allowed. First the two disputants present their sides of the story, and then other people ask questions, make suggestions and give advice. There is no hurry to these discussions and they often continue for several hours, until everybody is ready to agree on an outcome. If an agreement cannot be reached, then it is usual to set a date to meet again, until reconciliation is finally possible. When consensus emerges, the person in the wrong gets down on his knees and asks for forgiveness. First the person who has been wronged says that he has forgiven him and then the whole assembly generally extends forgiveness to everyone else. At this point the change in atmosphere is palpable, as people let go of their grudges and relax into friendly relations.

As discussed in chapter 5, *dere* assemblies used to be the locus of legal and political life in nineteenth-century Doko, and all manner of community issues and serious conflicts were discussed there, including murder, land theft and war. The assemblies had recourse to strong sanctions, including fines and expatriation, and they were the arena in which the community made decisions and exercised its will. Nowadays a great deal of political power lies with the state administration and the network of Peasants Associations, or PAs, that form its smallest units. In 1995 each of the small *deres*, such as Masho or Kale, had its own PA and the PA chairman could be a reasonably influential man. By 1997 the government had restructured things so that now two or three small *deres* were combined into one PA. In 1990s Doko these two political systems existed alongside each other, and it was not unusual, for example, to see the PA chairman addressing the community in a *dere* assembly.

The state administration is also now the centre of much legal power and the state-run courts in Chencha and Arba Minch deal with serious cases about murder, injury and theft. Many people in Doko resort to these courts if they cannot achieve the result they want from the *dere* assemblies, and it is not unusual for people to move between the two legal systems during one dispute. In the 1990s it was typically land disputes that proved the most intransigent and they were the reason for much toing and froing between the different legal systems. While in the 1960s the assemblies were dominated by debates about relations with the Amhara authorities, taxes and public work (Bureau 1981:179), the central issues in the 1990s were disputes between individuals, community affairs such as fixing the fences in the market place and cultural matters such as arranging this year's *halak'a* initiations or deciding how to perform a sacrifice that had not been done in the last twenty years.

Despite the changing content of the discussions and the new presence of political and legal alternatives, the form and the functioning of the assemblies seem to have remained more or less the same throughout the twentieth century. As the nature of the *halak'a* initiations has changed in Doko Masho, the role of the *halak'a* in the assemblies has changed a little, because there are now several *halak'as* rather than just one. But for the most part we can assume that the general form and functioning of the assemblies in 1990s Doko is more or less the same as it was in Doko throughout the past two centuries. The Doko assemblies are very similar to assemblies in other *deres* (see Bureau 1981:141–82 and Abélès 1983:41–56), and their workings can best be illustrated by a number of example cases that took place while I was in Doko.

Neighbourhood and clan assemblies

Minor arguments between household members and neighbours are common and they are usually resolved quickly by other household members and neighbours in informal assemblies at the house of one of the disputants. The following case is typical:

Kamba[14] and Kaltsa are father and son who live together in one compound. Kamba is a traditional elder, while Kaltsa is a Protestant who works as a carpenter. One day Kamba walked out of Kaltsa's new 'modern-style' house and slammed the door. Kaltsa told him not to break the door that he had worked so hard to make and implied that Kamba was stupid in not knowing how to open and close such 'modern' doors properly. Kamba was angry that his son should speak to him in this disrespectful way and hardly spoke to Kaltsa throughout the next day. There was bad feeling in the house and Assani, Kaltsa's wife, noticed it and asked what had happened. The next day she brewed coffee and invited around two or three of the close neighbours to make peace. Over coffee the neighbours first asked Kamba what the problem was and listened while he told his side of the story. Then Kaltsa got a chance to tell his version. Whenever one of them got off the point, perhaps bringing in old quarrels, the neighbours would bring them back to the case at hand. This case was simple and the discussion was quick. It became clear that Kaltsa was in the wrong to have spoken to his father in such a way about something so trivial. As this consensus began to emerge, it was somewhat thrust on Kaltsa, who accepted it quickly, if somewhat begrudgingly. The decision was unanimous, as it must be, and Kaltsa was found to be in the wrong. He got down on his knees and asked his father to have mercy on him. Kamba replied by saying that he forgave him and that he had stopped being angry with him. Then everyone generally forgave everyone else and the tense atmosphere dissolved into friendly relief.

These types of minor disagreements happen all the time, and are always quickly resolved in this manner. I was not spared this procedure and, on the few occasions when I got into arguments with my family or neighbours, I would always come home in the evening to find a crowd of people sitting around waiting to resolve the problem and restore peaceful relations. Stressful as this was at the time, it did mean that problems never blew up or got out of hand.

Arguments that are slightly less trivial are also discussed initially on a small scale in someone's house, and will only be taken to a more formal assembly if they cannot be resolved in this way. Good arbitrators, though, pride themselves in being able to bring even the most heated disputants to terms. Discussions will be longer and people can become angry, distraught and upset, but still the process of discussion until unanimous agreement is followed. Here is another case:

Adole, Gafo and Zida are all close patrilineal kin (second cousins). Gafo had accused Adole of hitting his wife, and had taken him to the local PA court, which had briefly locked him up. Zida's son had heard of this and had used his connections to get Adole released. As an ex-president of the PA, he had assured the current president that the family would sort it out. Thus a family assembly was held one night at Zida's house, as he was a senior kinsman and a respected elder and arbitrator. Adole came with his mother, and Gafo came with his wife. Two other close kinsmen and two neighbours also came, and Zida and his wife and son made up the group. Initially Gafo's wife was asked to present her complaint. She said that while Gafo was away weaving in Wolaita, Adole had come round to her house and had hit her and torn her cloth shawl. When she had finished Adole was asked to speak. He said this was completely untrue. He had gone round to Gafo's house to borrow something. He had called from outside and when he was told it was not there, he had not even entered the house. Everyone listened carefully to the two conflicting stories and Zida began to probe a bit. They knew of previous ill-feeling between Adole's mother and Gafo's mother, and as they questioned this indeed began to enter the picture. The discussion became extremely heated, Gafo started shouting and Adole's mother, an old woman, started crying. Adole kept protesting his innocence, and once or twice got up and tried to leave. The arbitrators tried to stay calm and to keep everyone involved in the discussion.

After three hours a consensus was beginning to emerge. Gafo's mother had been ill and Adole's mother had gone to visit her. There had been some quarrel and Gafo's mother was very angry. Then Adole had arrived, coming to borrow an axe. He had heard the women quarrelling and he had not entered the house. He had called out his mother and they had left together, the women's argument having not been re-solved. Gafo's wife had been so angry at some of the things Adole's mother had said, that she made up the story about Adole hitting her. (It was easier for her to accuse Adole, a young man in his early twenties, than his mother who is an old and well-respected woman.) Thus it was clear that Gafo and his wife were in the wrong. They both got down on their knees and asked forgiveness. Adole, still angry, had to be shouted at before he gave it. But eventually he did, and again the whole group generally forgave each other. Gafo and his wife sat down again. The heated atmosphere had now cooled down into friendly relief. Everyone sat and chatted for a while, as if there had never been any problem between them, and then got up and went home.

Other informal assemblies are held in the mourning period after someone has died. As kin and neighbours gather to sit in the compound of the deceased, they discuss any outstanding conflicts or arguments between his house and other people. Everything should be put in order after a death, and any unresolved matters are ideally brought to a close. There are also clan assemblies which discuss affairs particular to the clan. These can involve matters of ritual, such as when or how to perform a clan sacrifice, or can focus on other matters, such as land transactions or conflict resolution between clan members. All the assemblies, though, share the same basic form of open discussion until a consensus is reached.

Full neighbourhood assemblies also take place and they are most frequent during the agricultural season, when neighbourhood work groups are organised. These assemblies will generally take place at the house of the leader of the work group, or possibly at the house of the community sacrificer, if he lives in the neighbourhood. These discussions are mainly attended by men, and often take place in the evening while the women are preparing supper. Practical matters are discussed, such as whose land will be hoed when, and why so-and-so did not show up for work last Tuesday, and the assembly may impose fines on those who miss work.

Nowadays there are also assemblies organised by Protestants that deal specifically with conflicts between Protestants and traditionalists. These cases are increasingly common, and are frequently extremely fraught.

Wolk'a is having a dispute with his neighbourhood in Eleze. He is a Protestant, and the issue is overtly to do with conflicting interpretations of *dere woga*. There are, in fact, two cases, one concerning the neighbourbood work group, or *zurra*, and one concerning the Seniors' Feasts of this year's *halak'a*. Wolk'a is refusing to work with the *zurra* this year, in which one man from every house must participate. Wolk'a has not worked with the *zurra* this year, although he has done in previous years, but he is refusing to pay the customary fine, claiming that he does not have to because he has become a Protestant. He was also asked to donate a sheep for part of the initiation of this year's *halak'a* and again he refused on the same grounds. But he still thinks he has the right to eat at the Seniors' Feast, as he has provided the feasts himself in the past, when he became *halak'a* before he joined the church. So he is in deep conflict with the *dere*. Recently eleven of his sheep were stolen, and the conflict is escalating. I attended one of the many meetings in which reconciliation was attempted.

Early in the morning I went with the eight arbitrators to talk to Wolk'a. The arbitrators were all young men who are prominent in the church and included the preacher, the chairman of the Eleze PA, the secretary of the Masho PA, the doctor of the Doko Masho clinic, and Zida's son, the ex-president of the Masho PA whom we have met before. We all sat down in a little coffee house in the market place and discussed the case with Wolk'a. The arbitrators had discussed this case before and already seemed to have a clear idea of what needed to be done. They all felt that Wolk'a was in the wrong. He should still work with the *zurra* and he should not eat at the Seniors' Feast if he is a Protestant. But Wolk'a was adamant that he was in the right, and kept going on and on about his stolen sheep as if they weren't connected to anything else. He refused to change his mind and he began to drive the arbitrators mad. By midday it was time to go to discuss the case with the *dere*, but the arbitrators were annoyed that they had made no headway with Wolk'a. Two of them dropped out and said there was no point in bringing this to the *dere*. It was a waste of time and they went home. Two others almost dropped out, but were eventually persuaded to give it a try. And thus we went to meet the *dere*.

The assembly was too large to take place in a house, and by rights should have taken place at the Eleze *dubusha*. But since this was over two hours' walk from the market place, a compromise site had been chosen, the mourning ground of Dambo. This is not a traditional place to have assemblies and was not even in Eleze territory, but such matters did not trouble the Protestants. The people of Eleze came and sat in a long line, and after a gap Wolk'a sat at the end alone. The arbitrators and I sat in a line facing them. The discussion got under way.

People took turns to stand up in front of the assembly and say their views, and the others tried not to interject too much. It all became heated very soon and there was clearly a lot of anger. After four hours Wolk'a would still not change his tune and everybody was getting extremely frustrated. The arbitrators did their best to keep things calm, but they too were annoyed. More and more problems between Wolk'a and the *dere* came to light. Some time ago all the people of Eleze had contributed money to buy back some *dere* land that had been sold. Wolk'a had refused to contribute and eventually the *dere* had just let him remain apart. More recently, when the *dere* had called him to discuss the case about the *zurra*, he had refused to attend the assembly. After that the church called him and told him to attend the assembly and he still refused.[15] The list of complaints grew and grew. The arbitrators, all school-educated, tried to take each case in turn, while the *dere* men kept bringing them all together. Reconciliation seemed impossible.

Then the arbitrators threatened to leave. The case was impossible and this was useless. Only when they were on their feet did Wolk'a admit that perhaps he was in the wrong just a little bit. The arbitrators sat down. He should have come before when he was called to the assemblies and he was wrong not to have come. He got down on his knees and asked for forgiveness. The *dere* gave it and the discussion changed gear. Eventually the case over the Seniors' Feast was dropped, and Wolk'a agreed to pay the fine for not working with the *zurra*. Then the matter of the *zurra* feasts came up. Wolk'a said he had not been called to eat, and that he had the right to eat because he had worked with the *zurra* in previous years. The *dere* agreed that this was so and said that he had been called. Wolk'a retorted that he was only called by a small boy, and not in the appropriate manner. They argued for some time over this point of etiquette and eventually moved on.

What about Wolk'a's stolen sheep? Everyone knew that the *dere* had stolen them because of Wolk'a's behaviour, and the arbitrators reckoned that now the case seemed to be resolved the sheep would be returned. They also knew that because they were officials of the PA people would not admit anything in front of them, in case they got taken to prison for theft. They stressed that this discussion was for reconciliation and nothing else, but still the *dere* was silent. So the arbitrators suggested that the neighbourhood should meet among themselves and discuss the matter of the sheep. After they have done this they should come back to the arbitrators in a few days' time. Wolk'a was not very happy about this. He had admitted he was in the wrong and had knelt down before the *dere* to ask forgiveness. He had got forgiveness, but he had not got his sheep. Still, there was nothing more to be done today and the assembly disbanded and people went home.

Community assemblies

Community assemblies are larger and a little more formal than other assemblies and they always take place at special assembly places, or *dubushas*. *Dubushas* may be fenced or open, and some have little stone seats arranged in lines for people to sit on. Many *dubushas* have big old trees growing there and they are generally seen as sacred spaces. Community assemblies are open to all male *mala*. Women and *degala* may sometimes participate from the edges if they have something important to contribute, but they cannot bring their own cases to these assemblies. Community assemblies generally take place once a week, although the frequency will vary throughout the year and according to the general state of affairs. The Doko Masho assembly takes place at Pango *dubusha* in the market place every Sunday, while the Masho assembly takes place at Bulogars *dubusha* most Fridays.

Community assemblies are more formalised than other assemblies and there are certain ritualised conventions that must be gone through before the discussions can start. *Dere ades* come to the *dubusha* carrying their *horosos*, and *k'ach'ina* come carrying their walking stick, or *gufes*. As they enter the *dubusha*, they will stand their *horoso* or *gufe* in the ground in a designated space, and then pick a few pieces of grass and throw them in the direction of the assembled crowd and make a suitable blessing, such as 'be many!' (*dara!*), or 'sprout!' (*ach'a!*). The crowd will then reply 'welcome!' (*ahe!*). This blessing and response is common in everyday discourse, such as when entering a house or joining a group of people in a bar in the market place, but the throwing of the grass is extra and links in with the fertility symbolism of the *dubusha*.

As more and more people arrive, everyone takes their places, sitting in rows facing the front. The community sacrificer and one or two elders may have set seats at the front or at the side, but everyone else just sits where they like. In practice older men sit nearer the front, while younger men stay at the back. There is generally a calm and serious atmosphere while people wait for the proceedings to begin. Some of the younger men will make a fire, and hot embers will be used to light the bubble pipes that have been brought from nearby houses. The pipes are passed around the senior men during the discussions, and smoking is considered an essential part of *dubusha* activities.

Once there are sufficient people present, the blessings will begin. First the sacrificer gets up and collects his *horoso*. Standing in front of the assembly and holding his *horoso*, he then blesses for the fertility of the *dere*, as described above. At the end of each line everyone responds '*amen*'. Then the sacrificer returns his *horoso* and the herding *halak'as* collect their *horosos* and together bless the assembly. After this a few elders will collect their *horosos* and they too bless the assembly. Only after this can the discussions begin.

The person bringing the case will get up, collect his *horoso* or *gufe*, and stand calmly in front of the assembly. Speaking slowly and evenly, he will begin to bring his case. Most men will begin by praising the *dere* or the assembly before coming to the point, but the degree of circumlocution varies from person to person and from case to case. While rhetoric is very much a valued art in these assemblies, there are no formalised oratorical styles that participants must adopt.

If the case is a conflict between two people, the man will then return his *horoso* or *gufe* and sit down, and the second disputant will have his say. If other men have long speeches to make, they will take their turn standing in front of the assembly, holding their *horoso* or *gufe*. If they have smaller points or questions then they will call them out from their seats.

If the discussion is about setting a date for a sacrifice or ritual, then first one person will stand up and make his suggestion, then another and so on. It is extremely rare for more than one person to be standing in front of the assembly, although people may hover in the wings waiting to make their rejoinder. The case will be discussed until a unanimous decision is reached. If this is not possible, another date may be set and other relevant information may be asked for on that day. One of the herding *halak'as* may be asked to bring a new witness, or to take a message to some relevant person who was not present. If the assembly decides that a diviner needs to be consulted, or a sacrifice made to clear *gome*, then one of the herding *halak'as* may also be asked to do this.

Once the case is over for the day, the next case will begin. The next disputant will walk to the front, take his *horoso* or *gufe*, and begin. Some clever timing is required to get your case heard if there are many people with cases, and there seems to be a tendency for simpler cases to be heard at the beginning and more weighty cases to be discussed later on. In one sitting all manner of cases will be discussed. One Friday at Bulogars, for example, the Masho assembly discussed a suggestion about buying wood to repair the fence round the *dubusha*, and a case about someone cutting down trees from someone else's land. Then a young Protestant brought a case, asking why the *dere* had taken some of his land last year. After that the PA secretary, also a young Protestant, told the assembly that a new doctor was coming to the Doko Masho clinic and he needed a house to live in, and thus the *dere* would need to arrange for contributions of wood, thatch and labour. Finally the senior herding *halak'a* reminded people of the *gome* that had been found when reading the entrails of a sheep that he had sacrificed for the *dere* a fortnight ago, and there proceeded a long discussion about what this *gome* could possibly be and how they should clear it.

The Sunday assembly in the Doko Masho market place often deals with disputes in the market and also with inter-*dere* affairs. If the case is with another *dere* then the herding *halak'a* of that *dere* will present their case, occasionally accompanied by some elders from his *dere*. At the end of the day the *halak'a* will report back to his *dere*, and he will come with their response the next time the assembly meets. The following are my notes from one such case:

> The line of Doko *halak'as* stands in front of the assembled men, hold-ing their *horosos*. One by one they bless the assembly. Then they sit down and proceedings are set to begin. The good turn-out today makes me think that there must be an important case. There are a number of faces that I don't recognise, and I soon realise why. They are from

another *dere*, Ezzo, and they are indeed here to discuss a serious matter. The Ezzo *halak'a* steps up to the front and takes his *horoso* from where it is standing in the ground. He picks up some grass and throws it towards the assembled men. 'Be many!' he blesses. Then slowly and calmly he brings his case. He says that some Ezzo people saw a Doko man doing bad things in Ezzo. He gently comes to the point. This man was leaving a curse (*bitta*) and was seen putting down twigs and grass in Ezzo territory. The Ezzo *halak'a* sits down and waits to hear what Doko has to say.

The case has already been discussed a few times before and the Doko men have had some time to investigate. An elder gets up, takes his *horoso*, blesses, and begins to talk. He says how good relations have been between Ezzo and Doko and how he hopes they will remain so. The discussion goes on for some time, with men from both Ezzo and Doko speaking to the assembly. The Doko men explain that it is true that someone went to Ezzo, and they do not dispute the witness's allegations. But, they say, he was not doing *bitta*. A short while ago this man had hit a sheep too hard and it had died. This was *gome* for him and he had to 'clear his hands'. So, on the advice of a diviner, he took seven pieces of sheep excrement, seven pieces of a certain type of grass and some salty earth and mixed it all together. He then fed this mixture to a sheep in a different *dere*, Ezzo. This is all correct procedure to clear the *gome* and was not a *bitta* against Ezzo. The Ezzo men asked a few questions about this, and then said that they would have to report back to their own assembly and see what the *dere* thinks. It was agreed to meet again in two weeks' time to continue with the case.

Assembly attendance was fairly high while I was in Doko, although participation did tend to increase with age. As some of the previous cases show, even Protestants will attend *dere* assemblies if they have a case. They refrain from participating in the blessings and they do not smoke, but they respect the etiquette of the proceedings and will hold their *gufe* while standing in front of the assembly. While all men have an equal right to speak, age, status as either *dere ade* or *k'ach'ina*, and oratorical ability influence the extent to which they exercise this right, and certain key figures will generally influence the proceedings more than others. There is no leader, however, and debate is free and open, in much the same way as it is in smaller assemblies. While language may be a little less direct than it is in general conversation, there is little formalised oratory and few conventions of stylised speech. This, then, is how assemblies are organised in Doko.

Assemblies and cultural innovation

Now that we have seen how assemblies work in Doko, we can consider the ways in which assembly discussions can lead to communal decisions to change particular cultural practices. There are three main ways in which this can happen. First, creative solutions to inter-individual disputes can set a precedent for new ways to do things in the future. Second, interpretations of *dere* problems and diagnoses of *gome* can convince the community to reinstate old practices or to change practices in order to ensure they are doing them 'more correctly'. Third, and most importantly, the assembly can discuss new innovations and decide to implement them. While assemblies can also make decisions to keep things as they are, we will see that the particular organisation of the Doko assemblies is such that it tends to facilitate change and innovation.

It is not unusual for creative solutions to be found to difficult inter-individual disputes that have arisen out of new circumstances. Members of the assembly can see the implications of accepting one view over the other and thus decisions will generally be made that benefit most assembly members and do not have a vastly detrimental effect on anyone. A family assembly, for example, might accept that a man can put off taking the *kumets* payments to his father-in-law for another few years so that he can use the wealth instead to buy a loom and set himself up as a weaver. Or a community assembly, for example, might decide that two conflicting claims to a piece of land cannot be reconciled and hence decide to divide the land equally between the two disputants. In these and other ways, then, creative solutions bring about new outcomes which then set a precedent for future events.

Interpretations of *dere* problems and diagnoses of *gome* can lead to communal decisions to change a particular practice or to reinstate an old practice. A rather dramatic change of this nature took place in Doko Masho just before I arrived there.

Soon after the fall of the Derg, a community assembly was called to discuss the *gome* that was causing poor rainfall and illness in the *dere*. After lengthy discussions it was decided that the cause of the problems in the *dere* was the *gome* around the *degala*. During the Derg period they had been given land and had farmed together with the *mala* in communal work groups. They had also been buried together with the *mala* in the communal burial places, and they had had positions on the PA council. All of this was *gome* and was the cause of the *dere* problems. A decision was made to take back the land from the *degala*, to exhume and rebury their corpses, and to expel them from the PA council and the communal work groups. This decision was swiftly enacted, and the changes that the

Derg had forced upon the people of Masho were reversed in a matter of days.

We can see here how the organisation of the assemblies influences the type of decision that the assembly is likely to reach. In this case it is not at all hard to see how this particular decision would have come about. It is likely that many other possible causes of the *gome* would have been discussed, such as the sacrifices that had not been performed and the land that had been sown out of order. But while none of the *mala* participants in the assembly had anything to lose by taking back land from the *degala* and expelling them from the PA council and work groups, several of them would stand to lose economically and politically if the ritual order of sowing, for example, were reinstated. Since decisions are always reached by unanimous agreement, they would have been able to block any suggestions that they felt were disadvantageous to themselves. Their rhetoric would of course couch the issue in rather different terms, but the point would be clear. In this way the discussion would have gone round and round, and it is not hard to see how the decision about the *degala* would finally have been agreed upon.

Had the assembly had a different structure, then a different decision might well have been made. If the community sacrificer were the leader of the assembly, for example, or if membership were limited to only lineage heads, or if decisions were made by majority vote, then it is possible that those who stood to gain from the reinstatement of certain practices, such as the ritual sowing order, might have succeeded in pushing through a decision that the lapse of these practices was the cause of the *gome*, and therefore that they should be followed again. Or, had there been complicated styles of oratory, it might have been impossible for men to find the right terms in which to couch their disagreements with certain suggestions (e.g. Bloch 1971b). The very organisation of the assembly, then, influenced the type of decision that the assembly was likely to make.

Now that we have seen how the particular structure of the Doko assemblies influences the outcomes of assembly discussions, let us look at the third and most important way that assembly discussions can lead to incremental communal cultural change, namely by innovation. It is not unusual for people in Doko to come up with innovations that they feel improve a practice or make it more appealing in the current context. Any such innovations will be discussed at a communal assembly and if there is unanimous agreement then the innovation will be implemented.

As I have discussed in chapter 2, the period when I was in Doko was one of great flux, as people were in the process of trying to perform cultural practices that had not been performed for twenty years during the restrictive government of the Derg. Thus there were many assemblies taking place during which people were discussing whether or not to perform a certain ritual, and if so, how they should go about it. With increasing numbers of people joining the Protestant church, there was the additional problem of working out what to do if the sacrificer or the clan head joined the church and would no longer carry out his ritual role. In other cases changing demographic or economic patterns were forcing some communities to change the way they performed their rituals. This was a good time, then, to witness the mechanisms of cultural innovation.

Just before I arrived in Doko, the Woits'o assembly had decided to make a small change in the way they performed their *halak'a* initiations. Up until then they had not had a Beer Feast in a special beer *dubusha*, but had an *Uts'uma* Feast in the *halak'a*'s house, like they did in Shale (see chapter 5). But the number of *dere ades* was becoming so great that it was getting to be difficult to fit them all into one person's house. The crowded gatherings were becoming uncomfortable and an increasing number of men were not happy with the situation. Many of these men had participated in the *halak'a* initiations in some of the other *deres* of Doko Masho and had seen how pleasant it was to drink together in the *dubusha*. So someone had proposed the issue and it had been discussed at the assembly. A unanimous decision had been made to instigate the change and in 1995 and 1996 the Woits'o *halak'as* held Beer Feasts in the community *dubusha*.

Although many innovations get accepted like this, some proposed innovations get turned down and others become the focus of lengthy debate that can sometimes last for years. While I was in Doko, the Michamala clan were involved in one such protracted discussion. In the last few years certain members of the clan had suggested that the clan head should sacrifice a bull for them. Such a clan sacrifice had not taken place for around twenty years and they thought that it would be good for the clan if it were performed now. An assembly had been called and the suggestion had been made. At this assembly, however, the second most senior man in the clan, a character by the name of Sanka, had proposed an innovation which had divided the assembly. He proposed that he should hold the sacrificial spear jointly with the clan head and they should slaughter the animal together.

Sanka was having a lot of difficulty in persuading the others to accept his suggestion, and this proposed innovation was still being discussed two years later. The sacrifice could not take place until the matter was resolved because it was Sanka's role to collect the contributions, buy the bull, and present it to the clan head, and he was refusing to do this until his innovation was accepted. The result was a stalemate situation and the clan met every now and again to try to reach some consensus. One rainy

Friday in June 1996 I attended one of the clan assemblies at which the matter was being discussed.

> Once the pipes had been handed round and the blessings had been made, the discussion got underway. Since this was a continuing debate the problem was only briefly presented, and soon questions were focused on Sanka and the legitimacy of his suggestion. Sanka contended that his father had told him to sacrifice in this manner on his death-bed, and that he could not possibly go against his words. It would be *gome* not to respect your father, after all. Another man stood up and said that he had not heard Sanka's father say this, and were there any other witnesses? There was a general grumbling among the men that none of them had heard it, but then a close neighbour of Sanka stood up and said that he too had heard the words. Most of the men remained unconvinced, and argued that such suggestions must be made in front of many witnesses. And thus the discussion went on for several hours. There was clearly a lot of hostility against Sanka and much resistance to his innovation. But Sanka was remarkably tenacious and showed no signs of giving up. When dusk began to fall, the assembly had reached no consensus and they agreed that they would meet again to continue the discussion.

This matter had not been resolved when I left Doko over a year later and this stalemate may mean that the sacrifice never takes place again. As such it is also a tacit decision, but one that leads to cultural devolution rather than cultural transformation.

It is interesting to note in passing that innovations of this type had been accepted in Doko in the past. In chapter 4 I mentioned the case of the first sowing of the land by the community sacrificers in Masho and Kale. In Masho, you will recall, the community sacrificer hoed a little piece of land, buried the stomach fat of a sheep that he had just slaughtered and then sowed the first seeds. In Kale, however, the community sacrificer was accompanied by two other community seniors, the *maaka* and the *hudhugha*, and all three of them held the hoe together while working the land. This odd situation seems almost certainly to be the result of a similar discussion about who should hold the ritual implement. Such arguments are ultimately arguments about seniority, and in Kale the *maaka* and *hudhugha* seem to have successfully managed to enhance their status by claiming equality with the community sacrificer through the combined hoe-holding. It would seem that the people of Kale were convinced by their claims to seniority, while the Michamala clan have yet to be convinced by Sanka's attempt to enhance his status through a similar ploy.

These, then, are the ways in which clans and communities make decisions to change cultural practices incrementally. The organisation of the Doko assemblies, with their broad membership, relatively informal oratory and process of making decisions by leaderless discussion to consensus, facilitates open discussion, creativity and high levels of participation. The result is frequent innovation. As the social and economic context changes, the new circumstances lead to more and more inter-individual disputes and more and more cultural innovations. Through the resolution of small local issues, these innovations and creative solutions slowly bring about incremental cultural change. Each cultural innovation changes the local context ever so slightly, and thus slightly alters the patterns of tensions between people and the nature of the disputes and innovations that will next come about. In order to understand how transformatory change takes place then, for instance in the Doko Masho initiations, we need to try to follow through a chain of intended and unintended consequences that result from some of these incremental changes. We need to understand the 'chain reaction' that unfolds as one incremental change leads to another, which leads to another, which leads to another.

8   Transformation versus devolution: the organisational dynamics of change

We have seen how the changing production patterns in the nineteenth and twentieth centuries led to new social and economic realities in the lives of people in Doko and how people's individual strategies for change became translated into incremental cultural change by creative problem-solving and the innovatory ideas generated at the communal assemblies. It now remains to see how the cumulative effects of such incremental cultural change could result in overall structural change, or transformation. The primary aim, then, of this chapter is to show how the Doko Masho *halak'a* initiations could have transformed from the 'warrior' form to the 'wife' form. Having done this, we will need to return to the question of why the Doko Gembela initiations did not transform in the same way and also consider the more general question of why the practices of the sacrificial system seem altogether more resistant to transformatory change.

Cultural transformation: from warrior to wife

Let us quickly recap some of the major themes that have been developed in the previous chapters. We have seen that in the mid to late nineteenth century Doko existed as one unified *dere* and the groupings of Doko Masho and Doko Gembela did not exist. At this time most men were farmers and there was a very unequal pattern of land distribution such that genealogical seniors and the descendants of senior lines owned large amounts of land, which was farmed predominantly by slaves who had been captured in inter-*dere* warfare. A small number of men had an alternative source of income from the long-distance slave trade and many of these were also able to generate large amounts of surplus wealth. Throughout Doko these rich people would use their wealth to get initiated to the titles of *halak'a*, *hudhugha* and *dana*, and all these initiations were performed in something approximating to the 'warrior' form. Genealogical juniors had little chance of getting initiated because they were predominantly poor and for the most part their labour was exploited by the wealthy landowners through share-cropping or through communal work groups.

Then, in the late nineteenth century, *kawo* Toito came to power and Doko began to fragment. The small *deres* organised themselves into two groupings which became known as Doko Gembela and Doko Masho, and from then on there was no co-ordination in the *halak'a* initiations between these two groupings. Reasonably soon after that, the Gamo Highlands were conquered by Emperor Menelik and incorporated into the new nation state of Ethiopia. Both warfare and the slave trade were brought to an end and thus the rich landowners and the slave traders could no longer produce the huge amounts of wealth required to pay for the initiation feasts. The number of men becoming *dana* and *hudhugha* fell quite rapidly, and most attention became focused on the *halak'a* initiations.

Then, in the early years of the twentieth century, some men in the *deres* in and around Dorze began to take up weaving and get involved in the trade of imported consumer products which they bought in Addis Abeba and sold in the highlands. Involvement in these activities was open to all, and thus many young men and genealogical juniors found it a useful way of overcoming the economic disadvantage of their small landholdings. Men in Doko Gembela took up weaving and trading very rapidly, while those in Doko Masho, located just a little further from Chencha town and the road, took them up rather more gradually.

As the years went by more and more men took up weaving and trading in Doko Masho and this change in production patterns brought about a new situation whereby genealogical juniors were no longer dependent on their seniors, and wealth came to be much more evenly distributed. At this time genealogical juniors were keen to use their new-found wealth to become *halak'a*, because it enabled them to enhance their status and claim equality with their genealogical seniors. The demography of the Doko Masho initiations thus began to change, as genealogical juniors became initiated alongside their seniors.

The *dere ades* were also keen to encourage as many people to get initiated as possible, as they stood to gain from the feasts that the new *halak'as* gave. With most people in Doko Masho agreeing that initiation was a good thing, it would seem that the community assemblies agreed to make some small changes to the initiation process that would make it easier for people to get initiated. As the century progressed and Doko Masho became more integrated into the national economy, people began to find that there were all sorts of new alternative uses for their surplus wealth, such as buying consumer goods or paying school fees. In this new context it seems that the community assembly again agreed to instigate some more changes to the initiation process so that it would continue to seem an attractive option. All these changes that were made by the Doko Masho community during the twentieth century succeeded in maintaining the popularity of

the initiations. In the process, I have argued, it led to the transformation
of these initiations from the late-nineteenth-century 'warrior' form to the
late-twentieth-century 'wife' form.

How, then, did this take place? We have seen in general how the changing context exacerbated tensions between certain sections of the community and how the resulting disputes would have ended up being discussed
at an assembly. And we have also seen that new ideas and innovations
thought up in order to solve the new problems created by the new context would also have been discussed at the assemblies. Discussion at these
assemblies was organised in such a way that almost all sectors of society
could air their views, and decisions were made by consensus. This open
organisation led to the assemblies being the arena where the community acted together to resolve the changing structural tensions that were
threatening to blow things apart. Through discussion and compromise,
the community agreed to make small changes to many things, including
the initiation process.

Each time the community agreed to make a small change to the initiations there were ramifications beyond that one small change, as both
intended and unintended consequences followed from the initial incremental change. The social and economic situation was subtly changed
and the pattern of tensions in the community was slightly altered. Some
tensions were relaxed while others became accentuated, leading to new
discussions and more changes. And so the process would have gone on.

Because of the step-by-step nature of this type of change and the idiosyncrasies of the people involved, it is extremely difficult to piece together
a definitive historical account of how the transformation from 'warrior' to
'wife' actually occurred in twentieth-century Doko Masho. What we can
do, however, is construct a plausible model of how this transformation
might have occurred. In other words, with our knowledge of the initial
and final forms of the initiations, the forces of change and the mechanisms
of incremental cultural change, we can imagine how things might have
played out in Doko Masho. While it is likely that our resulting simulation
is only the outline of the actual transformation process – indeed it is
clear that other changes have taken place in Doko Masho which have not
been discussed in this book – such a simulation will none the less portray
the general picture. At the very least it will give us some idea of how
cumulative incremental change can result in overall structural change.

Let us start then with the 'warrior' form of the initiations. As you
will recall, in this form of the initiations one man is initiated at a time
and during his initiation he must feast the whole *dere*, both *ades* and
k'ach'ina. And because the *halak'a*'s wife must slaughter a sheep at some
point during the proceedings, men are always quite old when they get

initiated because a wife cannot perform this sacrifice until she has reached menopause and all the *kumets* and *gu?a* payments have been taken to her father. So in the 'warrior' initiations older men get initiated and they must spend a fortune in doing so.

As we have seen, this form of initiations was well adapted to late-nineteenth-century Doko life, as it allowed genealogical seniors and successful long-distance traders to use their wealth to buy community seniority. However, as the twentieth century progressed and production patterns changed, it increasingly became the case that many of the most wealthy people were young men. But because it was necessary for the *halak'a*'s wife to perform the sheep sacrifice during the initiations, it was not possible for these young men to become *halak'a*. Many of them would have wanted to and the *dere ades* would have had nothing to lose and much to gain by finding a way of letting them become *halak'a*. A young man who wanted to become *halak'a* might have suggested an innovation to the community, or the elders might have suggested an innovation in order to encourage these successful young men to distribute their wealth around the *dere*. One way or another, then, it seems likely that this issue would have been discussed at an assembly. And it seems extremely plausible that the community would agree to allow *halak'as* to get initiated without their wives having to perform the sheep sacrifice. This, then, would be the first incremental change.

This small change would have had a number of consequences. Most obviously, young men would be able to become *halak'a*. Some of them would still have had to wait until their father had become *halak'a* and they might even have had to contribute towards their father's initiation feasts. But none the less, as more and more young men began to become wealthy through trade and weaving, the average age of the *halak'a* would have started to fall.

Another consequence of this change would be that less wealthy men, particularly farmers, would have found it just a little bit easier to afford the initiation feasts because now they did not have first to complete all the *kumets* payments to their in-laws. Instead they could use this wealth to go towards the cost of initiation and put off the *kumets* payments until a later date. Such a strategy would have become popular with sons-in-law because getting initiated would have seemed a much better use of their surplus wealth.

Both of these consequential changes would have resulted in more men being willing and able to be initiated as *halak'a*. In such circumstances the *dere* would have initiated *halak'as* with increasing frequency. Instead of initiating one *halak'a* every two or three years, two or three *halak'as* may have been initiated in one *dere* during one year.

As the years went by these changes would have led to a changing demographic pattern in the initiations. The number of *dere ades* would have rapidly increased and the average age of these *dere ades* would have dramatically decreased. This demographic change would have led to the initiation feasts becoming more expensive. Although both *k'ach'ina* and *dere ades* were fed at the feasts, it was always the case that the *dere ades* had to be fed greater amounts of food. So as the proportion of *dere ades* increased, more food would have been required at the feasts.

Eventually it would have reached a point where many potential *halak'as* would have felt that the cost of the feasts was just too expensive. While they might have been able to afford it a few years ago, the greater number of *dere ades* now made it out of their reach. Some of them would very likely have been annoyed at this and would have raised the issue in one of the community assemblies. It is quite likely that the community would initially have just told them to work harder to produce more wealth. But if after a few years the number of men who were able to afford the initiation feasts began to fall significantly, then it is possible that these concerns would have gained weight and formed the locus of serious community discussion.

While all manner of solutions might have been thought of, one possible solution would have been to exclude the *k'ach'ina* totally from the Seniors' Feasts. This would significantly reduce the scale of the feasts and thus make them much cheaper. This small change would have had a number of consequential effects.

First, the number of men who were able to afford the feasts would have suddenly increased. Second, there would now have been an even greater incentive to become *halak'a* if at all possible, because otherwise you did not get to eat at the initiation feasts. The combined effect of these two factors would have led to huge numbers of men queuing up to be initiated. In such circumstances it is possible that the community would have decided to initiate several men together in batches, otherwise it would be quite ridiculous to have *halak'as* herding the *dere* for only a few weeks before the next one got initiated. In order to ensure that the changeover of *halak'as* did not get too fast they might also have decided to standardise the length of time that *halak'as* spent in office so that all men carried out a one-year term.

Having several *halak'as* at one time would have presented a number of issues that the community would have had to agree on. Which *halak'a* would carry out the *dere* sacrifices? In which order should they bless the assembly? Most of these issues would have been easily sorted out according to general Doko views about seniority, but some would have required more creative thinking. For example, if one *halak'a* out of the batch did something *gome* would all the *halak'as* have to be expelled from office or just the one who offended? This type of question must have been discussed at length in all the *deres* of Doko Masho, and different *deres* seem to have come up with different solutions.

For example, the Masho and Shale communities seem to have decided to instigate a ritual that symbolically links all the *halak'as* together on the day that they start to herd the *dere*, and then after that they will expel all the *halak'as* if one of them does something *gome*. Thus in these *deres* a sacrificer known as *maaka* passes a sheep over the shoulders of all the new *halak'as* and then slaughters it in front of them. The other six *deres* seem to have come to a different decision. They only expel the *halak'a* who has done the *gome* and they do not perform the sheep-over-the-shoulders ritual or anything akin to it.

In any case, the decision to initiate men together in batches would have led to the feasts becoming even cheaper in all the *deres*, as the new *halak'as* would have shared the costs of the feasts between them. This in turn would have enabled even more men to afford the feasts and thus the number of men getting initiated would have continued to increase.

As these changes panned out over the years the demography of the initiations would have changed even further. The majority of men would have become *dere ades* and the average age of these men might have fallen to only twenty or thirty. The old conception of *dere ades* as specially respected community seniors would no longer have really been appropriate. Parallel to this, the exclusion of the *k'ach'ina* from the feasts would have led to a feeling that the *k'ach'ina* were not really fully part of the *dere*. You only fully joined the *dere* once you had become a *dere ade* and could eat at the feasts. And thus gradually *dere ades* would have become to be seen as community members rather than community seniors, and the initiation process might have come to be seen as a process of joining, or entering, the *dere*.

This change in the conceptual nature of the transition might become mirrored in the symbolic form of the initiation. Since 'entering' is what wives do at marriage (indeed there is no separate word meaning 'to marry') and since communities are considered to be like houses, the similarities between a *halak'a* 'entering' the *dere* and a bride 'entering' her husband's house would most likely have been resonating in people's minds. This could have led to them slightly changing the nature of one of the initiation feasts so that it became more similar to the marriage feast.

The small *Uts'uma* feast which marks the end of the *halak'a*'s seclusion might have begun to change. It would have been normal practice at this feast for the *dere ades* in the neighbourhood to take the best seats by the fire in the main house, while the *k'ach'ina* made do with the seats nearer the door and in the other huts in the compound. However, as the demography of the initiations changed and the proportion of *dere ades* increased, it would have come to be the case that there would have been no room for the *k'ach'ina* in the main house and they would have all been relegated to other huts in the compound. This would also have fitted well with the new conceptual schema of the *k'ach'ina* as not being full *dere* members.

Given that now there would only have been *dere ades* in the main house, it would have come to be the case that the new *halak'a* could not himself eat in the main house because he was not yet a *dere ade*, and he would have eaten in one of the other huts with the *k'ach'ina*. Towards the end of the day, when the *dere ades* were satisfied with the quality of the feast, it is possible that they would have invited him to enter the main house since he had now proved his capability to be an *ade*. This would all have resonated so strongly with the marriage ritual that, either informally or by formal decision, elements of the marriage ritual might have been added to emphasise the importance of this transition and to indicate that the *halak'a* was now entering the *dere*.

An *Uts'uma* feast that contains many elements from the marriage ritual is indeed performed in contemporary Shale, and up until a few years ago was also part of the Woits'o initiations. In the Shale initiations, as mentioned briefly in chapter 5, there is a feast called *Uts'uma*, which takes place in the *halak'a*'s house. The *dere ades* eat in the main house and the *k'ach'ina* eat in the other huts. Late in the afternoon the *halak'a* enters the main house like a bride. The community sacrificer puts some butter mixed with *uts'uma* grass on the *halak'a*'s head and then feeds *kacha* to him and his wife, by handing him a gourd of wheat beer which they must drink together. Then the *halak'a* stands up and puts his right foot forward, over that of his wife, and if his parents are present they put their right feet above his. Then the sacrificer puts his right foot on the top of them all and pours wheat beer over them and blesses the *halak'a* to be well. This is what happens when a new bride steps over the doorway into her husband's house and the marriage symbolism is overt. In this form of the initiation the *halak'a* is beginning to seem more like a 'wife' than a 'warrior'.

As the number of *dere ades* continued to increase as more and more men got initiated it would soon have come to be the case that all the *dere ades* could not easily fit into one man's house. As the feasts became too crowded the men would have discussed what to do. Excluding the *k'ach'ina* and overflowing into the other huts might have been one option, but with the symbolic importance of the transition of the *halak'a* from sitting with the *k'ach'ina* to sitting with the *ades*, this might not have been popular. The *k'ach'ina* would also have protested against such a move as they then would not have been able to eat at any of the initiation feasts. Another option might have been to allow only those *dere ades* who lived in the immediate neighbourhood to attend the *Uts'uma* Feast. Yet another option might have been to move the feast to a more spacious location, such as an assembly place.

While Shale seems to have opted for the second option, thus retaining the feast in the *halak'a*'s house, the other *deres* seem all to have opted for the last option and have moved the feast to an assembly place. Since this has now become the day that the *halak'a* enters the *dere*, it also seems that these *deres* have turned this feast into the Beer Feast, and stopped having the Beer Feast on the Naming Day. Woits'o only made this transition in the early 1990s, as mentioned in chapter 7, and thus this particular change is actually grounded in known historical reality.

Even though the feast has been moved to an assembly place, the marriage symbolism has still been retained. In fact, the longer walk from the *halak'a*'s house to the assembly place is rather like the journey that a bride must make as she leaves her natal house and goes to her husband's house. The bride will not come of her own accord, but must be fetched by her groom and the intermediary known as *lazantsa*. And in many of the *deres* of Doko Masho we find that it is the initiation intermediary who brings the *halak'a* to the assembly place. And we also find that this intermediary is no longer known as an *u?e*, but is instead called a *lazantsa*, to add further to the marriage symbolism.

Further evidence for the historical reality of this stage of the transformation of the initiations can be inferred from a careful look at some of the details of the ritual. In both the Beer Feast and the Shale *Uts'uma* Feast certain spaces are used to stand for 'not community' and 'community' and the *halak'a* must make the transition from one to the other by the end of the day. In Shale the small huts in the *halak'a*'s compound are 'not community' and the main house is 'community', while in the *deres* that now do the Beer Feast the main house and compound together are 'not community' while the assembly place is 'community'. Following the logic of the marriage ritual, the *uts'uma* grass should be put on the *halak'a*'s head when he first enters the community space, as it is poured over the bride's foot just after she enters her husband's house. In Shale this would be in the main house, while in the other *deres* this would be in the assembly place. However, the reality is that the *uts'uma* grass is put on the *halak'a*'s head in the main house in all of the *deres*. This does fit with the structural symbolism of the Beer Feast and the most convincing explanation for this practice is that it is a left-over from when the feast used to take place in the *halak'a*'s house.

By now the form of the initiations has radically changed. With the *halak'a* now conceptually the *dere*'s wife, the symbolism of the spear and *kallacha* would no longer be appropriate and men would stop wearing them at their *sofe*. The initiations have now transformed from 'warrior' form to 'wife' form.

While I would hesitate to claim that this model of how transformation might have taken place in the Doko Masho initiations represents historical fact in all its details, I would suggest that it does portray the general processes by which the changing production patterns in the twentieth century led to changing practices in the initiations. The model makes sense of the contemporary variations in the initiations in the different *deres* of Doko Masho and it is supported by the little pieces of historical evidence about change that it has proved possible to ascertain.

On a theoretical level, this model of change has allowed us to imagine how the actions of individuals might have led to systemic transformation. The abstract model of change that we formulated in chapter 1 has been grounded in a real ethnographic case and we have seen how the series of disputes, resolutions and micro-transformations has iterated through the system to result in the overall transformation of that system. We have seen how the changing context provided certain individuals with new opportunities and how by acting on these opportunities they further changed the context and set up new tensions between various categories of people. As these tensions erupted into disputes they were discussed at the communal assembly and decisions were made to change the rules of the initiations ever so slightly. These changes to the rules further changed the context and opened up more new opportunities, and thus the cycle went round.

This analysis, however, has only partially solved the ethnographic puzzle with which we started this book. We have understood how the practices of the initiatory system transformed, but we still need to consider why the practices of the sacrificial system did not. Why did these two cultural systems change in such different ways? We have hinted at some of the factors that explain this difference in the preceding chapters, but it will be worthwhile to bring these points together here and see if we can take the analysis a little further. Before we turn to the sacrifices, however, let us first consider the initiations in Doko Gembela. The fact that these practices did not transform over the past hundred years or so might seem to problematise the distinction between the initiations and the sacrifices on which the original puzzle is premised. To show that this is not in fact the case we will need to extend our historical time-scale and consider how the Doko Gembela initiations might have changed before the beginning of the twentieth century.

Devolution in the Doko Gembela initiations

Let us first consider the changes that took place in the Doko Gembela initiations during the twentieth century. We have already suggested in chapter 6 the reasons why the Doko Gembela *halak'a* initiations did not transform like the Doko Masho initiations during this time, but these reasons can be usefully recapped here in light of the analysis presented above. In Doko Gembela the changes in production patterns that took place gradually in Doko Masho happened much more rapidly. Not only did men take up trade and weaving much more quickly, but they also became exposed to imported consumer goods and the temptations of urban life much earlier. By the early to mid twentieth century many men would already have chosen to spend their wealth on smart clothes and shoes and travel to Addis Abeba. More exposed to big city life they would have been less inclined to use traditional methods, such as the *halak'a* initiations, to increase their status in the community. As relatively rich and cosmopolitan individuals, their status would have been high in any case.

In this situation the *dere ades* and the genealogical seniors, who we will remember would have been mostly the same people, would have felt far more threatened by the changes taking place in the community. As a result, they would have been more likely to try to retain their senior status in any way possible. In this context very different discussions would have been taking place in the Doko Gembela assemblies. It is less likely that young men and genealogical juniors would have been wanting to become *halak'a* and it is less likely that the older men in the community would have been feeling particularly flexible about allowing changes. In the face of rapid change, it is not unusual for people to become increasingly conservative.

Rather than try to find ways to enable the newly rich men to become *halak'a*, it seems that the community instead began to 'catch' *halak'as* and force them to be initiated against their will. Older men who had got involved in trade or weaving and had already finished taking the *kumets* gifts would have begrudgingly become *halak'a*, but as they became more and more resistant the frequency of new *halak'a* initiations would have become less and less. By the 1940s or 1950s tensions would have been running very high in Doko Gembela. And by chance, this was the time that the first Protestant missionaries arrived there. Again, because of their proximity to Chencha town and the road, Doko Gembela received the missionaries a good few years before they arrived in Doko Masho. But in Doko Gembela the timing was perfect. The Protestant teachings provided a way to opt out of all the *halak'a* initiations and provided men with a justification to hold on to their new-found wealth. People joined in droves. In Doko Masho by contrast, people found Protestantism much less attractive around this time. The transformed *halak'a* initiations provided a way for most people to enhance their status in the community and thus the tensions between seniors and juniors were far less marked.

By the 1960s most of the people of Doko Gembela had become Protestant. In this context it was virtually impossible to find people who would become *halak'a*. The only people who were at all interested in the initiations were those who had already been initiated. They were not the locus of community discussion and debate, as most of the community had now joined the church. In this context we can see why the initiations simply devolved. With no debate there could be no innovation, and the initiations just fossilised. Men did not become *halak'a* and the last *halak'a* to have been initiated continued to herd the *dere* for years on end. The final straw came when the Derg government banned the initiations, and most of the *deres* of Doko Gembela have not initiated a new *halak'a* since then. The opportunities presented by the changing context in the twentieth century in Doko Gembela led to people opting out of the initiations altogether. In such a situation the initiatory system underwent devolution and not transformation.

In order to show that the twentieth-century transformation of the Doko Masho *halak'a* initiations was not a one-off anomaly, then, we need to consider how the initiations changed in earlier periods. Most importantly, we need to ascertain whether or not the Doko *halak'a* initiations underwent systemic transformation prior to the twentieth century. Although there is not enough data to piece together a precise model of the change in the initiatory system during the eighteenth and nineteenth centuries, there is however considerable evidence that the Doko initiations underwent significant systemic transformation during that time.

Transformation of the initiations prior to the twentieth century

The evidence for the earlier transformation of the initiations is twofold. First there are a number of inconsistent 'oddities' in the Doko initiations that would seem to be left-overs from when things were done differently in the past, and second there is great variation in the form of the initiations in all the *deres* throughout the Gamo Highlands. Our analysis of the 'warrior' to 'wife' transformation has shown us that both inconsistent 'oddities' and synchronic variation are very likely to be the results of temporal transformation.

For example, in many nearby *deres*, such as Chencha, Ezzo and Birbira, the contemporary form of the *halak'a* initiations is such that the initiation takes place in two stages, where men first get initiated to *atuma halak'a* and then afterwards get initiated to *bitane halak'a*. When they are *atuma* they carry out sacrifices for the good of the *dere*, and when they are *bitane* they become the messenger of the communal assembly. This form of the initiations is clearly quite different from either the 'warrior' or the 'wife' forms in Doko, and yet there is some indication that the Doko initiations may have had a similar two-stage form in the past.

We have already mentioned that the Kale *halak'a* is known as *gondale atuma*, or 'shield *atuma*', and this inconsistent 'oddity' is unexplainable in the twentieth-century context. We have not mentioned however that the two *halak'as* in Ch'ento are called *atuma* and *bitane*. Furthermore the *halak'a sofe* throughout the whole of Doko is often referred to as *atuma atso*, or 'making the *atuma*'. The notion of *atuma*, at least, has clearly been salient in past versions of the Doko initiations.

Evidence that the initiations used to take part in a two-stage form can also be found if we compare the basic form of the Doko initiations with those in neighbouring *deres*. In Chencha, Dorze and Ochollo and most other *deres* there is the basic rule in the *halak'a* initiations that every large feast is followed by a *sofe* – a status-changing event. Where there is one feast there is one *sofe*, where there are three feasts there are three *sofes*. In Doko Masho and most of Doko Gembela, then, the current position of the Seniors' Feast is thus anomalous. It is the largest feast that the *halak'a* must give and yet it is not followed by any *sofe* or change of status. The *sofe*-less Seniors' Feast in Doko might suggest then that there used to be a *sofe* and a change of status that took place after the Seniors' Feast.

This suggestion can be further supported if we take a very careful look at some of the variations in the form of the initiations in the *deres* of contemporary Doko Gembela. As we saw in chapter 5, in most of these *deres* the change-over of *halak'as*, where the new *halak'a* takes his place on the *halak'a* stone, blesses the *dere* for the first time and officially starts to 'herd', takes place on the Naming Day. This is the day of the first big feast, the Beer Feast, and it is followed by the *sofe*. However, one or two *deres* do it slightly differently. In Shaye the *halak'a* change-over and first blessing do not take place on the Naming Day, but instead take place at the Seniors' Feast. And in Kale, although the *halak'a* change-over takes place on the Naming Day, the first blessing does not take place until the Seniors' Feast. These variations would seem to suggest that the Seniors' Feast did once in fact mark a change of status. In which case it is very likely that it used to be followed by a *sofe*.

This very brief analysis might lead us to conclude that in the past the Doko initiations once had a two-stage form such that the Naming Day marked the transition of a man to *atuma halak'a* and then the Seniors' Feast marked his transition to *bitane halak'a*. Whatever the precise details of this form of the initiations, it is clearly quite different from either the 'warrior' or 'wife' forms found in the twentieth century. There would seem to be compelling evidence then that the initiations have transformed from this two-stage form to the 'warrior' form in the period prior to the twentieth century. The twentieth-century transformation of the Doko Masho initiations would thus not seem to be a one-off anomaly. Rather it would seem to be the case that the initiations have transformed many times in response to the continually changing context of the Gamo Highlands.

Devolution in the sacrificial system

The sacrificial system, on the other hand, seems to be incredibly resistant to transformation. Not only has there been no systemic transformation during the twentieth century, but there is also no evidence of any such transformation in the period prior to the twentieth century. Let us start by considering the type of change that the sacrificial system has undergone in the twentieth century.

It is tempting to understand the devolution of the sacrificial system in the twentieth century in much the same way as we have understood the devolution of the Doko Gembela initiations. We have seen that the changing production patterns in the nineteenth and twentieth centuries led to genealogical juniors becoming less and less dependent on their seniors as they found alternative non-agricultural forms of wealth production. At the same time genealogical juniors found a way to challenge genealogical seniority by using their new-found wealth to get initiated as *halak'a* and thus claim equal status with their genealogical seniors. As the structural tensions between the two competing conceptualisations of seniority became more marked at the turn of the century, the new movement of *Essa Woga* provided a way for people to opt out of the sacrificial system and participate only in the initiations. Many people became followers of *Essa Woga*, and those who did not none the less devoted less and less energy towards the practices of the sacrificial system. In this context we can see that the sacrifices, like the Doko Gembela *halak'a* initiations, were not frequently discussed at assemblies and were thus rarely the focus of innovatory ideas. Instead the practices were performed less and less frequently and the only change in the system was devolution.

Was this devolutionary change, however, a novel result of the twentieth century? Had the practices of the sacrificial system transformed like the initiations in earlier periods when they were more central to Doko life? There is compelling evidence that such transformations have not taken place. Instead the sacrificial system seems to have evolved or devolved in response to changes in the context of the Gamo Highlands. Overall systemic transformation does not appear to have taken place. Let us consider the evidence for this assertion.

First, there is very little variation in the general form of the practices of the sacrificial system throughout the whole of the Gamo Highlands. Most *deres* carry out the sacrifices in more or less the same way. We have already seen that the practices of the sacrificial system are carried out in much the same way throughout the whole of Doko, and they are also carried out in more or less the same way in the nearby *deres* of Chencha, Dorze, Birbira and others. My data from other parts of the highlands would suggest that there is a general consistency of form of the sacrificial system throughout the whole area. In short, the practices of the sacrificial system vary rather less than those of the initiatory system. Since synchronic variation is generally the result of temporal transformation, the lack of variation in the practices of the sacrificial system would seem to indicate that these practices have not undergone systemic transformation for a very long time.

This view is further supported by the fact that the practices of the sacrificial system in Doko do not include very many 'oddities' that would indicate that things were once done differently in the past. There are however one or two 'oddities' and little variations and a careful analysis of these will give us some more indication of the type of change that has taken place in the sacrificial system. Let us consider, for example, the joint hoe-holding of the sacrificer, *hudhugha* and *maaka* in the Kale first-sowing ritual that we mentioned in chapter 4.

This odd way of doing things would clearly seem to be the result of an innovatory incremental change, and if we remember the discussion that was taking place among the Michamala clan about joint spear-holding in the clan sacrifice, we can imagine how this incremental change could have come about. It would seem very likely that the first sowing in Kale used to be done more like it currently is in Masho, where the sacrificer holds the hoe and sows the seeds himself. At some point, however, it would seem that the sacrificer, *hudhugha* and *maaka* got involved in an argument about seniority, which they expressed in terms of their rights to hold the hoe at the first-sowing ritual. This argument would have been taken to the Kale assembly and discussed until everybody in the *dere* could agree on a solution. The solution in this case seems to have been the decision to let all three of them hold the hoe together.

Thus, as we have discussed before, the changing social and economic context led to inter-individual arguments and these arguments became translated into incremental cultural change by the innovatory solutions of the communal assembly. If such micro-transformations have taken place then why have the practices of the sacrificial system not undergone overall systemic transformation?

The reason, quite simply, is that these micro-transformations have not iterated. Isolated incremental changes have taken place over the years, in much the same way as they have in the initiatory system, but these incremental changes have not had a knock-on effect. They have not changed the context in such a way that new opportunities have been opened up to new people. Instead, an incremental change has taken place and that has been that. As we noted in chapter 1, not all incremental changes will iterate, but it is only through this process of iteration that overall systemic transformation can take place. And for some reason these changes tend to iterate in the initiatory system but not in the sacrificial system. In order to understand why this should be, and thus finally solve our ethnographic puzzle, we need to consider the effects of systemic organisation.

Systemic organisation and cultural change

In order to understand why incremental changes iterate in the initiatory system and not in the sacrificial system we need to start by looking at the pattern of linkages in the two systems. We need to consider why it is that incremental changes in the initiatory system often seem to feed back to provide new opportunities for individual action, while the incremental changes that take place in the sacrificial system seem to feed back to provide new contexts which do not offer such opportunities for action. To do this we need to look at the systemic organisation of the two cultural systems.

The systemic organisation of the initiatory system is rather like a network. There is a complex pattern of interconnections between the different elements of the system and most elements are linked up to several others. Most of the elements in the system are linked up to a similar number of other elements such that the density of interconnections is fairly evenly distributed across the network. There are no major junctions, or nodes, where everything comes together. In other words, power is distributed fairly evenly across the network.

Because of this pattern of connections, or distribution of power, change in any one element almost always has a knock-on effect on other elements.

Thus any incremental change almost always results in a cascade of change. This cascade is rather like the change that takes place when one domino in a network of dominoes is knocked over. The change ripples through the system, as the dominoes all fall over one by one, until a new stable state is reached, with all the dominoes lying on the ground. However, the organisation of the initiations is even more complicated than the domino analogy might suggest. For not only do incremental changes iterate like this, the network of interconnections is arranged in such a way that some of these iterations go round in loops so that the change becomes amplified each time. In other words, there are positive feedback loops which lead to the amplification of small changes and the transformation of the system into a new state.

The systemic organisation of the sacrificial system is rather different. First, the system is rather less complex and there are fewer elements and fewer interconnections between them. Second, the sacrificial system is not organised like a network, but instead it is organised like a pyramid. Some elements are more connected up than others. Those at the top of the pyramid are connected to large numbers of other elements, while those at the bottom of the pyramid are only connected up to a few other elements. There are several major nodes where interconnections are most dense. In other words, power is not at all evenly distributed in this system. However, these nodes are not themselves connected to each other and there is a pattern of interconnections such that pyramidal layers encompass each other.

As a consequence of this organisation, an incremental change made to one element in the system will often have very few knock-on effects to other elements. Changes made to elements in the lower part of the system will have very few knock-on effects as these elements are not connected to many other elements, while the knock-on effects of changes made to elements in the upper part of the system will dissipate quickly as they flow downwards. The organisation of the elements into encompassing layers results in each layer being reasonably independent from the other layers and so change in one layer generally has no effect in any of the other layers. Changing the practices between a segment head and his juniors, for example, has little effect on the practices between a lineage head and his juniors. Because of this pyramidal structure, incremental changes will at most iterate in the layer where the change was made but they will rarely have any knock-on effects beyond that.

It is this difference in the systemic organisation of the sacrificial system and the initiatory system that explains their different trajectories of change. Thus even when both sets of practices were central to Doko life prior to the nineteenth century, the changing political and economic contexts would have led to different types of change in these two systems. While the initiatory system transformed, the sacrificial system either evolved or devolved. And although the *nature* of the actual change would have been driven primarily by changing productive forces and brought about by individuals in discussion with the community, the *type* of change would have been determined by the organisation of the particular cultural system.

To move away from our particular ethnographic example for a moment, there would seem to be a general point here. If the systemic organisation of cultural practices influences the way in which they will change, then any general theory of change must take this into account. One cannot explain the way in which cultural practices change over time unless one specifies something about the systemic organisation of the practices concerned. Not all cultural practices will change in the same way. There will be different modalities of change for practices with different systemic organisations.

The practices of Merina circumcision analysed by Maurice Bloch (1986), for example, would seem to change in a way that is very similar to the practices of the Gamo sacrificial system. Changes in the political and economic context lead to changes in their function and they become more or less elaborated and take place at greater or lesser scales, but their symbolic form, or overall structure, remains remarkably constant. Like the Gamo sacrificial practices, the system evolves and devolves, but it does not transform.

While Bloch sees this modality of change, with changing function but stable symbolism, as something that is inherent to all rituals, my analysis would suggest a slightly different interpretation. It would seem that this modality of change is only characteristic of practices in cultural systems that have a pyramidal organisation. The anthropological literature is full of examples of such cultural systems, such as the Kachin *gumsa* or the chiefly systems of Polynesia (see chapter 1), and all these systems do indeed have a propensity for symbolic stability, or non-transformatory change.

Cultural systems that have a network organisation, however, will change in a very different way. Like the practices of the Gamo initiatory system, both their function *and* their symbolism can change. They can undergo overall systemic transformation. These types of cultural systems are far more sensitive to changes in the local context and the practices of neighbouring communities might transform in different ways as the result of tiny differences in their contextual situation. The practices of people who follow this type of cultural system will therefore often present the anthropologist with a case of phenomenal cultural variation, as in the case of the Gamo initiations and, for example, the practices of the Mountain Ok of Papua New Guinea (Barth 1987). This variation is a product of the network organisation of these cultural systems.

To conclude then, we have outlined a model of cultural change that has synthesised insights from both the individualist and systemic traditions in social theory. This model has combined an analysis of structure and agency, anthropology and history, event and process. And we have solved our initial ethnographic puzzle and explained why the practices of two different cultural systems in the Gamo Highlands have changed in such different ways. In doing so we have arrived at a general conclusion about the nature of cultural change: cultural systems with a pyramidal organisation will evolve or devolve, while cultural systems with a network organisation will transform.

Notes

1. However, in a later publication Barth writes 'all social acts are ecologically embedded... The social and ecological cannot, with respect to the forms of social events and institutions, be treated as separate systems' (Barth 1992:20).
2. *Ensete venticosum.* Differing from ordinary banana plants in terms of the form of the pseudostem, seed, embryo and chromosome number of the fruit, *enset* takes three to six years to build up a sufficient store of carbohydrates to be utilised as food. During that time it requires large amounts of manure or it will exhaust the soil. Despite this disadvantage, *enset* will support a greater density of population than cereal grains, has higher caloric yields per land unit, and is far more drought resistant (Hamer 1986:217–18).
3. During this time blacksmiths came from *mala* families. As ironworking became less lucrative in the early twentieth century most of them moved over to full-time farming and *degala* families took up ironworking.
4. Many of the *neftenya* in this area were in fact Oromo. However, since they spoke Amharic and were part of the national administration they were generally referred to as Amhara by the local Gamo people (Tadesse Wolde, pers. comm.).
5. In contrast, in the community of Dita, just 16 km from Dorze, only 9 per cent of males supported themselves from weaving (Olmstead 1975:91). It is likely that the numbers in Doko were about midway between these points.
6. *Kolts'o* is a vegetable that looks like a yellow potato, but stings to the touch. It must be ground and boiled before it is edible, and it is a low-status food.
7. *Stellaria media,* a common grass known for its abilities to grow well anywhere.
8. If *gu?a* is not taken then the relation between the houses of wife-givers and wife-takers can last up to four generations.
9. This seems the best translation for *angisa,* even though people in Doko do not think in terms of, or have a word for, lineages.
10. Women are also addressed using the teknonym. Thus Halimbe, Shagire's wife, was known as Assani Inde (Assani's mother).
11. If one man owned 8,000 units of land in the first generation, and he had three sons, who each had three sons, who each had three sons, then in the fourth generation the most senior descendant would own 1,000 units of land, while the most junior would only own 125.

12. Even if descendants of junior lines moved away in search of new land, as is probable, this would not vastly change the pattern of inequality in Doko landholdings.
13. A woman can only carry out this sheep slaughter if she has reached menopause and her husband has finished taking the *kumets* and *guʔa* offerings to her father. See chapter 3.
14. For obvious reasons, all names in this chapter have been changed.
15. It is possible to refuse a call to an assembly, but as this case shows, people will use all sorts of methods, such as stealing sheep, to ensure that the disputant finally attends.

Bibliography

Abélès, M. 1977. 'La guerre vue d'Ochollo', *Canadian Journal of African Studies* 11(3):455–70.

1978. 'Pouvoir et société chez les Ochollo d'Ethiopie méridional', *Cahiers d'Etudes Africaines* 18:293–310.

1981. 'In Search of the Monarch: Introduction of the State among the Gamo of Ethiopia', in Crummey, D. and Stewart, C. (eds.), *Modes of Production in Africa: The Precolonial Era.* Thousand Oaks, CA: Sage Publications.

1983. *Le lieu du politique.* Paris: Société d'Ethnographie.

1985. 'Ainesse et générations à Ochollo', in Abélès, M. and Collard, C. (eds.), *Age, pouvoir et société en Afrique noire.* Paris: Karthala.

n.d. 'Religions, Traditional Beliefs: Integration and Changes in a Southern Ethiopian Society, Ochollo'. Unpublished paper.

Abir, M. 1965. 'The Emergence and Consolidation of the Monarchies of Enarea and Jimma in the First Half of the Nineteenth Century', *Journal of African History* 6(2):205–19.

1966. 'Salt, Trade and Politics in Ethiopia in the "Zamana Masefent"', *Journal of Ethiopian Studies* 4(2):1–10.

1970. 'Southern Ethiopia', in Gray, R. and Birmingham, D. (eds.), *Pre-colonial African Trade: Essays on Trade in Central and Eastern Africa before 1900.* London: Oxford University Press.

1975. 'Ethiopia and the Horn of Africa', in Gray, R. (ed.), *The Cambridge History of Africa*, Vol. 4. Cambridge: Cambridge University Press.

Alemayehu Bekele. 1985. 'Marriage Systems of Borroda', BA dissertation, University of Addis Abeba, Department of Sociology.

Asmarom Legesse. 1973. *Gada: Three Approaches to the Study of African Society.* New York: The Free Press.

Awoke Amzaye. 1985. 'The Kore of Amarro', BA dissertation, University of Addis Abeba, Department of History.

Azais, R. and Chambard, R. 1931. *Cinq années de recherches archéologiques en Ethiopie.* Paris.

Bahrey. 1954 [1593]. 'History of the Galla', in Beckingham, C. and Huntingford, G. (eds.), *Some Records of Ethiopia 1593–1646.* London.

Bahru Zewde. 1991. *A History of Modern Ethiopia, 1855–1974.* London: James Currey.

Bailey, F. 1965. 'Decisions by Consensus in Councils and Committees', in *Political Systems and the Distribution of Power.* ASA Monographs 2, London: Tavistock Publications.

Bartels, L. 1983. *Oromo Religion: Myths and Rites of the Western Oromo of Ethiopia.* Berlin: Reimer.

Barth, F. 1959. *Political Leadership among Swat Pathans.* LSE Monographs on Social Anthropology 19, London: Athlone Press.

1987. *Cosmologies in the Making: A Generative Approach to Cultural Variation in Inner New Guinea.* Cambridge: Cambridge University Press.

1992. 'Towards Greater Naturalism in Conceptualizing Societies', in Kuper, A. (ed.), *Conceptualizing Society.* London: Routledge.

Basset, R. 1897. *Histoire de la conquête de l'Abyssinie (XVIe siècle) par Chihab ed-Din Ahmed ben 'Abd el-Qadar, surnome Arab Faqih.* Paris.

Beckingham, C. and Huntingford, G. (eds.). 1954. *Some Records of Ethiopia 1593–1646.* London.

1961. *The Prester John of the Indies: A True Relation of the Lands of the Prester John, Being the Narrative of the Portuguese Embassy to Ethiopia in 1520, Written by Father Francisco Alvares.* Hakluyt Society, Cambridge: Cambridge University Press.

Bloch, M. 1971a. *Placing the Dead: Tombs, Ancestral Villages and Kinship Organisation in Madagascar.* London: Seminar Press.

1971b. 'Decision-Making in Councils among the Merina', in Richards, A. and Kuper, A. (eds.), *Councils in Action.* Cambridge Papers in Social Anthropology 6, Cambridge: Cambridge University Press.

(ed.). 1975a. *Marxist Analyses and Social Anthropology.* London: Malaby Press.

(ed.). 1975b. *Political Language and Oratory in Traditional Society.* London: Academic Press.

1977. 'The Disconnection between Power and Rank as a Process: An Outline of the Development of Kingdoms in Central Madagascar', in Friedman, J. and Rowlands, M. (eds.), *The Evolution of Social Systems.* London: Duckworth.

1986. *From Blessing to Violence: History and Ideology in the Circumcision Ritual of the Merina of Madagascar.* Cambridge: Cambridge University Press.

1996. 'Structuralism', in Barnard, A. and Spencer, J. (eds.), *Encyclopedia of Social and Cultural Anthropology.* London and New York: Routledge.

Bourdieu, P. 1977. *Outline of a Theory of Practice.* Translated by Richard Nice. Cambridge: Cambridge University Press.

Braukamper, U. 1978. 'The Ethnogenesis of the Sidama', *Abbay* 9:123–30.

1980. *Geschichte der Hadiya Sud-Aethiopiens.* Weisbaden: Franz Steiner Verlag.

1984. 'On Food Avoidances in Southern Ethiopia: Religious Manifestation and Socio-Economic Relevance', in Rubenson, S. (ed.), *Proceedings of the Seventh International Conference of Ethiopian Studies.* Arlov: Berlings.

Bureau, J. 1976. 'Note sur les églises du Gamo', *Annales d'Ethiopie* 10:295–301.

1978. 'Etudes diachronique de deux titres Gamo', *Cahiers d'Etudes Africaines* 18:279–94.

1979a. 'Histoire contemporaine des Gamo d'Ethiopie', *Abbay* 10:201–4.

1979b. 'Une société sans vengeance? Les Gamo d'Ethiopie', *Ethnographie* 79:93–104.

1981. *Les Gamo d'Ethiopie*. Paris: Société d'Ethnologie.

1988. 'La mort du serpent: une nouvelle version d'Ethiopie méridionale', in Tadesse Beyene (ed.), *Proceedings of the Eighth International Conference of Ethiopian Studies*. Frankfurt and Addis Abeba: Institute of Ethiopian Studies.

1994. *Le verdict du serpent: mythes, racontes et récits des Gamo d'Ethiopie*. Paris: Centre de Recherche Africaine, Maison des Etudes Ethiopiennes.

Byrne, D. 1998. *Complexity Theory and the Social Sciences: An Introduction*. London: Routledge.

Cartledge, D. 1995. 'Taming the Mountain: Human Ecology, Indigenous Knowledge, and Sustainable Resource Management in the Doko Gamo Society of Ethiopia', PhD dissertation, University of Florida, Department of Anthropology.

Cerulli, E. 1956. *Peoples of Southwest Ethiopia and Its Borderland*. London: Ethnographic Survey of Africa.

Chiatti, R. 1984. 'Divine Kingship in Wolaita', PhD dissertation, University of California, Department of Anthropology.

Cilliers, P. 1998. *Complexity and Postmodernism: Understanding Complex Systems*. London: Routledge.

Comaroff, J. and Roberts, S. 1981. *Rules and Processes: The Cultural Logic of Dispute in an African Context*. Chicago: University of Chicago Press.

Crawford, O. 1958. *Ethiopian Itineraries, 1400–1524*. Hakluyt Society, Cambridge: Cambridge University Press.

D'Anglure, B. 1996. 'Lévi-Strauss, Claude', in Barnard, A. and Spencer, J. (eds.), *Encyclopedia of Social and Cultural Anthropology*. London and New York: Routledge.

Darragon, L. 1898. 'Le Sidama, l'Amara et le Konso', in *Comptes Rendus de la Société de Géographie*.

Data Dea. 1997. 'Social Stratification and Rural Livelihoods in Dawro, Southern Ethiopia', MA dissertation, Addis Abeba University, Department of Sociology and Social Anthropology.

1999. 'Trans-territoriality versus Variation in Ometo Identity: Comparative Cases from Wolaita and Dawro', Paper presented at the workshop on Cultural Variation in Southwest Ethiopia. Harris Manchester College, Oxford.

Davis, R. 1966. *Fire on the Mountains: The Story of a Miracle: The Church in Ethiopia*. Michigan: Zondervan Publishing House.

Dawkins, R. 1982. *The Extended Phenotype*. Oxford: Oxford University Press.

Dereje Feyissa. 1997. 'The Oyda of South Western Ethiopia: A Study of Socio-Economic Aspects of Village Inequality', MA dissertation, University of Addis Abeba, Department of Sociology and Social Anthropology.

Donham, D. 1985. *Work and Power in Maale, Ethiopia*. New York: Columbia University Press.

1986. 'Old Abyssinia and the New Ethiopian Empire: Themes in Social History', in Donham, D. and James, W. (eds.), *The Southern Marches of Imperial Ethiopia: Essays in History and Social Anthropology*. Cambridge: Cambridge University Press.

1990. *History, Power, Idealogy: Central Issues in Marxism and Anthropology*. Cambridge: Cambridge University Press.

1999. *Marxist Modern: An Ethnographic History of the Ethiopian Revolution.* Oxford: James Currey.

Donham, D. and James, W. eds. 1986. *The Southern Marches of Imperial Ethiopia: Essays in History and Social Anthropology.* Cambridge: Cambridge University Press.

Eve, R., Horsfall, S. and Lee, M. eds. 1997. *Chaos, Complexity and Sociology: Myths, Models and Theories.* Thousand Oaks, CA: Sage Publications.

Fancho Fanta. 1985. 'The Cultural History of the Borroda in the Late Nineteenth and Early Twentieth Centuries', BA dissertation, Addis Abeba University, Department of History.

Fargher, B. 1988. 'The Origin of the New Churches Movement in Southern Ethiopia', PhD dissertation, University of Aberdeen.

Feil, D. 1987. *The Evolution of Highland Papua New Guinea Societies.* Cambridge: Cambridge University Press.

Forster, J. 1969. 'Economy of the Gamu Highlands', *Geographical Magazine* 41:429–38.

Freeman, D. 1997. 'Images of Fertility: The Indigenous Concept of Power in Doko Masho, Southwest Ethiopia', in Fukui, K., Kurimoto, E. and Shigeta, M. (eds.), *Ethiopia in Broader Perspective: Papers of the Thirteenth International Conference of Ethiopian* Studies, Vol. 2, pp. 342–57. Kyoto: Shokado Book Sellers.

1999. 'Transforming Traditions: The Dynamics of Cultural Variation in the Gamo Highlands, Southwest Ethiopia', PhD dissertation, London School of Economics, Department of Anthropology.

Freeman, D. and Pankhurst, A. eds. In press. *Peripheral People: The Excluded Minorities of Ethiopia.* London: Hurst & Co.

Fried, M. 1967. *The Evolution of Political Society.* New York: Random House.

Friedman, J. 1975. 'Tribes, States and Transformations', in Bloch, M. (ed.), *Marxist Analyses and Social Anthropology.* London: Malaby Press.

Friedman, J. and Rowlands, M. 1977. 'Notes towards an Epigenetic Model of the Evolution of "Civilisation"', in Friedman, J. and Rowlands, M. (eds.), *The Evolution of Social Systems.* London: Duckworth.

Fujimoto, T. n.d. 'Oto Mana and Gita Mana in Malo', in Freeman, D. and Pankhurst, A. (eds.), *Peripheral People: The Excluded Minorities of Ethiopia.* London: Hurst & Co.

Gebre Yntiso. 1995. 'The Ari of Southwestern Ethiopia: An Exploratory Study of Production Practices', Social Anthropology Dissertation Series 2, Addis Abeba University.

Giddens, A. 1976. *New Rules of Sociological Method.* London: Hutchinson.

1984. *The Constitution of Society.* Cambridge: Polity Press.

Goody, J. 1962. *Death, Property and the Ancestors: A Study of the Mortuary Customs of the LoDagaa of West Africa.* London: Tavistock.

1971. *Technology, Tradition and the State in Africa.* London: Oxford University Press.

1976. *Production and Reproduction: A Comparative Study of the Domestic Domain.* Cambridge: Cambridge University Press.

Guidi, I. 1889. 'Le Canzoni Geez-Amarinna in Onore di Re Abissini', *Rendiconti della Reale Accademia dei Lincei* 4:53–66.

Haileyesus Seba. 1996. 'A Study of Social Change in Wolaita, Southern Ethiopia', MA dissertation, University of Addis Abeba, Department of Sociology and Social Anthropology.

Hallpike, C. 1972. *The Konso of Ethiopia: A Study of the Values of a Cushitic People*. Oxford: Oxford University Press.

1988. *The Principles of Social Evolution*. Oxford: Clarendon Press.

Halperin, R. and Olmstead, J. 1976. 'To Catch a Feastgiver: Redistribution among the Dorze of Ethiopia', *Africa* 46:146–66.

Hamer, J. 1970. 'Sidamo Generational Class Cycles: A Political Gerontocracy', *Africa* 40:50–70.

1978. 'The Origins of the Sidama: A Cushitic-Speaking People of Southwestern Ethiopia', *Abbay* 9:131–9.

1986. 'Hierarchy, Equality, and the Availability of Land Resources: An Example from two Ethiopian Ensete Producers', *Ethnology* 25(3):215–27.

Hansemo Hamela. 1992. 'D'irasha (Gidole): The Response to Social and Religious Change of a Community in Southwest Ethiopia', MA (Econ.) thesis, University of Manchester.

Harris, M. 1979. *Cultural Materialism: The Struggle for a Science of Culture*. New York: Random House.

1980. *Culture, People, Nature: An Introduction to General Anthropology*. New York: Harper and Row.

Harvey, D. and Reed, M. 1994. 'The Evolution of Dissipative Social Systems', *Journal of Social and Evolutionary Systems* 17(4):371–411.

Hassen, M. 1990. *The Oromo of Ethiopia: A History 1570–1860*. Cambridge: Cambridge University Press.

Hinnant, J. 1978. 'The Guji: Gada as a Ritual System', in Almagor, U. and Baxter, P. (eds.), *Age, Generation and Time*. London: C. Hurst.

Hodson, A. 1927. *Seven Years in Southern Ethiopia*. London: Hazell, Watson and Viney.

Huntingford, G. 1955. *The Kingdoms of Kafa and Janjero*. London: Ethnographic Survey of Africa.

1989. *The Historical Geography of Ethiopia, From the First Century AD to 1704*. British Academy, London: Oxford University Press.

Jackson, R. 1971. 'Periodic Markets in Southern Ethiopia', *Transactions* 3: 31–41.

Jackson, R., Mulvaney, P., Russel, T. and Forster, J. 1969. 'Report of the Oxford University Expedition to the Gamo Highlands of Southern Ethiopia', Oxford (mimeographed).

Keil, L. D. and Elliott, E. eds. 1996. *Chaos Theory in the Social Sciences: Foundations and Applications*. Ann Arbor: University of Michigan Press.

Knauft, B. 1985. 'Ritual Form and Permutation in New Guinea: Implications of Symbolic Process for Socio-Political Evolution', *American Ethnologist* 12:321–40.

1993. *South Coast New Guinea Cultures: History, Comparison, Dialectic*. Cambridge: Cambridge University Press.

Knutsson, K. 1967. *Authority and Change: A Study of the Kallu Institution among the Macha Galla of Ethiopia*. Etnologiska Studier 28. Göteborg: Elanders Boktryckeri Aktiebolag.

Kopytoff, I. ed. 1987. *The African Frontier: The Reproduction of Traditional African Societies*. Bloomington and Indianapolis: Indiana University Press.

Kuper, A., 1971. 'Council Structure and Decision-Making', in Richards, A. and Kuper, A. (eds.), *Councils in Action*. Cambridge Papers in Social Anthropology 6, Cambridge: Cambridge University Press.

ed. 1992. *Conceptualizing Society*. London: Routledge.

Kurimoto, E. and Simonse, S. eds. 1998. *Conflict, Age and Power in North East Africa: Age Systems in Transition*. Oxford: James Currey.

Lange, W. 1976. 'Dialectics of Divine "Kingship" in the Kafa Highland', Occasional Paper 15, African Studies Center, University of California.

1982. *History of the Southern Gonga (Southwestern Ethiopia)*. Weisbaden: Franz Steiner Verlag.

Leach, E. 1981 [1954]. *Political Systems of Highland Burma: A Study of Kachin Social Structure*. London: Athlone Press.

Lévi-Strauss, C. 1963. 'The Structural Study of Myth', in *Structural Anthropology*, Vol. 1. New York: Basic Books.

1994 [1964]. *The Raw and the Cooked: Introduction to a Science of Mythology*. London: Pimlico.

1981 [1971]. *The Naked Man: Introduction to a Science of Mythology 4*. Translated by John and Doreen Weightman. New York: Harper and Row.

Levine, D. 1974. *Greater Ethiopia: The Evolution of a Multiethnic Society*. Chicago: University of Chicago Press.

Lewin, R. 1993. *Complexity: Life on the Edge of Chaos*. London: Phoenix.

Lewis, H. 1966. 'The Origins of the Galla and Somali', *Journal of African History* 7(1):27–46.

1978. 'The Galla State of Jimma Abba Jifar', in Claessen, H. and Skalnik, P. (eds.), *The Early State*. The Hague, Paris and New York: Mouton Publishers.

McClellan, C. 1988. *State Transformation and National Integration: Gedeo and the Ethiopian Empire, 1895–1935*. Michigan: African Studies Center, Michigan State University.

Meillassoux, C. 1975. *Maidens, Meal and Money: Capitalism and the Domestic Community*. Cambridge: Cambridge University Press.

Merid Wolde Aregay. 1971. 'Southern Ethiopia and the Christian Kingdom 1508–1708, with Special Reference to the Galla Migrations and their Consequences', PhD dissertation, University of London, Department of History.

Mesfin Getahun. In press. 'Shashemene', in Freeman, D. and Pankhurst, A. (eds.), *Peripheral People: The Excluded Minorities of Ethiopia*. London: C. Hurst & Co.

Nadel, S. 1951. *The Foundations of Social Anthropology*. London: Cohen and West.

Nugent, D. 1982. 'Closed Systems and Contradiction: The Kachin in and out of History', *Man* 17(3):508–27.

Olmstead, J. 1972. 'The Dorze House: A Bamboo Basket', *Journal of Ethiopian Studies* 10(2):27–36.

1973. 'Agricultural Land and Social Stratification in the Gamu Highland of Southern Ethiopia', in Marcus, H. (ed.), *Proceedings of the First United States Conference on Ethiopian Studies*. Michigan: African Studies Center, Michigan State University.

1974a. 'Female Fertility, Social Structure and the Economy: A Controlled Comparison of Two Southern Ethiopian Communities', PhD dissertation, Columbia University.

1974b. 'The Versatile Enset Plant: Its Use in the Gamo Highland', *Journal of Ethiopian Studies* 12(2):147–58.

1975. 'Farmer's Wife, Weaver's Wife: Women and Work in Two Southern Ethiopian Communities', *African Studies Review* 18(3):85–95.

1997. *Woman between Two Worlds: Portrait of an Ethiopian Rural Leader.* Urbana: University of Illinois Press.

Orent, A. 1969. 'Lineage Structure and the Supernatural: The Kafa of Southwest Ethiopia', PhD dissertation, Boston University Graduate School.

Pankhurst, R. 1997. *The Ethiopian Borderlands: Essays in Regional History from Ancient Times to the End of the Eighteenth Century.* Lawrenceville, NJ: Red Sea Press.

Piot, C. 1995. 'Symbolic Dualism and Historical Process among the Kabre of Togo', *Journal of the Royal Anthropological Institute* 1:611–24.

Population and Housing Census. 1994. *Statistical Report on Population Size and Characteristics, Southern Nations, Nationalities and Peoples' Region*, Vol. 1, Part 1. Addis Abeba: Central Statistical Authority.

Rappaport, R. 1968. *Pigs for the Ancestors: Ritual in the Ecology of a New Guinea People.* New Haven: Yale University Press.

1979. *Ecology, Meaning and Religion.* Richmond, CA: North Atlantic Books.

Reed, M. and Harvey, D. 1992. 'The New Science and the Old: Complexity and Realism in the Social Sciences', *Journal for the Theory of Social Behaviour* 22:356–79.

Rey, P. 1975. 'The Lineage Mode of Production', *Critique of Anthropology* 1.

Richards, A. 1971. 'The Nature of the Problem', in Richards, A. and Kuper, A. (eds.), *Councils in Action.* Cambridge Papers in Social Anthropology 6, Cambridge: Cambridge University Press.

Richards, A. and Kuper, A. eds. 1971. *Councils in Action.* Cambridge Papers in Social Anthropology 6, Cambridge: Cambridge University Press.

Rodin, R., Michaelson, K. and Britan, G. 1978. 'Systems Theory in Anthropology', *Current Anthropology* 19(4):747–53.

Rowlands, M. 1979. 'Local and Long Distance Trade and Incipient State Formation on the Bamenda Plateau in the Late Nineteenth Century', *Paideuma* 25:1–19.

Sahlins, M. 1958. *Social Stratification in Polynesia.* Seattle: University of Washington Press.

1963. 'Poor Man, Rich Man, Big-Man, Chief: Political Types in Melanesia and Polynesia', *Comparative Studies in Society and History* 5:285–303.

1985. *Islands of History.* Chicago: University of Chicago Press.

Sahlins, M. and Service, E. 1960. *Evolution and Culture.* Michigan: University of Michigan Press.

Scott, H. 1952. 'Journey to the Gughe Highlands (Southern Ethiopia) 1948–9: Biogeographical Research at High Altitudes', *Proceedings of the Linnean Society of London* 2:86–189.

Shack, W. 1966. *The Gurage: A People of the Enset Culture.* Oxford: Oxford University Press.

Sperber, D. 1973. 'Paradoxes of Seniority among the Dorze', in Marcus, H. (ed.), *Proceedings of the First United States Conference on Ethiopian Studies*. Michigan: African Studies Center, Michigan State University.

1975. *Rethinking Symbolism*. Cambridge: Cambridge University Press.

1980. 'The Management of Misfortune among the Dorze', in Hess, R. (ed.), *Proceedings of the Fifth International Conference on Ethiopian Studies*. Chicago.

1985. *On Anthropological Knowledge: Three Essays*. Cambridge: Cambridge University Press.

1996. *Explaining Culture: A Naturalistic Approach*. Oxford: Blackwell.

Steward, J. 1955. *Theory of Culture Change: The Methodology of Multilinear Evolution*. Urbana: University of Illinois Press.

Straube, H. 1957. 'Das Dualsystem und die Halaka-Verfassung der Dorse als alte Gesellschaftsordnung der Ometo-Volker Sud-Aethiopiens', *Paideuma* 6:342–53.

1963. *Westkuschitische Volker Sud-Aethiopiens*. Stuttgart: W. Kohlhammer Verlag.

Tadesse Tamrat. 1972. *Church and State in Ethiopia, 1270–1527*. Oxford: Clarendon Press.

Tadesse Wolde. 1999. 'Entering Cattle Gates: Bond Friendship between the Hor and Their Neighbours', Paper presented at the workshop on Cultural Variation in Southwest Ethiopia. Harris Manchester College, Oxford.

Terray, E. 1974. 'Long Distance Trade and the Formation of the State', *Economy and Society* 3:315–45.

Thin, N. 1996. 'Environment', in Barnard, A. and Spencer, J. (eds.), *Encyclopedia of Social and Cultural Anthropology*. London and New York: Routledge.

Thomas, N. 1989. *Out of Time: History and Evolution in Anthropological Discourse*. Cambridge: Cambridge University Press.

Todd, D. 1977a. 'Caste in Africa?', *Africa* 47(4):398–412.

1977b. 'Herbalists, Diviners and Shamans in Dimam', *Paideuma* 23:189–204.

1978a. 'Aspects of Chiefship in Dimam, South West Ethiopia', *Cahiers d'Etudes Africaines* 18:311–32.

1978b. 'The Origins of Outcastes in Ethiopia: Reflections on an Evolutionary Theory', *Abbay* 9:145–58.

Tsehai Brehane Selassie. 1975. 'The Question of Damot and Wolamo', *Journal of Ethiopian Studies* 13(1):37–46.

Turton, D. 1975. 'The Relationship between Oratory and the Exercise of Influence among the Mursi', in Bloch, M. (ed.), *Political Language and Oratory in Traditional Society*. London: Academic Press.

Vanderheym, J. 1896. *Une expedition avec le Negous Menelik: vingt moins en Abyssinie*. Paris.

Vannutelli, L. and Citerni, C. 1899. *L'Omo*. Milan.

Vincent, J. 1986. 'System and Process, 1974–1985', *Annual Review of Anthropology* 15:99–119.

Watson, E. 1998. 'Ground Truths: Land and Power in Konso, Ethiopia', PhD dissertation, University of Cambridge, Department of Geography.

Wolf, E. 1985. *Europe and the People without History*. Berkeley: University of California Press.

Yalman, N. 1967. *Under the Bo Tree: Studies in Caste, Kinship and Marriage in the Interior of Ceylon*. Berkeley: University of California Press.

Index